RED KNIGHT

MICHAEL ASHCROFT
RED KNIGHT

THE UNAUTHORISED BIOGRAPHY OF
SIR KEIR STARMER

Biteback Publishing

First published in Great Britain in 2021 by
Biteback Publishing Ltd, London
Copyright © Michael Ashcroft 2021

Michael Ashcroft has asserted his right under the Copyright, Designs and Patents Act 1988
to be identified as the author of this work.

ISBN 978-1-78590-696-1

10 9 8 7 6 5 4 3 2 1

A CIP catalogue record for this book is available from the British Library.

Set in Minion Pro and Futura

Printed and bound in Great Britain by
CPI Group (UK) Ltd, Croydon CR0 4YY

MIX
Paper from
responsible sources
FSC
www.fsc.org   FSC® C020471

CONTENTS

AUTHOR'S ROYALTIES

Lord Ashcroft is donating all author's royalties
from *Red Knight* to charity.

ACKNOWLEDGEMENTS

A mong the scores of people who kindly agreed to be interviewed for this book, some asked not to be named publicly. For this reason, it is not possible to identify here everybody who deserves thanks; suffice it to say their background briefings were extremely useful.

The following people were notably generous with their time and help by assisting or advising in different and important ways: Prof. Bill Bowring, Sean Davey, Peter Burgess, David Jones, David Johnson, Mark Dixon, David Wharton, Michael Crick, Margaret Crick, David Griffith, James Hanning, Safia Bugel and the staff of Haringey Archive and Local History Centre.

Thanks must also go to the formidable Angela Entwistle and her team, as well as to those at Biteback Publishing who were involved in the production of this book. And special thanks to Kevin Culwick and to my chief researcher, Miles Goslett.

INTRODUCTION

Sir Keir Starmer did not want this book to be written. Indeed, it is no exaggeration to say that he actively obstructed it. It is important to make this clear from the outset, not by way of an excuse but by way of an explanation. As Sir Keir is the Leader of the Opposition and is therefore in charge of the government-in-waiting, readers have a right to know the context in which this examination of his life and career has been produced.

Out of courtesy, I first contacted Sir Keir through a mutual friend in the Parliamentary Labour Party in November 2020 to inform him of my plans for the project. Not having received any acknowledgement, I later wrote to him to clarify that although it is, technically, an unauthorised biography, it would be more accurate to describe it as an independent piece of work. With this in mind, I was able to assure him it would be objective, open-minded, factual, even-handed and without any political angle. Again, however, he did not respond.

By writing to him, I further hoped to gain confirmation from him that anybody who was approached as a potential interviewee – and who in turn sought his blessing in this regard – could be reassured by him that he had taken a neutral position on the matter. Such confirmation was not forthcoming. On the contrary, something else was revealed. Some friends of Sir Keir said they had been told by him that he was not 'comfortable' with this book, and that he would rather they did not participate in it.

At no point did I expect that Sir Keir would want to offer his personal co-operation by giving an interview, for example, but I was concerned that no obstacles should exist which would be detrimental to the book's progress either. While I am the first to accept that everybody is entitled to a private life, I also believe that any politician who wishes to present themself to the country as the Prime Minister-in-waiting should have a skin thick enough to be untroubled by a study of their character. Moreover, I had expected that Sir Keir would conclude there might even be an upside to some of those closest to him discussing their memories of him in the book. Seemingly, he had different ideas.

When the journalist Michael Crick embarked on a biography of Michael Howard shortly after he became leader of the Conservative Party in 2003, Howard let it be known that he was 'relaxed' about it. Despite being regarded by some as a controversial politician – and indeed although he had been described damagingly by his fellow Conservative MP Ann Widdecombe some years earlier as having 'something of the night' about him – Howard's attitude has always seemed to me to have been eminently sensible. Sir Keir's frame of mind would appear to stand in direct contrast to this.

It follows that by having such a prickly reaction to my decision to write this book, Sir Keir has arguably shown more of himself than he perhaps realised. Far from shrugging his shoulders or brandishing that most lethal of political weapons, a sense of humour, he has instead given every indication that he tends to be overly cautious and somewhat defensive. Furthermore, his response has done a fine job in convincing me that he thinks it would be perfectly acceptable for him to move into 10 Downing Street without a book of this kind asking some probing questions about him in a truly unrestrained way. Given that most of Sir

Keir's career has been spent outside elected politics – he was a barrister from 1987 until 2008; the Director of Public Prosecutions (DPP) from 2008 to 2013; and only became a Labour parliamentary candidate in December 2014 – this point cannot be dismissed.

Despite Sir Keir's wishes, I am pleased to be able to say that many people who have known him at various stages of his life were happy to help with this book. Some did so publicly; others preferred to do so anonymously. Given that Sir Keir may one day reach Downing Street, I am well aware that those in the latter category have perhaps decided that it would be unwise to upset the man who might be able to offer them a position in his government or in some other area of public life.

The job of Leader of the Opposition is often considered to be the worst in British politics. Neil Kinnock, who led the Labour Party from 1983 until 1992, once described it as 'purgatory', which is probably the only summary needed to illustrate how difficult a task it can be. To be so close to power and at the same time to be so far from it must surely be a form of torture for those who aspire to serve in the highest office in the land. In 2021, with the Labour Party going through a difficult period of self-examination, to be a Labour Leader of the Opposition is arguably harder still.

When this latecomer to elected politics arrived in the House of Commons in 2015, aged fifty-two, he had a profile that was significantly higher than that of most back-bench MPs and probably many frontbenchers, too. This came courtesy of his five-year term as DPP. He raised his profile further still by taking up the post of shadow Secretary of State for Exiting the European Union from 2016 until 2020, a period when his brief was the main focus of politicians and the media in Britain and around the world. That he was stubbornly against Brexit marked him out as a heroic figure for many around the country.

His climb up the greasy pole continued in April 2020, when he was elected leader of the Labour Party. To a degree, he dashed the hopes of some in Labour's ranks by achieving this goal; the desire for a woman to be in charge for the first time in the party's history was strong. Nonetheless, it was widely considered refreshing that Sir Keir, who had not rolled off Westminster's production line of career politicians, was taking the helm after only five years in the Commons. Furthermore, it was broadly welcomed that he had led a successful professional life outside of politics, much like many MPs of a bygone era.

Yet the truth is that Sir Keir, who is hard to read at the best of times, is easily portrayed as a man of contradictions. Having attended a fee-paying school and the University of Leeds, gone on to study for a year at the University of Oxford, become a successful barrister, then a QC, been appointed Director of Public Prosecutions, accepted a knighthood and finally entered the Commons, he is undeniably a member of the establishment. And yet despite having succeeded in life thanks to his own hard work, he seems always to be at pains to distance himself from the establishment by speaking so often of his 'working-class' roots and his socialism. It is as though he is worried that the public will think less of him for having done well off his own bat.

At the time of writing, a little over a year has passed since Sir Keir became Labour leader, and it is undeniable that some commentators have begun to wonder if the party's outlook under him is just too narrow. Others have questioned whether he is the right man to lead Labour. Some have even doubted if Labour itself has a future. Following an appalling set of local election results in May 2021, plus the loss of the parliamentary constituency of Hartlepool to the Conservatives in a by-election, Tony Blair, Labour's most electorally successful Prime Minister, attacked Sir Keir in the pages of the New Statesman for lacking a 'compelling economic message'. Blair added: 'And the cultural message, because he is not clarifying it, is being defined by the "woke" left, whose every statement gets cut-through courtesy of the right.' None of this has made Sir Keir's job any easier.

It is also only fair to point out that things were more straightforward for Blair. He became party leader at a time when the governing Conservative Party had been in power for fifteen years and, under John Major, had run out of road. Sir Keir took over Labour when the Tories had just won an eighty-seat parliamentary majority under their new leader, Boris Johnson (though, remarkably, the party had already been in power for almost a decade by that point). Moreover, there is irrefutable evidence that Labour's pool of parliamentary talent is shallower now than it was in the 1990s. Labour had close to 300 MPs when Blair took over the party; Sir Keir was one of only 202 Labour MPs to be returned to the House of Commons after the catastrophic electoral defeat of 2019. Another striking statistic that tells its own story is that whereas six of the twenty-one MPs in Blair's first Cabinet in 1997 represented a Scottish constituency, Labour had only one MP in the whole of Scotland at the time Sir Keir took the party's reins. British politics has changed significantly in the space of a generation. Without being able to rely on dozens of MPs in Scotland for support, the leader of the Labour Party has an even steeper hill to climb.

What may have made Sir Keir's challenge greater still is that, beginning with Blair in 1994, four of Labour's last five leaders were long-term residents of north London at the time they were elected to run their party. The last three of these men – Ed Miliband, Jeremy Corbyn and Sir Keir – live within a short drive of each other's houses, feeding the narrative that the bond between Labour's leadership and the provincial working-class vote on which the party was built is torn and frayed. It is not difficult to see why a view has taken hold that Labour has become a party run by and for people who embody the liberal and metropolitan elite. The question is whether Sir Keir's personality is big enough and well-defined enough to achieve the undeniable popularity that both Blair and Corbyn achieved in different ways, or whether he is more like Gordon Brown or Ed Miliband. This book sets out to explore Sir Keir's experiences and temperament with a view to seeing if he is equipped to make the tricky transition from his current predicament to Downing Street.

CHAPTER 1

'THE POSHER THE VOICE, THE MORE VULGAR THEY ARE'

Any mention of the county of Surrey tends to inspire in some people's minds the hackneyed idea that everybody who lives there owns a large house, works in the City of London and belongs to at least one members-only club. This stereotypical view, given credence by the label that the area is quintessential Stockbroker Belt territory, certainly has a ring of truth to it. Yet it is also undoubtedly simplistic. The upbringing of the self-declared socialist Sir Keir Starmer, who was raised and went to school in Surrey, serves as adequate proof that it has also always been home to people of more ordinary means, no matter how aspirational they are. The question becomes whether Starmer's background can be considered truly working class, as he has often been at pains to suggest when making his pitch to the electorate, or whether he is really a 'posh Trotskyist', as some newspapers have claimed.

Tracing his paternal line back to the early nineteenth century, it is clear that four of the five generations of Starmers that came before his were solidly working class. His great-great-great-grandfather, George Starmer, was born in Lincolnshire in 1819 and was a labourer there until his death in 1870. His son, also called George, began life as a farm labourer in the same county before marrying a servant, Matilda Buswell, and moving to Yorkshire in 1890, where he was employed as

1

a gamekeeper and then became a farmer. Their son, the colourfully named Gustavus Adolphus Starmer, who was Keir's great-grandfather, was born in 1882, also in Lincolnshire. He, too, was a gamekeeper though by 1907, he and his wife, Katherine, had moved south to the small Surrey town of Oxted. This began the Starmers' connection with the region, which continues to this day via Keir Starmer's younger sister, also called Katherine, who still lives in the Oxted area close to where she and her siblings were brought up.

During the First World War, Gustavus was a driver in the Army Service Corps. In 1917, he was found to be unfit for service because of heart disease. He was granted a gratuity of £35 and awarded the Silver War Badge, which was given to those who were honourably discharged due to wounds or illness. He died in April 1974, when Keir was eleven years old, and was still a resident of Surrey at that time. Gustavus's son – and therefore Keir's grandfather – was Herbert Starmer, known as Bert, who was born in 1905. Although he was born in Liverpool, he lived and worked in Surrey almost all his life. According to the 1939 Register, the national census compiled by the British government on the outbreak of the Second World War, he was at that time an agricultural wheelwright based in the village of Woldingham. Later, in the 1960s, he worked there as a mechanic at a garage. His wife, Doris, who was Keir's grandmother, was born in Surrey in 1907. The couple had four children – three boys and a girl. Their third son, Rodney, was Keir's father. He was born in 1934 and grew up in Woldingham. Rodney was certainly born into a situation most people would accept as being 'working class'. It is debatable, though, whether he can be described as having stayed in that social bracket throughout his life or whether, for reasons which will be shown, he managed to open a door through which his children could potentially make their way in order to live what would surely be thought of as a more middle-class existence.

Being overly critical of private individuals whom one has never met is never wise, particularly if, like Rodney Starmer, they are no longer alive to explain themselves. With that said, however, when researching this book, it has been noticeable that he was not considered by every interviewee who encountered him to be an easy man to know. On a visit in late 2020 to the street on the outskirts of Oxted in which he lived from 1963 until his death in 2018, for example, those neighbours who felt qualified to discuss his personality agreed to do so on an 'off the record' basis only. The reason for their polite reticence was soon clear. Speaking of an often scruffily dressed man, who wore a pair of shorts and a T-shirt on most days of the year and who sported an almost Victorian-era beard for much of his adult life, they variously described him as 'eccentric' and 'a bit of a strange character'. One neighbour said, 'The Starmers were staunchly Labour, and many others round here were Conservative. At election times their house would be plastered with Labour posters.' When asked if a clash of political views might have influenced their attitude to Rodney Starmer, they insisted this was not the case. With some reluctance, one of them added, 'He was just not very nice.'

An acquaintance of Rodney's also mentioned that he could remember receiving a round robin Christmas letter from him in December 2014 which contained at least one barbed comment – something he thought rather incongruous given the context. In the letter, a copy of which this person was willing to share, Rodney did indeed refer bluntly at one point to 'some of the residents in Oxted', of whom he clearly disapproved. In what sounds rather like a battle cry from a class warfare activist, he wrote of these residents: 'The posher the voice, the more vulgar they are.' As sweeping generalisations go, this one does seem to be somewhat gratuitous and may be said to shed some light on his personality and views, which those who knew him have all made clear

3

were unmistakably left-wing. To what extent such views shaped the outlook of his children is an open question, but it has to be considered at the very least possible that his judgement might have rubbed off on an impressionable young mind. Andrew Cooper, a childhood friend of Keir Starmer, says his recollection is that whenever Keir spoke of his father, 'He was always described as quite strict.'[1] Another friend, Paul Vickers, has said:

> Keir's dad was a very powerful, almost slightly intimidating, figure, a very big man and was always very principled. He was probably what you might call somebody from the traditional Labour left. I'm pretty sure that's where Keir picked up his first political insights: from his dad. His father ... would always ask you, and ask Keir, questions which revolved around politics. He expected us to be interested in politics.[2]

Tony Alston, a friend of Rodney's who knew him through their shared interest in competitive cycling, also suggested that his was a slightly unusual personality. '[Rodney] was what one might call a character,' Alston says.[3] 'He was one of those bluff but really kind-hearted people. He would turn up to a funeral wearing green plus twos and a baggy top. He was perfectly respectable; he was just unconventional.' Alston knew him mainly through the long-established Southern Counties Cycling Union, of which Rodney, a cycling enthusiast throughout his life, was president for several years. He suggested that some people who were involved in organising and running cycling events avoided getting on the wrong side of Rodney.

> I never argued with [Rodney] because I don't argue with people, but, if he had a view, he wanted it his way. Certainly, he would fight his

4

corner, but not in an unpleasant way as far as I remember. He was certainly popular in his own club, but he could be a trifle awkward if he thought he was right and you were wrong.

In view of the mixed feelings which Rodney Starmer seems to have generated among some of his friends and acquaintances, perhaps it is fairest to rely for a character reference on the man who spent more time with him than all those quoted: his eldest son. When he was interviewed on BBC Radio 4's *Desert Island Discs* in November 2020, Keir Starmer said: 'I don't often talk about my dad. He was a difficult man, a complicated man. He kept himself to himself. He didn't particularly like to socialise so wouldn't really go out very much, but he was incredibly hardworking.' He added: 'I understood who he was and what he was, but we weren't close.'

By contrast, his mother, Josephine, seems to have been far more popular. Those same neighbours who were so reluctant to talk openly about Rodney Starmer described his wife in glowing terms as a kind and friendly woman who was always cheerful. They were quick to add that they believed all four of her children had inherited her good nature. She was born in Woldingham in July 1939, four months after her parents' marriage and six weeks before the outbreak of war. Her father, Ronald Baker, who was also born in Surrey, was an electrical engineer. The 1939 Register records his profession as a driver and fitter for road passenger transport. The origins of her mother, Marjorie, are less clear, though it appears she died in Croydon, Surrey, in 1959. Looking back to the beginning of the nineteenth century, Josephine's forebears were employed in a wide range of jobs every bit as humble as those done by the Starmers. Records show that among her ancestors was an attendant in a Surrey County Council lunatic asylum, a printer, a miller, a general labourer, a servant and a laundress.

Josephine's path through life was far from straightforward. By the time she was ten years old, a recurring pain in her joints caused her parents to seek medical advice. Eventually, she was sent to Guy's Hospital in London for tests. There, aged eleven, she was diagnosed with juvenile idiopathic arthritis, also known as Still's disease; so called because the condition was first described by the English paediatrician George Still in 1896. This rare illness, the cause of which remains unknown, is characterised by fever and rashes as well as joint pain, and it can have a profoundly destabilising effect on those who live with it. The symptoms and frequency of episodes vary between individuals and are hard to predict. Sadly, Josephine was not spared the worst of what the disease is capable of inflicting.

According to the eulogy given at her funeral in 2015, she was quickly taken under the wing of the consultant who was in charge of her, Dr Kenneth Maclean. As Josephine was facing the prospect of being confined to a wheelchair for the rest of her life, Maclean was granted permission by her parents to, in effect, experiment on her with the new steroid cortisone. It had never been administered to children before the 1950s, but it had been shown to reduce swelling in the joints of adults suffering with rheumatism. In Josephine's case, it proved something of a wonder drug, enabling her to live a fuller life for much longer than might otherwise have been the case, albeit with consequences for her physical health as she entered middle age and beyond.

Josephine had to spend a considerable amount of time in hospital during her childhood, but that fact did not prevent her from passing the entrance exam to Whyteleafe County Grammar School for Girls in Surrey. It was while she was a pupil there, aged sixteen, that she first met Rodney Starmer, at a local dinner and dance being held by the cycling club of which he was a member. They struck up a close friendship immediately, despite a five-year age gap. By then, he had left

Purley County Grammar School, had completed two years' national service with the Royal Electrical and Mechanical Engineers and was apprenticed to a local toolmaking firm. After Josephine left school, she became a student nurse at Guy's Hospital, allowing her to maintain her contact with Dr Maclean, whose pioneering treatment improved her quality of life so markedly and guaranteed that she remained able to walk. Her friendship with this highly respected doctor had one further, significant benefit. When she and Rodney married in the late summer of 1960, he was a guest at their wedding. According to Rodney, who delivered the aforementioned eulogy, he took the couple aside at their reception and told them quietly that if they intended to start a family, the unknown side effects on Josephine of the cortisone treatment meant they should not wait. He also promised Josephine that if she ever had any children, he would arrange personally for her to give birth to them at Guy's.

In a demonstration of how robust Josephine remained as a young woman, she and Rodney took their honeymoon in the Lake District. There, Rodney wanted to share with his new bride his passion for climbing hills and mountains – an activity he had first enjoyed a few years previously when visiting the Dolomites in northern Italy. They stayed at the Dower House guesthouse in the grounds of Wray Castle on the western side of Lake Windermere and, not yet owning a car, made their way around the area by bus. Halfway through the holiday, and having already climbed eight mountains, they got into difficulties on Loughrigg Fell, a situation that was exacerbated by Josephine's lack of stamina compared to her husband. By chance, they soon came across a pipe-smoking middle-aged man who was sitting on a rock with a sketching pad. Showing some concern, he asked if they were alright and, noting Josephine's obvious exhaustion, advised them on the best way to descend the great hill.

The following day, they explained to Barbara Smith, the landlady of their guesthouse, the circumstances of this brief meeting. She told them that the man who had helped them was almost certainly her friend, Alfred Wainwright. He was already reasonably well known by then in Britain as a fellwalker, author and illustrator, but he would go on to become a television personality who sold millions of books, many of which are still in print today. The best known of these is *A Pictorial Guide to the Lakeland Fells*, a seven-volume series detailing the hills and peaks of the Lake District, which is still regarded by many walkers as the definitive guide to the Lakeland mountains. Mrs Smith arranged for the Starmers to see Wainwright again the following year when they returned to the area. They got on well, and this resulted in a friendship which lasted for the next thirty years, until Wainwright's death in 1991. The Starmers also remained on good terms with Wainwright's second wife, Betty, until she died in 2008.

Rodney Starmer believed that Wainwright – who, not unlike himself, had a reputation as a rather gruff man of few words – acted as a crucial beacon of hope to Josephine over those three decades. He was always kind to her and concerned about her condition, and he would write to her when her illness flared up and left her bedbound or, as was often the case, in hospital. He is also said to have inspired her to continue climbing as many of the Lake District's fells as she could by ending his letters to her with the words 'Get well, the hills are waiting for you.' Such was the respect the Starmers accorded Wainwright that Rodney confessed in *Encounters with Wainwright*, a book of tributes which was published by the Wainwright Society in 2016, that he and Josephine 'shed a tear' when they read his obituary in *The Guardian*. He also declared that both of them 'loved him like a father'.

It is clear that Cumbria itself became equally important in the lives of Rodney and Josephine Starmer, for they visited there at least once a year throughout their marriage until 2014, the year before Josephine's death. Despite her increasing incapacity, the couple managed to 'claim', or scale, 212 of the 214 Wainwright fells – an achievement which gave them much joy. This impressive statistic also features in *Encounters with Wainwright*, which, furthermore, includes a list of the health problems that dogged Josephine as the years passed by. They included her twice needing new knee and hip joints; her contraction of the MRSA superbug in hospital in 2000; and, finally, a fall in 2008 which broke a femur and resulted in her having a leg amputated just above the knee. In fact, this fall occurred while they were in the Lake District and required them to be driven by ambulance from there to London, where the operation was performed. Remarkably, thanks to Rodney's engineering ingenuity, even after the partial loss of a limb and when Josephine was confined to a titanium wheelchair, they continued to climb to heights of more than 2,000ft. The modifications Rodney made to the chair meant it could cope with the terrain. He also designed a walking frame for his wife.

Rodney and Josephine took seriously the advice offered to them in 1960 by Dr Maclean about having children as early as possible. Having married, Rodney took a job as a works manager at a large toolmaking firm at Ashford in Kent. In a sure sign that they were keen to upend their own working-class roots, the young couple secured a mortgage which allowed them to buy a bungalow on the edge of Romney Marsh. In June 1961, Josephine gave birth to their eldest child, Anna. On 2 September 1962, Keir was born. It has become standard practice in media reports to state as fact that he was named after Keir Hardie, a founder of the Labour Party and its first parliamentary leader, yet Starmer admitted in one interview in 2015 that he had no evidence for this because he had never discussed it with his parents.[4] Still, this idea has stuck, and he has never disabused anybody of it. Anna and

Keir were followed in March 1964 by twins Nicholas and, thirty-two minutes later, Katherine. Thanks to Dr Maclean, all the siblings were born at Guy's Hospital, despite the fact the family lived nowhere near the London Borough of Southwark, where it is situated. For any young woman in good health, the relentless nature of having to look after four young children who were born within three years of each other would be a challenge. That Josephine Starmer managed this task seems nothing short of extraordinary, particularly because her own mother was not alive to help her.

Shortly after Keir's birth, the family settled at 23 Tanhouse Road, a three-bedroom semi-detached house close to the commuter town of Oxted, which sits at the foot of the North Downs. The house was built alongside a few dozen identical properties between 1928 and 1930. With barely more than 1,100sq. ft of floorspace and only one small bathroom, it would have been cramped for a family of six, particularly as the children grew older. A two-plate Aga in the kitchen was perhaps the only outward sign of what might be thought of as anything approaching domestic luxury. The house had a driveway at the front, on which was eventually parked the family's Ford Cortina, and a back garden overlooking several acres of undeveloped land, meaning it was in an open and bright position. Today, Tanhouse Road is a reasonably busy thoroughfare, but its semi-rural location means it remains pleasant. Horses graze in the surrounding fields and a brook flows yards from what would have been the Starmers' front door. In the 1960s and 1970s, when there were fewer cars on Britain's roads, it must have been a relatively peaceful place in which to live. As a young boy, Keir had other children to play with locally, too.

Diana Watson, who was the same age as Starmer, says she can remember visiting him at home as a little girl about fifty years ago. 'I went to Keir's house for a birthday party or something,' she says.[5]

Their house was very modest. Even though Surrey is traditionally quite affluent, they came from a very modest background. Surrey is thought of as being very much part of the Stockbroker Belt, but east Surrey is really quite rural. It's near the Kent border. The Starmers were unpretentious. They were normal people.

She adds:

I remember his mother had curly brown hair and brown eyes, and I'm sure I remember noticing her hands were mis-shaped and asking my mother what was wrong with them, and she told me Mrs Starmer had arthritis. She had very kind eyes. I think they were quite like Keir's in a way.

Paul Vickers recalled visiting the house when Keir was in his teens and found it to be somewhat chaotic but friendly: 'I used to love going there. It was always like a building site and there were holes in the wall, there was bits of masonry missing. It was always as though they were trying to finish the house but never actually got quite around to completing the job.'[6]

Having moved to Tanhouse Road in 1963, Rodney Starmer continued to work in the toolmaking trade, but, due to his eldest son's ambiguous explanations, there has always been a certain amount of confusion as to his employment status. This uncertainty justifies examining the complicated question of whether he could objectively be thought of as working class or whether he was in fact a member of the middle classes. In March 2018, Keir Starmer gave an interview to BBC presenter Nick Robinson, in which he discussed his father's career. He said he 'was a toolmaker working in a factory and working every hour, basically'. He added:

My dad was a toolmaker, he was a very good toolmaker, but he had to live through the policies of Margaret Thatcher, and that decimated manufacturing. I remember distinctly, he went out to work at eight o'clock in the morning, came back at six o'clock for his tea, and went back to work till ten o'clock at night.[7]

The following year, he again talked about his father's occupation, telling the BBC Radio 4 *Today* programme that he 'worked in a factory' as a toolmaker.[8] And during a subsequent interview on *Desert Island Discs*, he returned to the pattern of his father's working day, this time changing the hour that his father returned home after his first shift, saying:

He worked as a toolmaker on a factory floor all of his life, and my enduring memory as a child was him, as he did, go[ing] to work at eight o'clock in the morning. He came home at five o'clock for his tea, went back at six o'clock and worked through till ten o'clock at night, and that was five days a week.

The inference that listeners to any of these broadcasts might have drawn is that Rodney Starmer was employed by somebody else, perhaps even in a lowly capacity, and may have been one of many toolmakers who toiled at a works. Yet the available evidence suggests this was not the case. For reasons best known to himself, Keir Starmer did not use any of these opportunities to explain that his father in fact ran his own business, the Oxted Tool Company. Initially, he operated from a unit on a farm in the Hurst Green area, close to where he lived. When this premises was no longer available, he moved to a light industrial estate at Gaywood Farm in the village of Edenbridge, just over the nearby county border in Kent. Nicky Kerman, who still runs the site, says he can recall Rodney Starmer well because he was a 'cheerful chap with a big beard', who was one of the first people to rent a workshop there.

> He was in Unit A, which is probably about 1,500sq. ft in all, and he almost always worked alone, to the best of my knowledge. He gave it up to look after his wife in the 1990s, as far as I'm aware. I think he specialised in making tools for other people. I remember he had a lot of machines and was clearly very good at his job.[9]

A Companies House representative said that, as of January 2021, no records of the Oxted Tool Company exist in its historical files. This makes it difficult to assess how successful Rodney Starmer's business became and indicates that he may have remained a sole trader – as opposed to running a limited company – throughout his working life. Keir Starmer did specify that money was tight when he was growing up, saying in 2019 that 'there were many times when the electricity and the telephone bill didn't get paid'.[10] This suggests that the business may have struggled at times. It is thought that if he did ever employ other people, he did so only on a small scale or on an ad hoc basis. He was certainly more than an ordinary labourer, however. Indeed, his friend Tony Alston says Rodney Starmer told him he had once secured a piece of work from a government department. 'Rodney was a precision engineer,' says Alston.

> At one time he was very left-wing. His company won a job working for the Ministry of Defence. I don't know if it's true, but he always used to say, 'I rang them up and pointed out I was left-wing,' and they said, 'We know exactly what you're like, Mr Starmer, and we've offered you the contract,' so he took the contract.

Alston adds: 'He used to do jobs that people couldn't get done elsewhere.

It was machine work, high-quality stuff. I'm under the impression that he employed other engineers from time to time.'

While it is fair to say that a person's own sense of who they are and of the class they feel they belong to certainly matters, it is hard to accept that Rodney Starmer was a straight-up-and-down member of the working class, as his son has often suggested. This poses the important question of how Keir Starmer regards himself. When, in December 2019, he hinted publicly that he was considering standing to succeed Jeremy Corbyn as Labour leader, he tackled this topic by telling the BBC Radio 4 *Today* programme:

> And as for the sort of middle-class thrust, as you know, my dad worked in a factory, he was a toolmaker, and my mum was a nurse, and she contracted a very rare disease very early in her life that meant she was constantly in need of NHS care, so actually my background isn't what [people] think it is.

Technically, everything he said on that occasion in relation to his father is true, of course. Yet as a skilled manual worker who was self-employed and who owned a house (albeit with a mortgage), it is certainly arguable that Rodney Starmer would be thought of by some social scientists as being a cut above other toolmakers who *did* work in factories for other people. None of this would matter in any way, of course, but for the fact that Keir Starmer has not been totally explicit about it when asked, presumably for self-protective reasons.

Aside from their cycling and walking hobbies, Rodney Starmer and his wife enjoyed opera and classical music, and they would regularly attend plays and concerts all over Surrey, especially at the Barn Theatre in Oxted, which is known for amateur dramatics. Its chairman,

Bruce Reed, describes them as 'a lovely couple' who would often attend the same musical two or three times because they enjoyed it so much. He says, 'Rod would do anything for anyone. They were both salt of the earth.'[11] He also remembers that, in 2005, they posed happily for a photograph at the theatre with the Duke of Kent, the Queen's first cousin, to mark the occasion when he opened a £300,000 extension containing a new wheelchair lift. In view of Rodney's previously mentioned comments about a 'posh voice' being indicative of a 'vulgar' person, it is amusing to reflect on Reed's account of the reverence Rodney showed the visiting royal. Reed adds: 'Rod usually insisted on wearing shorts, apart from the one day that the Duke of Kent visited. He told me he'd been out and bought a pair of trousers especially for the occasion. He was a shorts and sandals and socks man throughout the year otherwise.'

Family holidays were always spent in the Lake District, though, perhaps oddly, the Starmers never took their children to meet Alfred Wainwright during these visits, fearing they would intrude on his privacy. Another of Josephine's enthusiasms was keeping donkeys, and from the 1970s, they usually had at least two of these beasts living in their back garden. Rodney even became a director of the Donkey Breed Society, a national charity. They also offered a home to dogs that had been abandoned or needed to be rescued. All this was fitted in around Josephine's thirst for knowledge and education. In the mid-1970s, she enrolled with the Open University and received a degree after three years of study. Religion is not thought to have played an especially prominent role in the lives of the Starmers, though Josephine is understood to have attended a local church into her eighties. Keir has been open about being an atheist, telling one interviewer in April 2021 when asked if he believes in God: 'This is going to sound odd, but

I do believe in faith. I've a lot of time and respect for faith. I am not of faith; I don't believe in God, but I can see the power of faith and the way it brings people together.'[12]

As a result of Josephine's illness and Rodney's unsociable working hours, there were few adult visitors to the house during Keir's childhood. The family lived under the appalling shadow of Josephine suddenly having to be admitted to a high-dependency unit. Such was Rodney's devotion to his wife that he stopped drinking alcohol so he would be able to accompany her to hospital at any hour of the day or night if need be. There, he would remain with her for as long as necessary, sleeping in a chair if it came to it. He became so well versed in her illness that he knew exactly what symptoms to watch out for and what combination of drugs she was to take depending on her state. Keir has even recalled a time when he was aged thirteen or fourteen, and his father rang him from a hospital to warn: 'I don't think your mum's going to make it. Will you tell the others?'[13] Such unwanted and painful responsibility, placed on his shoulders at a young age, certainly forced him to grow up quickly and perhaps to take life more seriously than most of his peers. Inevitably, as shall become clear, it left its mark on his personality as well.

The four Starmer siblings were all sent to a primary school in the village of Merle Common, approximately four miles from Tanhouse Road. It was a small, Victorian building with only about fifty pupils and is described by Diana Watson, who lived next door to it and was an exact contemporary of Keir Starmer, as 'rather sweet and idyllic'. It has long since closed. She says: 'It was an old, purpose-built village school with an outside toilet block and a little village hall over the road where we would go for dancing and other activities.' She says one abiding memory she has of this time is that Keir was 'very protective' of his younger brother, Nicholas, who was apparently prone to 'making mischief'. Starmer has also discussed his brother in passing, once saying:

> My brother struggled at school, whereas I did alright, and I remember my parents instilling in me that we were both as successful as each other and that you always measured what people were dealing with in front of them, and so they never singled me out as a golden boy. They were proud; they wanted me to do what I did; but they always brought it back to, 'And your brother's doing just as well in what he's doing,' so now I never use the word that someone is 'thick' or 'stupid' or not able to do things. I hate that language. Or that people are 'bright'. I see it completely differently: that people are very good in different fields at what they do, and we measure them in that way.[14]

Nicholas has lived in the north of England for some years and has worked as a mechanic. Of his other siblings, Katherine is married and lives in Oxted with her husband and children. Anna is believed to have worked in the NHS.

When they were aged eight, Keir and his classmates moved to the newly built Holland Middle School nearby. Diana Watson joined him there and, like him, sat the 11-plus examination in order to determine whether, from September 1974, they would attend the local comprehensive school, Oxted County School, or one of Surrey's grammar schools. Diana says that she has no memory of the school forcing them to work particularly hard in order to prepare for this rigorous test, perhaps because there was less competition for it at the time. In any case, she says, Starmer's work ethic and attention to detail was already on show by then, in contrast to the vast majority of his classmates, suggesting that he did not need to be pushed. She says:

Holland Middle School was in a bigger catchment area, so there were kids from Hurst Green who went there as well. It was the feeder for Oxted County School, a comprehensive which at that time was less desirable than it is now. Keir was quite hardworking and serious. In our year, probably four or five pupils got into a grammar school. Keir was one of them; I was another.

There is no question that his passing the 11-plus was a source of great pride to his family, not least because his elder sister, Anna, did not go to a grammar school. Indeed, of the four Starmer siblings, Keir would be the only one to take this academic route through his senior school career. His parents decided that he would go to Reigate Grammar School, some twelve miles from their house – a distance long enough to require him to catch a bus every day. It is striking that it was on these bus journeys that he would forge some of his thoughts about politics, religion, justice and equality, therefore marking not just the beginning of the next phase of his life but also the birth of his belief system.

Having considered Keir Starmer's background, perhaps it would be most accurate to say that it was neither 'working class' in the strictest sense nor 'posh', as some journalists have attempted to prove, but was instead closer to what some sociologists and academics would in years gone by have called petit bourgeois. This French term, akin to lower-middle-class, is one that would undoubtedly be well understood by Starmer, whose deep interest in Marxist theory was to fill hundreds of hours of his time as a young man.

CHAPTER 2

SCHOOLBOY SOCIALIST

When Keir Starmer entered Reigate Grammar School in September 1974, it was on the cusp of great change. Having been founded in 1675, it was one of the oldest and most traditional educational establishments in the country. Set in grounds close to the centre of the market town of Reigate, it was not a particularly grand place, but it did bear many of the characteristics of a public school. It was academically selective; it was open to boys only; it operated a house system; masters wore gowns; rugby took precedence over football; there was a thriving Combined Cadet Force; corporal punishment was standard practice; and a steady stream of alumni went to Oxbridge. Such outward projections of exclusivity might have appealed to a certain type of parent in Surrey, but, for a host of reasons, one would not have thought automatically that Rodney and Josephine Starmer would be among them. Not only did they support Labour, a party whose ideological opposition to such institutions was well known, but the school was in fact fee-paying for most of the time that their son was a pupil there – something many people in left-wing circles considered to be beyond the pale, even if they could afford to educate their child privately. In the recent past, Starmer has been accused of deliberately concealing his attendance at Reigate Grammar, so, given the level of public comment his apparent defensiveness over his secondary education has attracted, it is worth examining how this toolmaker's son ended up at an independent school before considering the impact of this experience on his life and career.

One of the biggest political battles being fought during Starmer's schooldays related to the very path on which his parents set him: the fairness of selective education in England and Wales. This vexed question had dominated British politics for decades. Rodney Starmer's assumed political hero, Keir Hardie, had even spoken about the issue during the previous century. It was reported in the *Westminster Gazette* on 1 August 1896 that Hardie had attended an international conference of socialists, and he was quoted afterwards as saying that he believed everybody should receive a full education which was 'free at all stages, open to everyone without any tests of prior attainment at any age – in effect, a comprehensive "broad highway" that all could travel'.[1] Attitudes towards the 11-plus examination specifically and grammar schools in general had only intensified since the 1950s, and many radicals and progressives considered the entire system to be nothing short of immoral. A central charge was that grammar schools created a publicly funded elite whose members were destined for university, while those children who did not attend them had to make do with lesser expectations. All this was said by detractors to reinforce social divisions.

This was the backdrop to the decision in 1965 by Harold Wilson's Labour government to instruct all 163 local authorities in England and Wales to close the 1,200 or so grammar schools which existed and replace them with non-selective comprehensive schools. Although this comprehensivisation process picked up speed during its first five years, its rhythm was interrupted in June 1970, after the Conservative Party won the general election. The new Prime Minister, Ted Heath, appointed Margaret Thatcher as his Secretary of State for Education and Science.

As the product of a grammar school herself, Thatcher believed in academic selection as the best way for bright children from poorer backgrounds to advance through life. Although she accepted the idea of non-selective education (indeed she approved 3,286 comprehensives during the forty-four months she held the Education brief),[2] she also wanted to protect good schools. In this vein, her first act as Education Secretary was to overturn Labour's policy and issue what was known in her department as Circular 10/70. This directive meant that no education authority should be forced any longer to subscribe to the blanket policy of comprehensivisation. Education therefore became a matter of choice at a local level, potentially allowing some grammar schools to determine their own fate rather than having change thrust upon them. The importance of a common education for everybody may have been dear to many within the Labour Party, but Rodney Starmer was on Thatcher's side of the argument when it came to the schooling of a member of his own family. He believed in having options rather than adhering to diktats.

The headmaster of Reigate Grammar School throughout Starmer's seven years there was Howard Ballance. He had been in post since 1968 and was of a conservative frame of mind. Some boys nicknamed him 'Slimey' because, according to one former pupil, 'he had a habit of creeping about and peeping through classroom windowpanes and then caning anybody who was misbehaving'. Whatever his charges may have thought of him during their schooldays, however, Ballance is remembered as a man who was devoted to his job. He was of the generation of schoolmasters which had served in the army during the Second World War, but that didn't mean he was an authoritarian figure. For example, he made a point of memorising the Christian names of all 700 pupils in his care at a time when most teachers referred to boys by their surnames only. He was also aware that as the head of a county grammar school, he was responsible for boys from every social background, some of whom were less privileged than others. He would even liaise with the local police if a boy got into a scrape which might have led to him being charged with an offence, persuading officers to allow him to deal with the problem. He cared deeply about the ethos of his grammar school and the success of those in it. During his fourteen-year stewardship, Reigate Grammar prospered, with improved exam results, greater sporting success and more emphasis on drama, music and the Duke of Edinburgh's Award. Most crucially of all, however, Ballance is credited with saving Reigate Grammar School from being incorporated into the comprehensive system and with setting it on a new course, of which Keir Starmer was a direct beneficiary.

Reigate Grammar School was set up in the seventeenth century by Henry Smith, an alderman of London, when he bequeathed £150 towards the purchase of land for a 'free school'. Later, it was linked to the local parish church of St Mary's, until the mid-nineteenth century when it was reformed as an independent establishment. After this, it developed and expanded, leading to a Victorian building programme, the results of which still stand today. In the early twentieth century, the county began paying for able boys to attend the school as well, but by the time of Starmer's arrival, it stood at a crossroads. Three decades earlier it had opted to be taken over by Surrey County Council under the terms of the 1944 Education Act. This meant it became a voluntary-controlled school. The school's foundation owned most of its land and buildings and appointed some of the school governors, and the local authority funded the school and employed the staff.

Although Surrey County Council was dominated by the Conservatives, there was great enthusiasm among its reform-minded members for scrapping Reigate Grammar and creating a new comprehensive school and a new sixth form college in Reigate. When Ballance learned of this in March 1971, he took legal advice from a London law firm, Blyth Dutton, about how to break free of local authority control and, through Mrs Thatcher's adjustment, revert to independent status. Two months later, on 23 May, the chairman of the school's governors, Albert Channing Owens, wrote to Thatcher explaining that, following a vote, the governors wished to apply to discontinue as a voluntary-controlled school and become fee-paying. This request was made under Section 14 of the 1944 Education Act. The letter stated that the school had made financial arrangements with the Crusader Insurance Company Ltd, of Reigate, to buy from the local education authority any property and equipment not already owned by its foundation. Noting that it was bound to give two years' notice to disentangle itself from the tentacles of Surrey's education authority, it was also made clear that Reigate Grammar hoped to reopen as a fee-paying school in September 1973. Owens summarised the decision as follows:

> The governors feel that there is a place and a need in the educational system of this country for grammar schools and that a school such as Reigate, approaching the tercentenary of its foundation, has much to offer that cannot be found in other types of educational establishments. It is the governors' opinion that in view of the County Council's proposals the essential nature of the school can only be preserved for all time by its becoming independent.

This move by a voluntary-controlled school was considered worthy of national attention. *The Times* picked up the story a few days later, quoting the chairman of the governors as saying:

> We feel there is a great need in our part of Surrey for the sort of

education we offer. There are 700 boys in the school, which is about the right number. The governors have agreed to the plan and now have been told that the teachers are 100 per cent behind it. Indeed there is absolutely no doubt that many would go elsewhere if we went comprehensive.

It seems highly unlikely that anybody in Surrey who took an interest in education at that time would have been unaware that the future of Reigate Grammar was being fought over, and that, one way or another, it was on course to become a very different kind of school. Interested parties would almost certainly have included Rodney and Josephine Starmer, because their eldest son's 11-plus exam was beginning to show on the horizon.

Surprisingly, more than two years passed before any meaningful response from Thatcher was forthcoming. Then, on 21 June 1973, a representative of hers in the Department for Education wrote to Owens to explain that the Secretary of State could not accept the application. The department's letter stated that 'after full and careful consideration of all the information before her, [Thatcher] is not prepared to grant the leave sought'. The reason given for this decision was that Thatcher considered the application to be 'inappropriate at the present time'. The school was advised that a second application could be made but 'only in association with proposals submitted by the local education authority under Section 13 relating to other maintained schools which would, if approved by [Thatcher], have the effect of leaving no place for the school in its present form'. The plans of Ballance and the governors were frustrated, forcing them back into talks with Surrey County Council.

Just over six months later, in February 1974, a snap general election was called by Ted Heath, which resulted in a hung parliament. Labour, still led by Harold Wilson, returned to government and Thatcher was replaced as the Secretary of State for Education by the Labour MP Reginald Prentice. By this point, Keir Starmer had passed his 11-plus. Then, in June 1974, three months before he started at Reigate Grammar, the *Surrey Mirror* reported it was 'almost certain' that the school would become fee-paying after the council's overtures had been met with 'total rejection' by the governors. By the time of Starmer's first day in the school, Ballance was working six and a half days a week to secure the necessary funds to make it viable as a private institution.

David Jones taught languages at Reigate from September 1975 until July 2011. One of his first pupils was Keir Starmer, to whom he gave French lessons. He says that Starmer's first few terms would have been overshadowed by its unclear future but that many parents stepped in to help Ballance. 'A very active, very accomplished parents' committee was formed to promote and attain the independence of the school,' Jones remembers.[3] Their collective efforts paid off.

As Ballance negotiated a hefty loan with the local branch of Barclays Bank, teaching staff were promised a 5 per cent pay increase if they agreed to stay on at what he hoped would be the new fee-paying school. At the same time, provisions were made to take extra pupils – including girls in the sixth form – to increase revenue. Donations from wealthier parents were sought as well. Ballance's second application to become independent, in line with Thatcher's advice, was finally approved by Prentice in May 1975 – that is to say at the end of Starmer's first year. It was decided that the changeover would take place on 1 September 1976, the beginning of Starmer's third academic year. Ballance became the first headmaster of a voluntary-controlled school in England to achieve the status of independence. Not only that but Surrey County Council eventually agreed to cover the fees of every pupil who had entered the school via the 11-plus for the duration of their stay – a figure which ran to more than £300,000. Only the parents of new pupils arriving from September 1976 would have to pay fees.

This was the convoluted process by which Starmer came to spend five years at a fee-paying school, albeit free of charge. Ultimately, his good fortune was made possible by Margaret Thatcher's decision to issue Circular 10/70, giving grammar schools some say in their destiny. As David Jones says, 'Mrs Thatcher had approved the loophole through which the school squeezed to become independent in September 1976.' Jones says he remembers the period with a certain amount of affection:

> It was quite an exciting time, in a way. The school had to build its resources and establishment pretty much from scratch. Howard Ballance was a tremendous force for good through all of that. I suppose that forged some of the spirit of the time, because at that point all the boys were 11-plus pupils and there was tremendous gratitude for the substantial undertakings that were given and there was enormous parental commitment as regards extra-curricular help and, indeed, fundraising.

There is no doubt that Rodney and Josephine Starmer knew before their son joined the school that fundamental change in its status was on the cards, but they obviously believed that the prospects it offered him trumped the beliefs of progressive-minded politicians. Not only is it normal for every parent to want the best for their child, but it is equally true that no child can be responsible for decisions taken by their parents about their schooling. With this in mind, it is noteworthy that when the *Daily Mail* discovered in September 2009 that Starmer had omitted to mention Reigate Grammar School in his *Who's Who* entry, it concluded that this was a piece of chicanery which reflected badly on his character. By then, he was the DPP, and the *Mail* was deeply unimpressed. 'Despite the fact that the school almost certainly made him the man he is, it didn't fit with his image as a man of the people,' it thundered in a leading article. 'Those who utter small lies invariably tell big ones as well. Don't such small acts of deception tell us something significant about these public figures?'[4]

As with the questions raised in the previous chapter about what Starmer has had to say regarding his father's profession, the fact that he attended a grammar school which became a private school should not matter to anybody. A more interesting point is why he should feel any sensitivity about it. Conceivably, he may have regarded it as somehow compromising that, in a way, he owes his schooling – and everything that sprang from it, starting with his attendance at a good university – to Margaret Thatcher, a politician he has repeatedly criticised in public. Alternatively, it could be that he feels some misplaced sense of guilt at being the only one of four siblings who was given a grammar-school-style education. Whatever the true explanation, it is striking that after the *Mail* took him to task in 2009, he updated his *Who's Who* entry by confirming in its pages the name of his alma mater in Surrey. It would have been strange if he had not done so, because it is quite obvious that he flourished there.

*　　*　　*

Travelling from Tanhouse Road to the town of Reigate every morning involved Starmer having to leave home early to catch a bus. The twelve-mile journey took more than half an hour each way. He was not the only boy in his year to use public transport to get to school; several of his exact contemporaries did as well, including Andrew Sullivan. Although it would soon become clear that their politics were very different, Sullivan says he and Starmer always had a friendly rivalry. Sullivan also sat directly behind Starmer during their first three years at school, until they were aged fourteen, giving him a ringside seat on Starmer's early years. In retrospect, he likens them to two characters from Alan Bennett's play *The History Boys*, which is set in a fictional northern grammar school in the early 1980s. 'The thing that made us different was that we lived quite a long way from the school,' Sullivan says.[5]

> He and I were both on the other side of the county. I actually lived in Sussex, so we both got the same bus every morning. Generally speaking, over the years we just got into this fight. We would constantly argue. It was like something out of *The History Boys*. It would have looked like that to most people. It was the 1970s, so everything was quite political. These were the years of Wilson, Callaghan and Thatcher. She was elected Tory leader in 1975 and that, I think, is when the arguments really started. On most days we would have some kind of knock-down argument on the bus, and it would often continue through the day at school. We would pick up other people along the way. It became a bit of a performance after a while. Someone told me recently they had vivid memories of these arguments, including me at some point debating Keir about Thatcher.

Another exact contemporary on those journeys was Andrew Cooper. 'He got on at Oxted; I got on at Godstone,' remembers Cooper.[6]

> It was about a half-hour bus ride either way that we shared most days with relatively few others on that bus. He was very popular and likeable and widely liked. He was quite sporty. He was very into sport, certainly in the early years. He was bright but was not the very brightest. Nor was I. He was in the upper echelons. He was a very funny guy; a jokester. His personality is much more relaxed

and light-hearted than comes across. If there was a group of teenage boys on a bus larking about, Keir would always be at the heart of that. He was charismatic. He stood out as having a personality and would initiate jokes and conversations and was at the heart of things, I'd say. There was a lot of Top Trumps played to begin with and then, as we got older, political discussions. Andrew Sullivan was often on the same bus. We were untypically interested in politics from a young age.

Sullivan, now a political commentator who has lived in America since the 1980s, attributes his and Starmer's 'precocious' interest in politics to both of their families having had strong political opinions. 'His parents were very socialist and committed to the left, and it was clear that he was already committed there,' he says. But he remembers that their discussions were not restricted to politics:

It was also a fight about religion, too. I was a pretty devout Catholic and happy to argue about transubstantiation and abortion with anyone at the age of twelve; he was an atheist. At school there were some very bright kids, and these sorts of conversations were going on. We would have fights about it. He remembered last time we got together, actually, that he would even go into the Christian Union, where I would go after class, to pick a fight with me there, just to keep the argument going. We got it into our heads that we were at war.

During Starmer's first year, the boys were split into three forms, each consisting of about thirty pupils. As he moved up the school, a new system developed in which forms were reorganised according to which house a pupil was in. There were eight houses, each named after a local geographical feature or area. The house system was not pastoral and existed primarily for the purposes of competition on and off the sports field. Each house had two assemblies a week, which were held in two small classrooms. Starmer was put in a house called Linkfield. In the sixth form, pupils were again divided into sets depending on the A-Level subjects they were studying. As would be expected for a selective school, academic matters were paramount, with Howard Ballance pushing the boys to do their best at all times by encouraging rigour.

In addition to termly reports, monthly reports were issued in a process overseen by Ballance personally. Andrew Cooper remembers that these assessments were posted on a classroom wall, meaning there was no hiding place for anybody who had performed badly. 'You'd be graded one to five for effort as opposed to achievement, with a one being excellent and a five being poor,' he recalls. 'If you got a four or five you had to go to the headmaster. From a schoolboy point of view, those monthly reports were how we judged one another's ability. You had to get your parents to sign them.' He says that, certainly during their first three years in the school, 'I would guess Keir was in the one to three range.'

Peter Wheatley, a physics teacher at the school from 1975 who taught Starmer at A-Level, says that the academic ability of most boys of Starmer's vintage was never in question anyway, whether they were being put under pressure or not. 'When the school was a proper state grammar school, the ability level of the pupils was amazingly high,' he says.[7]

In forty-three years of teaching, I never taught classes as bright as those proper grammar school classes at Reigate. They were outstandingly good. It was because the school covered such a big catchment area. The boys were so intelligent. The brightest boy I ever taught was one year older than Keir. He was ridiculous. His dad was a jobbing builder, and he went to read maths at Cambridge. When we went independent, for the first few years it was more about who had the biggest purse. There was a hell of a change of standard. That wouldn't have affected Keir. He got in as a proper grammar school entrant, so he was in one of the seriously bright years.

Starmer had several close friends as he moved up the school, including Mark Adams, Paul Vickers, Steve Wheddon and Geoffrey Scopes. He was not able to spend all his spare time gadding about with them, though. From the age of fourteen, he was encouraged by his parents to get a holiday job working on a farm, so he could earn his own money. Another friend in his year was Quentin Cook, subsequently known as Norman and by his DJ name Fatboy Slim. They took violin lessons together, though Cook left Reigate Grammar aged sixteen, and they appear to have lost touch thereafter. Music remained a very important part of Starmer's life as a schoolboy, however. He also played the flute, the piano and the recorder. Mark Dixon began his teaching career at Reigate Grammar in 1978 and rated Starmer's musicianship highly. 'He was a very good flute player and played in the school orchestra,' he says.[8]

I ran an early music group [at Reigate]. We were a group of recorder players and crumhorn players. He got quite keen on this. He used to come along at lunchtimes. He and a boy called Gary Stevens were the senior members of the group, and we had some junior members as well. We performed at various concerts and competitions. I remember we once played our recorders in a competition in Redhill and won. The judge was hugely complimentary and quite moved by our performance. His parents were also very keen. They were kind enough to invite the group to tea at their place in Oxted. They were very supportive of the school and his musical interest. I also took him one weekend to meet a university friend of mine who played the baroque flute professionally, so that he could see what it was like. He was very enthusiastic.

In fact, Starmer was good enough at the flute to be an exhibitioner at the Junior Guildhall School of Music, which was linked to the main Guildhall School of Music, one of Europe's premier conservatoires. Every Saturday morning, at the insistence of his parents, he would travel to London to attend lessons given by staff who played in professional orchestras. The expectation was that most of the students would go on to study music at undergraduate level before turning professional themselves. Surprisingly, the Guildhall claims to have destroyed the records of many former students, and Starmer's file would appear to be among them, making it difficult to assess just how good a musician he was. He did volunteer in a 2015 interview that he realised at the age of seventeen that while other students at the Guildhall were 'hugely talented' he 'just practised hard', suggesting he never harboured ambitions of making a career out of playing music.[9] Yet he put his talent to use. His flute teacher, Deirdre Hicks, died in 2020, but the archives of Reigate Grammar record that during his sixth form he set up and ran a wind ensemble which featured on a float during the 1980 Lord Mayor of London's procession. He also played lead flute during school productions of *Joseph and the Amazing Technicolor Dreamcoat* and *Oliver!*, and he would perform in local concerts in Surrey with Ms Hicks. As a teenager, he also toured Malta with the Croydon Youth Symphony Orchestra, one of south London's leading amateur orchestras, which performed concerts several times a year.

Reigate Grammar had a reputation for being a strong sporting school in the 1970s, and Starmer was a keen partaker. During the autumn and spring terms, rugby was the main game, though hockey and cross-country running were also on offer. Sixth formers could play football if they preferred. In the summer term, it was a choice between cricket, tennis and athletics. Alan Reid was in charge of the cross-country and athletics teams and remembers Starmer as a decent middle-distance runner. 'From my point of view, he was quite a quiet lad,' he says. 'I've dealt with a lot of extroverts, but he was a quieter boy. My recollection is that he was in the school athletics team until he was about fifteen.' The school magazine, *The Pilgrim*, also notes that in his lower sixth, between 1979 and 1980, he was part of the 1st XI football team. He played in the midfield position and was rated as a 'talented ball player' who 'increased in stature as the season progressed', doing well enough to win his colours. In his final year, he won his colours again and was awarded the Paul Lynch Cup for being the player of the year. Graham Best, who was in charge of the team, is nothing but complimentary about his ability. 'Keir was a very skilful and keen footballer at school and always played with great energy and commitment,' he says.[10] 'Although the team was not hugely successful, Keir captained the side in his last year and proved a good leader both on and off the field.'

In another non-academic department he was just as determined to succeed, completing his Duke of Edinburgh's Gold Award aged seventeen. In order to achieve this goal, he had to undertake a series of five self-improvement exercises over a period of at least a year, including volunteering in the community. The award culminated in planning and completing an adventurous journey in Britain. For that final stage, he was among a group of fourteen pupils who went on a five-day camping and hiking expedition during the summer holidays in

1980. Dartmoor was the chosen location. Mark Dixon, who helped to oversee the scheme at Reigate, was one of the masters who supervised the trip. 'They would have covered fifty miles in four days carrying all their equipment, including tents and food, with them, so it was pretty arduous,' he says.

Each group was expected to do a project during the hike. Over the years, most chose the flora, fauna or geology of the region, but Keir's group showed considerable originality by choosing 'the psychology of the group'. They will have kept a log of how the dynamic of the group developed over the four days, which would have been amusing and was certainly a novel approach to the project.

In a report Starmer wrote about the trip for *The Pilgrim*, he noted that there were 'minor disagreements about map-reading' between himself and his friend Steve Wheddon, adding, 'But I was always right!' It seems his desire to lead was already on show – a suggestion which chimes with Dixon.

During Starmer's top year in the school, he was made a prefect and was considered the ideal candidate to write – again for *The Pilgrim* – a summary of the results of his house in the various inter-house competitions. Once more, his serious and sensible side was apparent, as was a politician's skill for giving the impression that mediocre achievements sounded more positive. 'This year saw Linkfield do very well in most House competitions,' he wrote, 'and there is a genuine feeling of being part of a team when we assemble for House prayers. Although we did not actually top the list in many competitions, we were nearly always in the top three, and congratulations must be given to everyone who took part.' He was pleased to announce that Linkfield had come second in the speaking competition – something he called 'a really good result' considering it was 'a House with no outstanding orators'. He was also proud of the results of the quiz and chess teams and the cross-country and hockey teams. Rugby and basketball were less successful, he admitted, 'but the spirit was there for both and that's what counts'. He went on: 'To sum up, I think we can now look at Linkfield as a House of dedicated young people who can be relied upon to put a fine effort into anything they are called upon to do.'

These unblemished accounts of his youth don't quite do Starmer justice, however. One contemporary says he can remember a prank Starmer played at school which also reflects a fun streak that existed within him:

> I think we once had a school photo using a camera which rotated from one side to the other, and I think it was Keir who figured out that if you were positioned on the extreme left-hand side, once you'd been in the photograph you could run round the back and appear on the right-hand side as well. The fact that I think it was Keir who did this is indicative of the kind of personality he was.

The culture of Reigate Grammar started to change after it became an independent school. Not only was this because the number of children who had to sit the 11-plus had diminished; it was also because of the arrival of girls in the sixth form. 'By the time we got to the sixth form [in September 1979] there were perhaps twenty girls,' says Andrew Cooper. 'He was very popular among the girls because he was funny and charismatic. I don't think he had a girlfriend from among those girls; he did have girlfriends, but I don't remember a steady girlfriend from that period.' Groups of friends including Starmer would meet at weekends and during school holidays. 'It would usually be at someone's house or more probably in a pub,' says Cooper.

We would often meet either in the Reigate area or sometimes at points roughly halfway between Reigate and Oxted, like Nutfield. There was a village hall there, which was sometimes used as a venue for parties. I'm sure we were all guilty of drinking beer under the age of eighteen but nothing more dangerous than that.

Andrew Sullivan says that, inevitably, Starmer's personality changed as he grew older. Whereas he remembers himself being 'uptight and ordered' and someone who 'wore his school cap at all times and said thank you to the bus driver', Starmer became 'much more one of the lads'. He goes on:

> People liked him. He was quite popular. But he always seemed a little angry about the world. There was a rough edge to him. He was physically more rough and ready, and he was not totally conformist. You got the impression he did not like the school very much. He certainly wasn't going to go down the Oxbridge route. That was a big difference [between us]. At some point, he didn't seem to be doing the conventional thing, but he was obviously very clever.

This non-conformist dimension to Starmer's character was certainly in evidence outside school. He became active in left-wing politics, joining the East Surrey Young Socialists – the youth wing of the Labour Party – when he was sixteen years old. Andrew Cooper, who was a Conservative member of the House of Lords and now sits as a crossbencher, was at the forefront of this organisation before Starmer joined it. He says there was little formal debating at school, and, if there had been, it wouldn't have been very dynamic anyway.

East Surrey was obviously a very Conservative area, and our school was, by 1976, a private school. Most of the students probably reflected the politics of their parents, so there weren't very many Labour-supporting people there. I grew up in a Labour-supporting house and got involved when I was not quite fourteen, in 1977. The Labour Party Young Socialists group was already well established by then. It was chaired by Guy Morris, who became quite a good friend of mine and who lived not far from Oxted. The secretary was Jane Robinson.

Nobody seems to know definitively why Starmer became involved in the group, beyond acknowledging the obvious reason: his parents voted Labour. Cooper says he can recollect one early conversation about politics on the bus to school before Starmer joined. 'I remember him being very supportive of the fire brigade pay strike [between November 1977 and January 1978]. I remember having a discussion with him about it upstairs on the bus. I was less sure about it; Keir was very strongly supportive of it.'

Despite his parents' devotion to Labour, it is interesting to note that he has said that his father was too busy to get involved in the party locally. 'He wasn't active because he was a toolmaker working in a factory and working every hour, basically, so he didn't have time for activism, but he was a strong Labour supporter,' he told the BBC in 2018. Neither was the schoolboy Starmer force-fed left-wing doctrine by his parents. In the same interview, he was asked if politics was talked about at home, or whether he was ever taken out by his parents to campaign. He answered, 'No, no... [my dad] wasn't there during the week for those [political] conversations.' Even when pressed on *Desert Island Discs* to state what exactly sparked his interest in politics as a teenager, he did not answer the question directly.

It seems likeliest that, having inherited some political beliefs, he had the intellectual curiosity to explore them. He was not usually forthright in expressing his opinions as a teenager, according to Cooper, though he did discuss his father sometimes. 'He did talk about his dad quite a lot but not his mum. Rodney was always described as quite strict. He never shared the fact that he had those challenges [relating to his mother's illness] in his home life. I don't recall him often expressing strong personal views on everything,' Cooper says. 'But I don't remember a time when I didn't know Keir was a Labour person through and through.'

Nationally, the Young Socialists was considered to be in the grip of the Trotskyites in the late 1970s, but the picture in east Surrey was different. Cooper goes on:

> For reasons I was never able to make sense of, the Labour Party in east Surrey – which was obviously in a Conservative-supporting area – was on the other fringe of the Labour Party altogether and was affiliated with a group called the Campaign for a Labour Victory (CLV), which was the forerunner of what became the Social Democratic Party.
>
> One of the first Labour Young Socialists meetings I went to had a speaker from the CLV. I remember it vividly because Labour HQ, who ran the Young Socialists nationally, were so perturbed that this group wasn't aligned, they sent a speaker down to talk to us and try to whip us into line.

Cooper became chairman of the East Surrey Young Socialists in 1978, and it is from this point that he can clearly remember Starmer's active participation in the group. Meetings would usually be held in the top-floor room of an outbuilding at the back of Cooper's parents' house, which was on the village green in Godstone.

I certainly remember Keir coming to those meetings. I think it's true that I was in the Labour Party before he was, and I remained in it until I went to university in 1981. I sometimes joke that perhaps it was me who brought Keir into the Labour Party, though probably that's not true.

The group met every four to six weeks, but it was a very social kind of socialism, and they would invariably seek out refreshments when the serious business of politicking was over.

We didn't just meet to pass motions. Mostly we would sit around and natter about politics for a bit and then go to the pub. Keir definitely had a passionate, positive belief in equality. I don't think I had at the time a great sense of to what extent he was an out-and-out socialist, as opposed to a moderate, but if we argued with people about the Conservatives, the arguments were good natured. There was no animus. If you'd looked around the room at that time and said, 'One of you will one day be Labour leader,' you wouldn't have thought it would obviously be Keir, but certainly he would have been on the shortlist.

The Young Socialists also helped the local Labour Party when it came to canvassing and campaigning. A small number of Labour councillors sat on the district council, elected by wards in Caterham and Oxted. Cooper says Rodney Starmer's connections may have been influential in fostering his son's political activities, as there were two centres of left-wing activity around Oxted, each dominated by a personality faction.

Keir knew from his father, I think, the leading Labour figures from the Oxted camp. One was Robin Harling, who was the chairman of

East Surrey Labour Party for most of the time that I was in it. He had a brother called Jim. They both lived in Oxted, near Keir. And there was also a legendary figure called George Cornish, who was a very popular Labour councillor. Keir knew the Harlings, who were a big Labour force. Keir then became involved with a few people from school [in the Young Socialists]. I think there were ten or twelve of us in the Young Socialists. Not that many. I think we were quite highly valued because we were willing to go out canvassing.

The constituency Labour Party was supportive of Tony Benn at the time.

They found us quite puzzling because they expected us to be more left-wing than them, and we were less so. I remember somebody from the regional Labour Party came to see us. They were checking up on the Young Socialist groups because they were worried about extremism, and he wrote me a letter afterwards saying we were like a ray of light because we were so mainstream.

Cooper left the Labour Party to join the SDP when it was founded in March 1981 by the so-called 'Gang of Four' Labour politicians, comprising Shirley Williams, Roy Jenkins, David Owen and Bill Rodgers, but Starmer stayed on.

Jon Pike, who lived in Caterham, a short distance from Oxted, was a few years Starmer's junior. Through his interest in left-wing politics, and because his mother knew Starmer's mother, he got to know Starmer and also joined the Young Socialists. According to him, nobody was off-limits to the group – not even the local Conservative MP for East Surrey, Sir Geoffrey Howe, who was at the time Margaret Thatcher's

Chancellor of the Exchequer. 'We ran jumble sales and held public meetings and poked fun at the Tories', Pike has recalled.

> We weren't always politically or socially astute. One time, we found out that Geoffrey Howe was starting a fun run in Oxted. We all signed up so as to go to the start and heckle him. Heckling done, it then dawned on us that we had to actually run the course. A certain amount of walking and smoking of fags may have occurred.[11]

One wonders what the teenaged Starmer would have said if he had been told that in the future he, just like Howe, would go on to be called to the Bar by Middle Temple, would become a QC, would be elected as an MP and would also accept a knighthood for his abilities as a lawyer.

Despite having a fairly packed extra-curricular life, those who taught Starmer remember that he did not ignore his studies. The consensus is that he was academically solid, if not brilliant. He is understood to have chosen physics, chemistry and maths as his A-Level subjects. Mark Dixon taught physics and occasionally came across him in lessons. 'Keir was a very well-meaning lad with a good sense of humour, with an occasional hint of mischief', he says. 'He was always very organised at school, very lively, versatile and wide-ranging. Academically he was pretty sound. He was not absolutely at the top of the pile, but he was in the top set. He was pretty sharp.' His parents took a close interest in the progress of his studies as well. Dixon adds:

> I remember at parents' evenings, they always came and always wanted to have a chat and were fully supportive and thankful for what one had done for their son. They very much appreciated everything that was being done for him and talked about how he was having a great

time at school and getting the most out of it. It doesn't surprise me he's got to where he has.

Peter Wheatley, who also taught Starmer physics at A-Level, concurs. 'They were all very bright,' he says.

> He's not one of those names that leaps out as having been absolutely outstanding, but he was in a very outstanding year. The proper grammar school pupils were sharp and highly motivated. They were good fun to teach. Typical of them would be if I set them a selection of questions at the end of the chapter in a textbook for homework, several members of the class wouldn't just do the eight or ten questions I'd asked them to do, they'd do all twenty or thirty questions. It was hard work for me, but it was quite interesting to come across kids so highly motivated. As I say, the catchment area was so big that the school was able to be very selective.

In his final term at school, in the summer of 1981, Starmer did well enough in his A-Levels to win a place at the University of Leeds. Before he left school, he was, with three other pupils, a recipient of the CE Deacon Prize for Service to the School, illustrating the esteem in which he was held. There is no doubt that his secondary schooling was successful on all fronts – socially, academically, in terms of handling responsibility and also in getting the most out of the extra-curricular activities that were on offer. All these achievements were a tribute to him but also to his parents, especially his mother. Making them proud mattered to him very much. Going to Reigate Grammar also afforded Starmer his first independent taste of left-wing politics, thanks to his friendship with Andrew Cooper. And yet despite all this, a fundamental contradiction remains.

Starmer has stayed close to Reigate Grammar since leaving it. Not only are some of his best friends today also his former schoolmates but it seems he has always been happy to lend his support to the school when required. Former member of staff David Jones recalls that he has regularly put in an appearance at events when asked. 'Certainly during his time as DPP, he was always outstanding when it came to attending functions at the school to which he'd been invited. He not only attended the functions but he would always come and have a pint with us afterwards,' he says. In February 2014, Starmer also delivered the Henry Smith Lecture to pupils at the school.[12] That year, a new organisation, the Henry Smith Club, was established. It is aligned with a Reigate Grammar bursary campaign which pays the fees for five children whose parents cannot afford to fund a private education. Starmer has willingly backed this charitable initiative and, indeed, has played an active role in it. At least once, in 2017, he was the guest of honour at its fundraising dinner, held at the East India Club in London. On that occasion, he 'spoke of his fond memories of his time at school, and of the first-class education he received, which laid the platform for his successful career'.[13]

Notwithstanding all that he has achieved courtesy of a selective grammar school education, however, he has also made it plain that, ultimately, he rejects the system through which he came. 'I don't agree with separating children at eleven, because I think children develop at different ages,' he said during an event at the Labour Party conference in 2019. 'I also profoundly disagree that you're either, as it were, a talented child, or a not-talented child. Everybody is good at different things.' Instead, he has said he would advocate a comprehensive system in which pupils are put into streams according to their ability. This would, he believes, create a state education system that is so strong that private schools would become 'irrelevant'.

As proof of his commitment to the state sector, his own children have not been educated privately, and he is adamant that they never will be. 'Going to a grammar school allowed me to have that focus, but I still don't think it's the right thing to have done,' he said. 'I didn't have a lot of choice about it at the time.'[14] All of which prompts the question: why bother to help raise money for less-well-off pupils to attend the fee-paying school of which you were a beneficiary if you do not believe such institutions should exist in the first place? Perhaps enquiries of this nature, which demand a proper explanation, throw some light on the reason why Reigate Grammar School was omitted from Starmer's *Who's Who* entry until the *Daily Mail* picked up on it.

CHAPTER 3

KING OF MIDDLE-CLASS RADICALS

The idea of taking a year off between school and university was less commonplace in 1981 than it is today, but one early adopter was Keir Starmer. Forty years ago, many young people who did decide to have a gap between receiving their A-Level results and becoming an undergraduate often chose to go in search of adventure by backpacking around Asia or South America, or perhaps doing voluntary work in Africa. Others wanted to sample the world of commerce by working in an office somewhere in Britain. In a move which says much about his character as a young man, Keir Starmer trod an altogether more altruistic path by spending several months in Cornwall looking after disabled people and then going to work in his father's toolmaking business.

The place to which Starmer went first was Churchtown Farm Field Studies Centre. It had been established in 1975 by the Spastics Society, which is now known as the charity Scope. It was located in idyllic countryside in the village of Lanlivery, close to Bodmin Moor, and was primarily intended to encourage nature studies and outdoor pursuits. In the late 1970s and early 1980s, there were very few operations in Britain, or, indeed, in Europe, like it which were devoted solely to those with physical, sensory or learning disabilities. It catered for all ages, from young children to middle-aged adults all the way up to those who were in their nineties. Clients came from both the UK and other countries, including France, Germany and America.

Churchtown's overriding philosophy was that learning should be fun. It was quite normal for a child in a wheelchair, for example, to be immersed – in their chair – in a large pond in the centre's grounds, so they could get as close as an able-bodied person to insects and plants, which they would then be taught about. Some visitors to the centre lived for most of the year in residential hospitals, meaning that a trip to Churchtown was for them a holiday. Others were at school or college studying for O-Level or A-Level exams in biology or geography, and the type of fieldwork on offer at Churchtown was considered essential to their progress. Clients were also taught about farm animals and were able to learn practical tasks, such as how to milk a goat or groom a horse. Outdoor activities including rock-climbing, orienteering, hiking, swimming, fishing and birdwatching were on offer, too, as was sailing on the river at the nearby town of Fowey or day trips to the seaside.

David Griffith was the bursar and administrator at Churchtown in 1981 and says that it was in many ways a revolutionary place. 'At that time, we were in the forefront of taking disabled people out of doors on field trips and outdoor pursuits. Now it is the norm, but then it wasn't,' he says.[1]

We were nominated [by the European Economic Community] as the centre to go to in order to learn how to take the disabled out of doors in educational terms, and we ran courses for politicians abroad about special needs education and on how to do that. We were the only organisation Europe-wide that was doing some of this pioneering work.

In 1981, the village of Lanlivery consisted of a church, a pub, a school and a few houses. Churchtown was based in disused farm buildings which had been converted for use by those in wheelchairs. It employed its own professional care staff, but it always needed non-professional voluntary assistants. Its status meant there was no shortage of offers of help throughout its busiest months, from May to November, and it was not even necessary for it to advertise. 'Bearing in mind we were a centre for students from special schools throughout the country, the word of mouth that generated in educational establishments promoted the enquiries we got,' adds Griffith.

Most volunteers were selected because of what their CV suggested they would be able to contribute. Some had knowledge of geographical or environmental studies, others had some experience in caring for a disabled person and the rest had a background in outdoor pursuits. It is thought that some voluntary work with the disabled, which Starmer had done as part of his Duke of Edinburgh's Gold Award, probably recommended him for this unpaid role. A maximum of eight Churchtown assistants could be accommodated at any one time, most of whom had quarters in a manor house that was just over the road from the central site. 'The minimum age for volunteers was eighteen,' says Griffith.

> We didn't encourage people to stay longer than six months because part of the ethos of the centre was that the enthusiasm that young volunteers brought was important. That's why the turnover was high. I can recall having a conversation with Princess Anne, in which she wanted to know that sort of detail of what made Churchtown tick, and that was one of the things we told her.

In spite of the beauty of Cornwall's countryside, decamping to such a remote area to care for strangers with a range of complicated conditions would not be the first wish of every teenager straight after leaving school. Demonstrating admirable strength of personality, however, Starmer stuck with it. The work would have been relentless and demanding for a non-professional volunteer like him. The number of clients visiting at any one time varied according to their disability. A maximum of seventy mentally disabled but ambulant clients and visiting staff could stay there at once, though if a group comprised individuals who were primarily physically disabled and required a wheelchair, that number shrank to about thirty. Courses lasted for one week and ran from Wednesday to Wednesday. 'Voluntary assistants didn't get involved in personal care, but their core function was to support our clients at mealtimes and, most importantly, to be additional pairs of hands while out in the field in various activities,' says Griffith. 'They would have had an interest in either environmental studies or in outdoor pursuits so that they could get stuck in with abseiling or rock-climbing or sailing.'

Although hundreds of volunteers worked at Churchtown during the years Griffith spent there, he says that he and another member of staff can recall Starmer. According to them, he volunteered with two other young men from the London area and looked after disabled girls and boys from mid-summer 1981 until the end of the year. Griffith says Starmer was well suited to the work, and his time there was considered a success. 'I remember three of them came down,' he recalls.

There are certain people who stand out in a crowd. I think it's probably that there were three of them together that triggered memories. They had a stronger presence than an individual coming to stay with us; they had that bigger impact. I remember they were very good with the clients. I remember in the evenings we always had social activities, and very often we would encourage the volunteer assistants to lead in entertainment if they could, whether it was a quiz or whatever. We had a piano. This group of three were quite good at entertaining our clients in the evening. [Starmer] had a classical musical interest and would have been fully involved in the life and work of the centre.

Starmer returned home in time for Christmas and had a further nine months of freedom at his disposal before he began studying for his degree at the University of Leeds. Surprisingly, however, he did not stray far from Surrey for long during this period. While others in his situation might have got a job with a view to making enough money to go on an extended holiday, for example, he spent six months working alongside his father, learning how to operate a production machine in Rodney's factory workshop.

Based on his various accounts of the straitened circumstances in which the Starmer family often lived, it is fair to assume that he would not have been paid much money by his father in exchange for his time, if he was paid at all. The fact that he was content to devote himself to this experience rather than escaping his parents' clutches as soon as possible suggests that he was either a very dutiful son or that he felt pressurised into remaining in Oxted, conceivably for financial reasons. Who is to say that his father did not expect him to pull his weight if he was about to become a full-time university student requiring some level of support? Whatever the explanation, Rodney Starmer did later acknowledge that the period they spent together might not have been regarded by his son as the most fruitful or interesting use of his time; he admitted that he knew Keir had found it 'dead boring'.

Little did either of them know then, however, that there would be one upside to Starmer's stint in the toolmaking business. Thirty-seven years on, in 2019, he was able to tell members of the Labour Party who he hoped would elect him as their leader that he was not the middle-class man some might assume but in fact had working-class roots. He cited as evidence the experience of this dull manual work. 'I actually had never been in any workplace other than a factory until I left home for university,' he said in 2019. 'I had never been in an office. The idea that somehow I personally don't know what it's like for people across the country and in all sorts of different circumstances is just not borne out.'² He had been able to make exactly the same point during an interview at the Labour Party conference three months previously.

In September 1982, not long after his twentieth birthday, Starmer finally travelled north to start the next phase of his life. Leeds is one of the original redbrick universities, founded in the early twentieth century, and it has long been regarded as one of Britain's better seats of learning. It is a campus university which is based in the heart of the city, guaranteeing its popularity with students who feel they can enjoy the best of both worlds. In the early 1980s, Leeds was still associated in many people's minds with the murders carried out there by serial killer Peter Sutcliffe, dubbed the Yorkshire Ripper. Indeed, Sutcliffe's last known murder victim, Jacqueline Hill, was a Leeds University student who was killed in November 1980, and the month before that another young woman, Maureen Lea, had been attacked by Sutcliffe in the grounds of the university. The case had only been resolved in May 1981, when Sutcliffe was jailed, and the shadow cast by his unspeakable crimes was painfully long.

Yet as a metropolis and as a university, Leeds was always considered fun and lively. It had a thriving social and sporting scene and the era's best-known bands, such as The Undertones, The Cure and The Smiths, visited regularly to play gigs. The Rolling Stones also played in Leeds just a few weeks before Starmer's arrival. With a population approaching 1 million, this West Yorkshire urban centre was a world away from the small Surrey town where Starmer had grown up, and he is known to have had a happy time there.

He was the first person in his family to attend university, and his parents were adamant that he should not waste the opportunity. There is more than a mere suggestion that they exercised a certain amount of control over his university career, despite him being an adult. Originally, Starmer had expressed an interest in reading politics.

Given his devotion to the Young Socialists, this was unsurprising. Furthermore, the politics department at Leeds was held in high esteem by many at that time. For example, Ralph Miliband, the prominent left-wing intellectual and father of Starmer's two future friends, the politicians David and Ed Miliband, had been professor of politics there until 1978. Yet in a sure sign that Rodney and Josephine Starmer expected their son to gain a degree in a subject that would equip him to enter a profession after he graduated, they insisted that he should read law instead. Starmer acquiesced, even though this subject is notoriously time-consuming even at undergraduate level, and despite his legal knowledge being minimal when he began the course. As he has admitted, despite being twenty years old when he arrived at Leeds, he had never met a lawyer before; he didn't know what lawyers did; and he didn't know the difference between a solicitor and a barrister. Over the ensuing nine terms, spread over less than thirty-six months, he had to grasp an enormous amount of information.

In the early 1980s, Leeds was considered a good institution at which to read law. One former tutor of the era says that it was 'not generally thought by those in academic circles to be in the first rank, but it was proudly in the second rank'. Most of those studying alongside Starmer would have been undergraduates for whom Leeds was their second choice after Oxbridge, UCL, Bristol or perhaps Manchester or Birmingham. The tutor recalls that the course at that time involved getting to grips with the standard subjects used by every respectable law faculty in the country, except at the universities of Oxford and Keele.

In the first year, four compulsory subjects were taught: contract, tort, English legal system and constitutional law. In the second year, there were two compulsory subjects: land law and crime. In the third year, trusts and jurisprudence were obligatory. During years two and three, students had to choose three further subjects to achieve the requirement of five subjects. The list of options available to them was Roman law, legal history, European law, international law (peace), international law (war), family law, employment law, revenue law, social security law and conveyancing. The course was arranged to ensure that graduates had a Qualifying Law Degree for the purposes of entry to the profession. With very few exceptions, subjects were taught by a combination of two lectures per week – making a total of forty for the year per subject – and one tutorial group consisting of a lecturer plus four students, which met once a fortnight, making a total of ten tutorials per year per subject. By the standards of many undergraduate degree courses, this was a rigorous regime which made fairly sizeable demands on a student's time.

During his first year, Starmer lived in a room in Charles Morris Hall on the university campus. Luckily for him, at least one friend from Reigate Grammar School, Geoffrey Scopes, was also at Leeds, giving Starmer an immediate advantage over other new students who had arrived knowing nobody else. Starmer has said that he was prone to drinking pints of snakebite, a notoriously intoxicating lager–cider mix, in the union bar. He was apparently a regular attender of the university's Thursday night disco and an enthusiastic football player. He also made an attempt to remain engaged politically. One of his first acts on arriving at Leeds was to become a member of the university Labour Club, which was chaired by a third-year student called John Erskine. 'I do remember signing [Starmer] up to the Labour Club at the freshers' fair,' Erskine says.[3] 'The name does stay with you. I signed him up. I took the money. It cost £1. We were quite busy, so he moved on, but I ran into him at subsequent Labour Club meetings.'

Leeds Labour Club was one of the biggest university Labour clubs in the country, with several hundred members. Erskine had secured the chairmanship in June 1982 by beating the Militant tendency, the

Trotskyist faction which dominated Labour politics at the time. 'The alliance with which I took the Labour Club [from Militant] was made up of radical lesbian feminists, Jewish students and Labour moderates,' he says. The battle with Militant continued throughout Starmer's first year and beyond, as the club sought to cement itself into a position that was firmly on the democratic left rather than anything more radical.

Yet despite the intriguing challenge that this fight represented to some, including Erskine, there is no suggestion that Starmer had much appetite for it. Frankly, there is little evidence that he had any inclination towards becoming too heavily involved in any aspect of student politics. Certainly, he did not hold any official position within the club. 'We did try and make contact with [Starmer] about internal Labour Club elections, and he was a bit circumspect about taking on Militant in the way that I would have,' Erskine says. 'Even then, he was quite legal about things. In those days I was not above cutting corners in terms of dealing with Trotskyites. I was also always committed to taking people on, whereas I think he was more measured.'

It was not only Militant's presence that made politics so diverting during Starmer's first twelve months at Leeds. With Margaret Thatcher's Britain beginning to take shape; curbs on the trade unions becoming a fact of life; the 1983 general election proving disastrous for the Labour Party; and Michael Foot's resignation triggering a leadership election, there was no shortage of engrossing matters to occupy the Labour Club. 'It was a time of great energy,' says Adam LeBor, who also belonged to the organisation during Starmer's first year.[4]

It galvanised everyone. I was also active in the Union of Jewish Students (UJS) as well. Both UJS and the Labour Students spent a lot of time fighting the Trots and the Socialist Workers Party, politically speaking. It was a time of massive political awakening. I had always been a Labour Party supporter, and there was such a range of people in the Labour Club, some from working-class backgrounds, some quite posh people, some from everyday middle-class backgrounds. It was great. I learned so much about politics. It fizzed with energy.

Despite this atmosphere, neither Erskine nor LeBor has any memory of Starmer being notably active or showing any zeal for political debate. The club met in a lecture theatre for an hour every Wednesday at lunchtime, and meetings would be overseen by Erskine. Guest speakers would be invited, or student discussions would be held. The South African social campaigner Denis Goldberg was one well-known figure who addressed the club, and the human rights campaigner Peter Tatchell was another, as was the veteran Leeds MP Denis Healey. Erskine says he strived to get a variety of speakers from different backgrounds, as long as they were of the non-Trotskyist left. Starmer apparently showed less interest in these meetings than might have been expected. 'Keir wasn't that regular an attender of the meetings,' says Erskine.

I'd say he'd come to every two or three. I don't remember him being particularly regular [in his first year]. Looking back on it, he was someone who was obviously very thoughtful and intelligent and concerned about behaving in a legal kind of way. The one speech I remember him making was quite measured and concerned with what was happening in the party.

LeBor adds that he 'can't remember Starmer at all', although he is at pains to stress that almost nobody's powers of recall are perfect four decades later. Still, it is as if Starmer saw things in black-and-white terms, simply believing there were no enemies on the left. Matt Tee, who ran the

Labour Club between 1983 and 1984, when Starmer was in his second year, also says he has no memory of meeting him at that time.

The student union is another arena in which many national Labour politicians who have attended university often forge their debating skills and mould their principles. Again, though, there is no hint that Starmer showed any serious intent in this context. From June 1983 until June 1985 – the year Starmer graduated – Erskine became a convenor for the National Union of Students in Leeds, placing him at the heart of the union. He says he does not remember Starmer putting forward motions or participating in any set-piece debates at union meetings and events. It seems that even though Starmer's student days covered what is now regarded as a seismic period in Britain's political history – including the 1984–85 miners' strike, which began in Yorkshire, and the struggle to rebuild the Labour Party under its new leader, Neil Kinnock – whiling away endless hours in coffee bars and pubs talking politics was not for him.

As well as being active politically, Adam LeBor also edited the student newspaper, the *Leeds Student*, between 1983 and 1984, when Starmer was in his second year. Again, LeBor says he has no recollection of Starmer showing any interest in journalism during his editorship and does not believe he was well-known enough within the university to be written about in the paper either. The *Leeds Student* was an independent newspaper that represented those who attended Leeds Polytechnic, as well as those who were at the University of Leeds, though its principal focus was the university. It was printed weekly each term, meaning that it published approximately twenty-four editions every academic year. Each one was sixteen pages long, with sections covering news, comment, arts, music and sport at both institutions. Approximately 4,000 copies were printed in each run. Having examined all seventy-two editions that were produced during Starmer's time at Leeds, it is clear that student politics received a wealth of coverage, from reports on rent strikes to the manifestos of Union Council and NUS candidates. The activities of the Labour Club also featured fairly regularly, either because of its ongoing row with Militant, or through its involvement with campaigns such as 'anti-fascist week' (October 1982), or for its call for a mandatory £20 weekly grant for students (February 1983). Starmer, however, was not mentioned or pictured in relation to any of the reports on the Labour Club between 1982 and 1985. Moreover, he never wrote for the paper and was not named or quoted in any other articles.

In order to locate his name in the *Leeds Student* for the purposes of this book, it was necessary to scour every single corner of the publication. It did crop up – just once. The paper ran a 'Personals' section, where students could leave birthday greetings or, sometimes, more obscure messages and wisecracks for each other. This was all good clean fun. In the edition published on 27 January 1984, somebody left an anonymous note for Starmer, which was cryptic but, in its way, rather telling. It read: 'Keir Starmer, King of Middle-Class Radicals.' This was almost certainly an in-joke between friends, but, if nothing else, it proves that since he was twenty-one years old, this former Surrey grammar school boy has been fending off accusations of being more bourgeois than he would care to admit.

When it came to his involvement in student politics at Leeds, Starmer could be described as the man who wasn't there. He did not seek the spotlight but was instead cautious, modest and restrained. Why should this have been so? John Erskine believes he knows the answer to that question: 'At the time it might have annoyed me that someone with a bit of talent [like him] was like that,' he says.

I wished he'd get stuck in. I wished he didn't have the scruples he did. But I can see it as being of a piece. He was someone who was serious about getting a good law degree and not letting down his parents. The law department at that stage was very good. People like Brian Hogan taught there. They cracked on and expected people to deliver academically, so I'm not surprised [to find] that he concentrated most of his efforts on his studies.

At the start of his second year, Starmer and Scopes were among six students who rented a terraced house together at 22 Chestnut Avenue in the Hyde Park area of the city. The others were fellow law student John Murray, Simon Head, Alison Jenkins and Deborah Bacon. It was from this point that Starmer began to show a deeper interest in his degree. The law faculty at that time was based in buildings in Lyddon Terrace, away from the main campus, and was in a sense self-contained, in that it had its own common room and study area. There was also an active university Law Society. As there were only about 100 law students per year, many of them knew each other quite well and didn't necessarily mix much with students who were reading other subjects.

Leeds had a strong criminal law element and some well-regarded professors, including Charles Drake, Brian Hogan and Horton Rogers. Among its senior lecturers was Peter Seago, who was also a Justice of the Peace. This environment may have fostered in Starmer, some of whose future career was spent working as a criminal barrister, an interest in criminal law. Yet he has often said that his attraction to working in an international human rights context was developed as an undergraduate, when he made up his mind to become a barrister and eventually to specialise in this branch of the law. 'I became absolutely fascinated with the idea that at the end of the Second World War and the atrocities of the Second World War, the countries around the world came together and made commitments to each other to honour human rights,' he has said. 'I became fascinated and really taken with the idea behind human rights, really. It's not so much the individual rights, but it's the human dignity that sits behind human rights, how we treat individuals, how we treat them fairly, equally.'[5] Having taken up this cause, he began to study harder than ever – and not only in order to keep his parents happy.

One of his principal tutors at Leeds was Clive Walker, who became a lecturer there at the start of Starmer's second year and is now professor of criminal justice studies. He has always thought Starmer was one of the most capable students he has ever taught, and, according to another of Walker's former students, he was always convinced that Starmer would succeed in the law. As he is not significantly older than Starmer (Walker graduated from the University of Leeds with a law degree in 1975), their relationship was perhaps less formal than many other student–tutor associations are, and they remain in close contact. In light of this, it was somewhat surprising that Walker refused point-blank to talk about Starmer for the purposes of this book. 'My role demands *uberrima fides*,' Walker said by way of explanation. Assuming that I know no Latin, he then kindly added: 'Which is lawyer-speak for "my lips are sealed".'[6] It remains unclear why Prof. Walker should consider his role in Starmer's life to be strictly off-limits. He and Starmer even worked together on two law books in the 1990s. The first of these, *Justice in Error*, was published in 1993, and Walker and Starmer are credited as co-editors. It comprises a series of essays by academics and campaigners concerning aspects of the criminal justice system which have resulted in the conviction of innocent people. The second, *Miscarriages of Justice*, follows a similar theme and was published six years later.

There is no doubt that Starmer worked extremely hard at university. By his own admission, his studies were at the centre of his life, and he spent much of his time with his head in his books because he is naturally driven and industrious. Nobody was surprised when, in the summer of 1985, he took a first-class degree in law. It is worth saying that in the mid-1980s, achieving this result from a decent redbrick university was still considered unusual enough to be fairly impressive. One former member of staff says Starmer was among only three or four people in his year to have reached this height. He has certainly always been thankful for the platform which his tertiary education provided for him. And as is the case with Reigate Grammar School, he has been careful to maintain strong links with the University of Leeds, opening its new law faculty building in 2011 and serving as a member of its advisory board.

Having enjoyed academic success as an undergraduate, Starmer was not entirely sure which direction to take, though it was quickly apparent that he was in no mood to rest on his laurels. One source familiar with the set-up at the University of Leeds at the time says they believe that Prof. Horton Rogers may have advised him to have a word with another academic, Adrian Briggs, in order to help him reach a decision about next steps. Briggs had worked in the law faculty at Leeds between 1979 and 1980, and by 1985 was based at St Edmund Hall, Oxford. Rogers and Briggs had stayed in close touch, meaning talented students who were leaving Leeds were well-positioned to be given a steer on what the University of Oxford might have to offer them, specifically in relation to a graduate course called the Bachelor of Civil Law (BCL), Oxford's postgraduate law degree. No sooner had he finished his business at Leeds than Starmer was accepted onto this course, joining St Edmund Hall (known affectionately as 'Teddy Hall') for the academic year 1985–86 as a mature student on a scholarship.

According to the lawyer Ken Macdonald, himself an alumnus of St Edmund Hall who went on to become the Director of Public Prosecutions in 2003 before taking up his current post as warden of Wadham College, Oxford, only the most able students are accepted onto the BCL course. 'The BCL is probably the best graduate law degree in the common law world,' he says. 'It's very competitive to get on. The brightest graduates in law from around the UK and the Commonwealth tend to compete to get on that degree, and [Starmer] got on it.'[7]

A senior member of St Edmund Hall staff during Starmer's year there agrees, explaining:

The BCL is a graduate degree, but it's not an ordinary graduate degree. It's not a doctorate. It insists on a fair coverage so that when you leave you haven't been sitting in the law library by yourself hunting out one particular subject. You're expected to be prepared on a range of subjects. It's a tough course.

Starmer's time in Oxford was academically unrelenting and, when examined, really quite brief. He studied there for just twenty-four weeks, spread over three eight-week terms. He barely had time to appreciate his surroundings before he had left, let alone to make much of an impression on other students there. St Edmund Hall is located on Queen's Lane, just off the High Street, and occupies a small site based around a quadrangle. In the 1980s, it had a strong sporting reputation and, having begun admitting female students only a few years earlier, was known as a college with a fairly masculine atmosphere.

During Starmer's period of study, the University of Oxford was awash with future front-rank politicians. David Cameron, Michael Gove and Jeremy Hunt were all students there at the time. And in early 1986, Boris Johnson, then in his penultimate year at Balliol College, was elected president of the Oxford Union, the influential debating society. (There is no known evidence that the two ever met at this point.) Some future Labour Party MPs were also undergraduates while Starmer toiled away on his postgraduate course, including Ed Balls, David Miliband and Stephen Twigg. It was natural that Starmer should have wanted to join them in signing up to be a member of the Oxford Union Labour Club (OULC), and it is certainly known that he and Miliband became friendly at this time. Perplexingly, no official OULC records from the period survive, but one person who is familiar with the history of the club says it is 'highly unlikely' that Starmer would have held any sort of executive role, partly because the OULC has always been much more of an undergraduate phenomenon.

As Starmer had done at Leeds, he kept a low profile otherwise. With that said, he did become friendly with one left-wing undergraduate, Ben Schoendorff, who was the chairman of the OULC in the year before Starmer arrived. As shall become clear in the next chapter, their friendship would endure beyond Starmer's Oxford career.

In contrast to its right-wing equivalent, the Oxford University Conservative Association, the OULC rarely made the student or national press in 1985 or 1986, perhaps in part because it chose to boycott the Oxford Union at that time. Instead, anti-Apartheid activism was the principal means by which it captured the attention of the student press, especially in relation to the activities of Barclays Bank in South Africa. For example, on one occasion in November 1985, some OULC members – including Stephen Twigg – were at the forefront of a sit-in at the entrance to the Randolph Hotel in Oxford, in protest at a Barclays 'milkround' recruitment event being held in the city. A few months later, David Miliband, then the president of the Corpus Christi Junior Common Room, stopped the college from banking with Barclays. These were the issues which appear to have taken precedence at the time, and Starmer seems to have had little opportunity to join in with them. He worked hard enough to gain what has been described by his friend Geoffrey Robertson, a leading barrister, as a 'goodish' BCL in the summer of 1986.[8]

Starmer, who is now an honorary fellow of St Edmund Hall, has spoken of his memories of this period of his life in refreshingly frank terms. 'When I arrived at St Edmund Hall, I had a first-class degree from Leeds University behind me, but I was still not clear what path I should take next,' he has said. 'My time at St Edmund Hall – an intense year studying for the BCL – confirmed me in my choice of pursuing a career as a human rights advocate, both here in the UK and abroad. From then on, I did not look back!'[9] Having originally thought of becoming a solicitor – a job which some in legal circles believe would have suited him just as well because it does not usually require any public speaking skills – Starmer has claimed that he became convinced at Oxford that he wanted to present arguments in court instead and, therefore, to be instructed as a barrister by a solicitor. For a young man who had hitherto shown little, if any, interest in debating in any formal context, this was surprising to say the least. One lawyer who would work with Starmer years later casts doubt on his suitability for his chosen route. 'The BCL is quite competitive to get on to, but if you do your homework, you can get on it,' they say.

> Keir can read what the law says and apply it, but that's not what being a human rights lawyer is all about. Anyone can do that. Human rights law – or any legal practice that's pushing the boundaries – is not about accepting the status quo and trying to take the path of least resistance, but about trying to battle new frontiers.

Could Starmer open up new horizons in a legal sense? His first challenge was to gain a place at Bar School in London. With two solid academic qualifications to speak of, this presented no problems at all.

CHAPTER 4

ALTERNATIVES

An idea has taken hold that when Keir Starmer first moved to London in 1986, he lived above a brothel. This is not quite true. To be strictly accurate, it would appear that he rented a room in a flat above a sauna. The flat in question was on the top two floors of 285 Archway Road, part of a parade of shops located directly opposite Highgate Underground station. The brothel story is not without basis, however. In August 1985, the year before Starmer's arrival, Victor Mehra, the owner of a business called the Highgate Sauna Centre, which was indeed based at 285 Archway Road, was found guilty at the Old Bailey of living off the earnings of prostitution. *The Times* reported that Mehra received a sentence of nine months in prison.[1] A sauna supposedly continued to operate from the same shop in 1986, though it is not clear who ran it. The premises had apparently ceased to be a house of ill repute by the time Starmer moved in. According to some accounts, though, it remained a fairly insalubrious place.

Starmer came to be living in these surroundings thanks to his old school tie. His exact contemporary at Reigate Grammar School, Andrew Cooper, had lived in the flat until late 1984 while attending the London School of Economics. Another school friend, Paul Vickers, had taken on the digs from Cooper. 'Waves of people then started to live there, including Keir,' says Cooper.[2]

It was an unbelievably grubby place. We used to joke about the fact that we lived above a brothel. It was a massage parlour, very sordid, with a reception area on the ground floor and stairs down to the basement where there were just rooms with dirty mattresses on the floor. We joked about it until the landlord went to prison, at which point we realised it really was a brothel.

Starmer's only comment on what type of sauna it was when he lived there after Cooper is that it 'kept interesting hours'. The hole in the kitchen floor and the broken windows which Cooper remembers must have been repaired at some stage, and some other improvements made, because, according to the electoral roll, Starmer remained at that address for at least four years, until 1990, and some of his later flatmates were young women. It seems unlikely that they would have been happy to live above a den of vice.

Initially, Starmer shared the flat with Vickers – who later worked for the BBC and *Private Eye* magazine – and another old Reigatian, Mark Adams. Stephen Bunyan made up the quartet. Of this period, Vickers, who died in 2017, once observed: 'Keir was one of the more important figures in the social whirl. He was a great party animal. He was very keen on Desmond Dekker, and I think his favourite record was *The Israelites*, which we would have to listen to dozens of times a week.' He added: 'Keir's politics were hard left and with that hard leftness came responsibility, so any decision that was made had to be made collectively, but of course Keir, as the strongest personality in that collective, usually got his own way.'[3]

By day, Starmer, who had turned twenty-four in September 1986, attended the Inns of Court School of Law at Gray's Inn Place in Holborn. There, he took what was then known as the Bar Vocational Course, the obligatory nine-month professional training course for would-be barristers in England and Wales before they began their pupillage. All aspiring barristers must belong to one of the four Inns of Court, the ancient professional associations whose appearance and characteristics are much like some Oxbridge colleges. Starmer was fortunate in that his Bar School fees were partially covered by the Inn he had joined, the Honourable Society of the Middle Temple. Having been interviewed by some of Middle Temple's senior members, he had been awarded a Queen Mother Scholarship, which is considered one of the most prestigious bursaries on offer and is usually given in recognition of academic excellence.[4] According to the recipient of a similar award at about the same time, it might have been worth approximately £1,500.

In order to be called to the Bar so that he could eventually begin practising as a barrister, Starmer also had to attend twelve dinners in Middle Temple's fabulous Elizabethan dining hall. These formal dining sessions were mandatory and were considered an important part of a barrister's education, though many in legal circles regarded this tradition as something of an anachronism. Starmer was lucky in one way, though. While studying for the BCL at St Edmund Hall, he had got to know Anthony Metzer, who was at that time in his final year at Wadham College, where he was reading law. They had struck up a friendship. Metzer then attended Bar School with Starmer and had also joined Middle Temple, guaranteeing that at least one friendly face would be in the Inn's dining hall.

In tandem with his legal studies, Starmer continued to put his energy into a very different sort of endeavour, with which he had been preoccupied since leaving Oxford: namely a magazine called *Socialist Alternatives*. Over a period of about a year, from July 1986 until August 1987, five editions of this Marxist journal were produced on what could be described as a professional-amateur basis. In other words, the title gamely took a dive into the choppy financial waters of the commercial publishing business, but the end product appeared to be somewhat hastily cobbled together and was often as error-strewn as a local parish newsletter. Given the relative youth of those behind it, its inexpert appearance was probably unsurprising. Starmer was a member of its seven-strong 'editorial collective', which was led by Benjamin Schoendorff, who was at the time in his final year of a PPE course at Oxford. As explained in the previous chapter, he had been chairman of the Oxford University Labour Club between 1984 and 1985, and Starmer had first fallen in with him while he was a mature student at St Edmund Hall. The periodical listed as its address 22 Charles Street in Oxford, a house which, by coincidence, had been owned until 1984 by the future publisher and Labour MP Derek Wyatt and was rented to students thereafter. Most members of the editorial collective studied at Oxford during the magazine's brief existence. It has never been clear who put up the money to fund it, nor how it was sustained.

Socialist Alternatives was inspired partly by the thinking of a Greek revolutionary commonly known by the moniker 'Pablo'. His real name was Michalis Raptis, or Michel Raptis, and during his life he was a leading member of the Fourth International, a Trotskyist organisation whose aims are to overthrow capitalism and establish world socialism. Raptis, who was born in 1911, is said to have met and got on well with Fidel Castro, Che Guevara and Ayatollah Khamenei, and after the Second World War he established himself as one of Europe's more prominent left-wing radicals. A common misconception is that *Socialist Alternatives* was a Trotskyist magazine, but according to Richard Barbrook, one of its unpaid contributors, this is wide of the mark. 'I met Jane Alexander, who was on the editorial board of *Socialist Alternatives*, at a party,' says Barbrook.[5]

I think I was the only person at this party who had heard of the Pabloites. Jane invited me to some of their meetings and got me to write this article. People say Keir was a Trotskyist, but he wasn't a Trotskyist. That's the mistake they make. They assume that merely because Michel Raptis, who was the leader of this little faction, had been a Trotskyist, but he stopped in the 1960s. He then got really into self-management and red–green politics. It would be completely accurate to say that Keir was a member of a group that had been founded by an ex-Trotskyist.

Having ditched Trotskyism in the 1960s, Raptis also turned his attention to women's liberation. He developed a cult following, especially in Paris, and the left-wing clique which pored over his essays and discussed his philosophy became known collectively as the Pabloites. *Socialist Alternatives* was, in effect, the London franchise of the Pabloite movement. Barbrook says that he can recall attending some of their meetings at a flat in Hampstead 'near where George Orwell had worked in a bookshop in South End Green', and at which it is possible that drugs may have been smoked on occasion. 'We used to sit around; we used to talk,' he says.

> I'm pretty sure we smoked dope but [Keir] was a lawyer, so I know lawyers at the time used to avoid doing that. He was a very committed lawyer. That's what I knew him as. We probably broke the Misuse of Drugs Act, but I wouldn't think he did. It's so long ago I can't remember. I don't even know if he was in the room when that happened. Keir struck me as straight shooter who mixed with a bohemian crowd that he didn't really suit.

Its first issue, vol. 1, no. 1, published in July 1986, had a cover price of 90p

– roughly the price of a pint of beer at the time – and introduced itself as 'a journal with a difference'. The opening editorial declared: 'Thatcherism is rapidly loosing [*sic*] its hold over British politics and yet the Left finds itself in such a mess that it appears unable to present a coherent socialist alternative.' It went on to outline its vision of socialism as 'the generalised self-management of society as a whole' and claimed it was 'concretely working towards a radical extension of popular control over wealth and power' by 'building a new kind of alliance from the bottom up integrating both the traditional wing of the labour movement and the new social movements'. It spoke of 'sexual', 'racial' and 'economic' oppression and exploitation and also criticised the Labour Party's right wing for its 'unholy alliance' with the 'realigned left' over the expulsion of Militant Tendency members from the Labour Party.

For reasons best known to himself, Schoendorff, despite being the magazine's de facto editor and the driving force behind the enterprise, sometimes wrote under the pseudonym 'Harry Curtis'. In middle age, Schoendorff has claimed that the views he held when he was involved with *Socialist Alternatives* remain important to him, commenting in 2019: 'I remember Keir very well … we were radical anti-imperialist ecosocialists. My personal stance hasn't changed much since.'[6] In an attempt to explain what it was all about, Starmer once told the BBC:

> [*Socialist Alternatives*] was an organisation looking at how you grow politics from the bottom up rather than the top down, and there was a lot of interest at the time in self-management and how you change the economy through that, so that was the next [political] phase that I went through when I went to college.

On that occasion he did not, however, manage to explain what self-management is. For the avoidance of doubt, others have defined it as a social and economic model instituted by the Communist Party of Yugoslavia from 1950 until 1990, which was advocated by President Tito, among others.

The first edition of *Socialist Alternatives*, which was thirty-six pages long, featured an article on Marxism by Raptis himself. Another contributor was the Labour MP Tony Benn, whose recent speech to the Brussels Conference was reproduced. Starmer's principal piece in the magazine's opening offering argued for the expansion of trade unions in light of the ongoing Wapping dispute – the printworkers' strike held between January 1986 and February 1987 that was sparked by Rupert Murdoch's decision to relocate his British newspaper operation from Fleet Street to east London. Starmer then endorsed the idea of handing greater control over the economy to trade unions, opining:

> These are important examples of how trade unions can begin building horizontally within and beyond the union, thus extending the challenge from simple workplace control to control over industry and community ... the challenge of control can only be met if unions are radically enlarged to encompass the political elements of control throughout society.

A second piece by Starmer took the form of a critique of a campaign launched by Neil Kinnock, called Freedom and Fairness. In the article, Starmer took issue with what he regarded as its pro-capitalism approach, writing, 'Freedom and Fairness, like its industrial counterpart [Jobs and Industry], presumably safeguards the freedom of capital in Britain whilst showing little regard for the freedom of the workforce and community to extend their political control.' He went on:

> The 1979 defeat can be seen as a rejection of corporatism and statism

by the electorate. It is unfortunate however, that Freedom and Fairness should interpret this as a reaffirmation of market values coupled with an extension of home ownership ... Unfortunately, by turning back to the market economy, it misses a third alternative, that of participatory socialism based on democratic planning.

The next edition, published in October 1986, anticipated the 1987 general election and stated that 'Socialist Alternatives will continue to argue for a radical extension of popular control over wealth and power'. In it, Starmer co-wrote an article with his close friend Alex Harvey, another member of the editorial collective, assessing the recent TUC conference. By the third edition, the magazine's editorial page covered what it saw as a world 'ecological crisis' and spoke of how 'capitalism feeds on all forms of oppression'. A few paragraphs later, it was reduced to begging its readers for 'material' and also for 'financial' help, presumably to stay afloat.

Starmer's contribution to this issue again saw him back on the trade union beat, this time devoting three pages to what he called 'a new type of industrial pluralism' to combat the 'authoritarian onslaught of Thatcherism'. The degree of Starmer's brain power this type of article used up was discussed many years later by his flatmate Paul Vickers, who recounted that on one occasion two burglars walked into their flat in Archway Road while Starmer was working at his desk and stole their television and video recorder. The thieves arrived and left without Starmer realising, bumped into Vickers on the stairs, dumped the electrical items and ran off. Starmer, apparently lost in thought, was oblivious to the crime. 'He was so obsessed with the books, he was so buried in his texts, that he didn't notice these two burglars walking round ... helping themselves to our stuff', said Vickers.[7]

Perhaps Starmer's proudest Socialist Alternatives moment came in

April 1987, when he interviewed Tony Benn at his Holland Park Avenue townhouse for the fourth issue of the magazine. While firing questions at Benn in his kitchen, he was invited to sit on one of Benn's prized possessions: a wooden chair that had been owned by Keir Hardie. The subject on which they reflected concerned whether the Labour Party needed to be 'refounded' if it was to survive. At one juncture, Starmer asked Benn: 'Would you say then that overall the Labour Party should become the united party of the oppressed, rather than the party of any one section of the oppressed, for example the working class?' Although Benn's answer was characteristically fluent, the very fact that Starmer asked him this captured the eye of the political journalist Nick Robinson more than thirty years later. When he challenged Starmer about it during a BBC interview in 2018, Starmer sounded somewhat defensive. 'Well, that's very much how it felt to me and in the era of Thatcher and as I say this searing sense for me that manufacturing was being destroyed, that the economic model was wrong and that there needed to be radical change,' he said. He added: 'Well, that was obviously me thinking I had cracked all the answers at an early age; language which doesn't make much sense, actually.' At the time of their meeting Tony Benn may well have agreed with Starmer's subsequent critique of his own position, for their encounter failed to merit a mention in Benn's assiduously kept diary for 1987.

The fifth edition of the magazine, produced in August 1987, was in large part devoted to an examination of the recent general election, in which Thatcher had claimed a third successive victory. (Incidentally, in this election Starmer's own MP in north London, Sir Hugh Rossi, a Conservative, had also held his seat.) Starmer's byline appeared on four articles, indicating that he was spending an increasing amount of time on the magazine despite having to revise for his Bar exams. Richard Barbrook is not surprised at the level of his devotion to the cause. 'He was the guy who got the magazine done,' Barbrook recalls.

The thing I remember is that he got all the articles in, he got it laid out, he got it to the printers and he got it back from the printers and distributed it at the bookshops, and that's what I remember he was like. The rest of them probably sat around and talked about it and had interesting ideas. [Starmer] wasn't the leader, this other guy, Benji Schoendorff, was the leader. [Starmer] was the number two, the organiser basically. The other guy knew Raptis.

Despite Raptis apparently ditching his Trotskyist leanings, there is no doubt that *Socialist Alternatives* continued to plough a furrow that made it unashamedly hard left. It condemned the Labour Party under Neil Kinnock, lambasting the 'Labour right's hopeless neo-Keynesian economic programme'; it called for a 'radical extension of common ownership over wealth and power'; it argued in favour of prisoners' rights; and it pushed for the working week to be cut to thirty-two hours. Starmer also queried police activity in the context of the dispute between printworkers at Wapping, whom he supported and where he had attended the picket lines as a legal observer. He wrote of 'paramilitary policing methods' and said: 'This leads to the question of the role the police should play, if any, in civil society. Who are they protecting and from what?'

Yet Barbrook believes that, for all its presentational faults, the magazine, which he describes as 'avant-garde', was in fact visionary. 'I think it was ahead of its time,' he says.

They were really ahead of their time on green issues. The trouble is, it was too green for the reds and too red for the greens. If Keir dusted off all his old issues of *Socialist Alternatives* and studied them, he would be a much better leader of the Labour Party.

Another reader of the magazine who got to know him at this point was Peter Tatchell, the human rights activist. 'Socialist Alternatives was radical left but democratic and modernising enough to embrace human rights, ecology, feminism and LGBT+ equality,' Tatchell says.[8] 'It was very anti-Stalinist, libertarian and anti-statist. I'd describe Keir as being on the radical, thoughtful, questioning left. He was always very open to explore new ideas and perspectives. Unlike some people on the left, he was not at all dogmatic or sectarian.'

It is certainly true that one of its major preoccupations, environmental matters, enjoys mainstream press coverage now. At the time, though, it must have felt to Starmer that he was fighting an uphill battle. Each issue of Socialist Alternatives is thought to have had a print run of between 500 and 1,000 copies. It was sold mainly in left-wing bookshops, including Collet's on Charing Cross Road and the Camden-based shop Compendium, and had a limited readership. Paul Vickers even said dismissively that because the magazine consisted of nothing more than 'dense political theory' it was 'totally unreadable'. He added: 'As a result, we used to sit [in the flat] surrounded by boxes of thousands and thousands of unsold copies of Socialist Alternatives.'

To what extent Vickers exaggerated its poor sales for effect is not clear. What is more certain is that Starmer cannot be faulted for trying to maximise the magazine's chances of success. Not content with distributing it via bookshops, he made sure it was also available to those who attended meetings held by the Socialist Society, a radical organisation of activist intellectuals founded in 1982 that was independent of the Labour Party and committed to making 'socialism the common sense of the age', in the words of its founding statement. Among its members were the left-wing academic Ralph Miliband, the future Labour leader Jeremy Corbyn, and Caroline Benn, author and campaigner on education, who was married to Tony Benn. Another principal figure was Hilary Wainwright, who made a couple of contributions to *Socialist Alternatives* herself, including giving Starmer an interview for the April 1987 edition.

Wainwright recalls that some members of the magazine's editorial collective managed to get themselves voted onto the Socialist Society's steering committee. The significance of this is that the Socialist Society was instrumental in helping to co-organise with the Campaign Group of MPs an annual Chesterfield conference. The inaugural Socialist conference was in October 1987, a meeting of 2,000 radical left activists in Tony Benn's Derbyshire constituency. These conferences were sometimes attended by the leader of the National Union of Mineworkers, Arthur Scargill and, among others, the Labour MPs Ken Livingstone, Bernie Grant, Audrey Wise and Eric Heffer, another occasional *Socialist Alternatives* contributor. Its purpose was to build a broadly based movement against Thatcherism in the wake of the defeat of the miners and the abolition of the Greater London Council. This confirms that key players within *Socialist Alternatives* were tangentially linked to national politics.

'There was a group of boys in the Socialist Society from *Socialist Alternatives*,' Wainwright says.[9]

I think they were still students. I think they'd all come from Oxford. I remember one was called Alex Harvey. They must have turned up at a Socialist Society AGM and got themselves elected to its steering committee. We were quite a significant organisation, but not a huge one. We had quite a big paper membership – maybe 500 or so. We were mainly a group of politically active intellectuals, politically active inside and outside the Labour Party. That inside–outside theme was important. We rejected the notion the big division on the left was about whether to be inside or outside of the Labour Party.

There was a significant group inside the party who shared a lot of ideas with people outside the party; through the Socialist Society we created a space where the most important point wasn't whether you were in or out of the Labour Party but rather whether you were committed to working in a non-sectarian way on developing new ideas and promoted political education. We produced three or four Penguin books like *What Is to Be Done About Health?* and *What Is to Be Done About Education?* and we would have educational conferences. Our members were mainly teachers at schools and universities and polytechnics and higher education colleges, as they were then, and also journalists. So it was a body of socialist intellectuals of a committed and practical kind.

Starmer's ties to the Socialist Society continued for several years. For example, in 1989, he and another barrister, Robin Oppenheim, participated in drawing up the socialist policy review document for the third socialist conference, as an alternative to the Labour Party policy review of the same year. The event was sponsored by Tony Benn and the Campaign Group of MPs, and the policy review was published in the Socialist Society's journal, *Interlink*. Oppenheim and Starmer's contribution, titled 'The Judiciary and the Legal System', featured ideas on a new democratic constitution and on human rights. Andrew Coates, a Marxist writer who met Starmer in the 1980s, says:

Socialist Society meetings were monthly at one point. Meetings were held all over London in various university buildings. [Starmer] was a very committed, serious person, quite amiable. Some of his comrades were quite annoying, but he wasn't. Benjamin Schoendorff was what we call a faction leader, and he was just a bit annoying. They were formally on the steering committee, but they weren't very intensely involved in it and they were just a group who were trying to press this thing about 'the alternative' and it was the forerunner of green–red politics. [Starmer wrote] pretty serious stuff on legal reform and human rights. He was pretty respected in that sphere already. He was active for quite a long period of time.[10]

The Socialist Society has been defunct for almost thirty years, having held its last meeting in 1993. This long passage of time perhaps helps to explain why Hilary Wainwright has no vivid memory of Starmer. As with Barbrook and Coates, however, one of Starmer's colleagues – Schoendorff – did lodge in her mind, leading to the impression that Starmer was more of a background personality. 'I remember the guy who led *Socialist Alternatives*, Ben Schoendorff, was quite a dynamic character,' Wainwright says.

He rather dominated their contributions. When Keir became DPP [in 2008], people said, 'Do you remember he was in the Socialist Society?', and then I became aware that he had been, but I can't say I remember him sitting across the table from me. I haven't had anything to do with him since. He didn't strike me as a distinctive political figure at the time. In a way, this accords with the situation now, which is that whatever are his forensic skills, he doesn't have a recognisable political vision either for himself or for the Labour Party. Obviously there's a danger in retrospective projection, but he had no memorable political profile that I can recall.

As for the magazine, Wainwright says,

I probably would have read *Socialist Alternatives*. I can't say that I can remember any good ideas [in it]. I would have taken it seriously, as

I would have any publication coming up with interesting new ideas. Through Schoendorff it had quite a strong French connection which could have been quite interesting. It wouldn't be a reference point, but occasionally I would read it.

* * *

By the summer of 1987, Starmer had completed his Bar Vocational Course. His final stage of preparation to be a barrister required him to secure a pupillage. In effect, this is a twelve-month training contract in a set of barristers' chambers. As the profession is so oversubscribed, and each set takes on only a few pupils every year, clearing this hurdle is notoriously difficult. In the 1980s, the legal world remained pretty traditional, and it was still tilted in favour of those who were white, male, had been to a private school and had attended Oxbridge. Starmer, of course, ticked all these boxes, whether he would care to admit it or not. His academic qualifications, and his acquaintance with a string of well-placed academics from the universities of Leeds and Oxford who could vouch for him, meant that he was at least as well equipped to succeed as most of his rivals. In light of the set of chambers he eventually ended up in, however, his background probably served him less well than did his political beliefs.

Aspiring pupils could apply to as many sets of chambers as they wished. At that time, the process required them to write a personal letter to a chosen set explaining why they wanted to be in pupillage there. If they were lucky enough to be asked for an interview, they would be seen by two senior members of chambers, usually on a Saturday. They might then be invited to return for a second and possibly a third grilling before a final decision was taken. It seems appropriate at this point to quote the late barrister and author John Mortimer, creator of *Rumpole of the Bailey*, who once wrote of 'the splendid miseries' of being a pupil in a barrister's chambers. Mortimer was by no means the only legal figure to have regarded this early stage of a young lawyer's career in such agonising terms, but he would have been better placed than most to monitor Starmer's progress. For at the age of twenty-five, Starmer was accepted as a pupil at 1 Dr Johnson's Buildings, a mixed common law set in the legal district known as the Inner Temple. Mortimer was still an associate tenant of these chambers, despite his various literary triumphs. Situated in a handsome Grade II-listed nineteenth-century property close to the Royal Courts of Justice, it was well-regarded and, crucially for a young man with Starmer's politics, less stuffy and more liberal than other sets. Indeed, several young left-wing barristers were already in situ there, and, as we shall see in the next chapter, Starmer had already got to know them.

One of those who conducted Starmer's pupillage interview was Gavin Millar, whose sister, Fiona, is the partner of Alastair Campbell, Tony Blair's former press secretary. Another was Stephen Irwin, a medical negligence specialist who became a High Court judge in 2006 and who was appointed a Lord Justice of Appeal in 2016, a role which he relinquished in 2020. The third was Peter Thornton, who would go on to become the Chief Coroner of England and Wales. It is said that the interview did not go as smoothly as Starmer might have hoped. There is a story that during it he quoted the maxim 'property is theft' – which is attributed to the nineteenth-century French socialist Pierre-Joseph Proudhon – while explaining why he thought non-violent burglars should not necessarily have to go to prison. This remark apparently caused some consternation among some of the senior barristers at 1 Dr Johnson's Buildings when they later heard about it. Allegedly, it was Stephen Irwin who came to Starmer's defence, saying he was clearly 'absolutely brilliant' and should be taken on.[11] Without explaining why,

Irwin would not be drawn on the veracity of this tale when asked about it for the purposes of this book. He did become Starmer's pupil master, however, and his refusal to take the opportunity to deny that he did utter Proudhon's words suggests the story may be true.

The head of 1 Dr Johnson's Buildings in the autumn of 1987 was Lord Hooson, a Welshman who was among the last of a dying breed that had been active in both the law and politics simultaneously. He had been a barrister since the late 1940s and was also, from 1962, a Liberal MP. He remained in the House of Commons for seventeen years until losing his Montgomeryshire seat at the 1979 general election, whereupon he was elevated to the House of Lords. His legal career was no less high-profile. He was perhaps best known for having defended Ian Brady, the Moors Murderer, at his trial at Chester Assizes in 1966. Other notable personalities in the set were Louis Blom-Cooper, a fierce opponent of the death penalty; Alex (now Lord) Carlile, one of the youngest QCs in the country, having taken silk a few years earlier aged thirty-six; and Geoffrey Robertson, an Australian who had acted for the defence in a string of newsworthy cases such as the *Oz* magazine trial and who at that time dated the future television cook Nigella Lawson. Starmer must have counted himself lucky to be rubbing shoulders with such colourful figures as he negotiated the foothills of his chosen occupation, for others of his vintage would have found themselves working in comparatively drier and dustier environments. Some of the younger members of the set at 1 Dr Johnson's Buildings may not have been as glamorous as their elders, but, as alluded to already, they certainly shared the same trenchant left-wing opinions as Starmer, and he was well known to them.

Pupillage is usually split into two terms, each lasting six months, which are known as 'sixes'. Pupils work under a pupil master or pupil mistress. First, they operate in a non-practising capacity and must watch and learn by shadowing their superior in court and helping them in chambers as necessary, for example by assisting with research or by drafting skeleton arguments. During their second six months, they are allowed to begin handling their own cases and clients, albeit at a low level. Over the course of their year-long traineeship, they are assessed by the seniors in their set. They are then invited to apply for a permanent position, known as a tenancy, which enables them to base themselves in chambers as a self-employed barrister. If their face fits after a year in pupillage, they are likely to become a tenant, but this is by no means guaranteed. Generally, tenancy is awarded only after a vote of all members of chambers, including the clerks, who distribute most of the work.

Colin Wells was a pupil alongside Starmer between 1987 and 1988. Another pupil was the aforementioned Anthony Metzer, Starmer's friend from his spell at Oxford. All of them, according to Wells, were 'centre-left', which defused the situation immediately. 'In those days there was a lot of competition to get [a pupillage], but the three of us got on very well,' says Wells.

> Hundreds of people applied to that set. They had a very good reputation. If you were accepted for an interview, you might be in competition with 100 or so other people. I had a good reference. I suppose being politically active in the Labour movement helped. The chances of me getting anywhere were quite remote because I went to a polytechnic, I was working class and I have a strong accent.

Despite the fact that he and Starmer were both ultimately gunning for a tenancy, Wells says that Starmer was always friendly towards him. 'He could look at things from left field,' he recalls.[12]

He was always someone I could discuss cases with. He's a very bright guy, very intelligent but humble as well. He would help out. When you're pupils, you're thrown together for quite an intensive twelve months or so and tend to live in each other's pockets, but you have to get on with the work.

As is the case with many young barristers, Starmer's legal career began in earnest with minor criminal briefs. The hours were long, and the work was often hard. 'You have to remember, when you're doing a pupillage, you're probably putting in twelve- to fifteen-hour days and commuting all over the country doing court appearances,' says Wells. Occasionally, he recalls, they might have a quick drink of an evening, but there was not a great deal of time for socialising. In any case, Starmer had a laser-like focus on his work, and his public-spirited approach to the job was apparent from the word go. 'He was someone who was very well prepared to get his hands dirty, roll his sleeves up and get involved,' remembers Wells.

It wasn't just for his career. It was a true commitment to representing those who'd been wronged. That's the impression I still have of him to this day. I was delighted when he became leader of the Labour Party because everyone asked me what he was like and I was able to say he's a true socialist. He's a political animal in that sense, not just a careerist. He actually genuinely believes in it. You can't say that for a lot of politicians. You can't say that about a lot of barristers, either.

During the summer of 1988, Starmer, Metzer and Wells all applied for tenancy at 1 Dr Johnson's Buildings. Of the three, Wells was not accepted, but he was allowed to 'squat' there temporarily and apply again later. Metzer and Starmer were taken on, but just as had been the case the year before when vying for pupillage, Starmer's interview did not exactly go swimmingly. His senior colleague, Geoffrey Robertson, who considers himself to have been Starmer's mentor, once said that he 'looked about fourteen, was nervous and awkward in the interview and (worst of all, for my colleagues on the panel) was poorly dressed'.[13] The item of clothing they found particularly disagreeable was, apparently, his cardigan. In retrospect, the idea that Starmer thought it sensible to attend such a formal meeting wearing something which in the 1980s was most closely associated with the breakfast television presenter Frank Bough did show a complete lack of *savoir faire* on his part. Robertson added, 'It needed all my powers of persuasion to get [Lord Hooson] to accept him.' A glowing reference from one of his better-known tutors from his days at Leeds University was apparently crucial to his success.

Having become a tenant, Starmer could start to earn his first self-generated income by running his own cases and by acting as junior counsel to some of his older colleagues who were able to take on bigger briefs. Six years after becoming a law student at Leeds, he was finally on the move. By this time, his personal life was looking up as well, insofar as his girlfriend, Angela O'Brien, whom he had first met at Leeds, had moved into his flat at Archway Road. She was one of three young women living there with Starmer and the aforementioned Mark Adams and Paul Vickers. She would go on to become a clinical psychologist, and there is no doubt they were serious about each other. Starmer had even published a piece written by O'Brien in the final edition of his beloved *Socialist Alternatives*.

CHAPTER 5

SOCIALIST LAWYER

Socialist Alternatives was not the only left-wing publication to pre-occupy Keir Starmer during 1987. Although he devoted a considerable amount of energy to pushing the message of the Pabloites that year while he was working long hours as a law student and later in pupillage, he also found time to become a member of the editorial committee of another new magazine, called *Socialist Lawyer*. It is the official journal of the Haldane Society of Socialist Lawyers, which was founded in 1930 and describes itself as 'an organisation which provides a forum for the discussion and analysis of law and the legal system from a socialist perspective'. Independent of any political party, its membership consists of lawyers, law teachers, law students, legal workers and trade unionists. Starmer's link to the Haldane Society has rarely been mentioned outside of legal circles, and he has never advertised his involvement in it – for example, it is not listed in his *Who's Who* entry. For professional and personal reasons, however, it was an important part of his life, and this phase of his career warrants examination.

Starmer's contemporary at 1 Dr Johnson's Buildings, Colin Wells, who was also a Haldane member in the 1980s, says that the group was considered a key platform for barristers and solicitors on the left at the time. 'If there were strikes and industrial disputes, we would help out in a legal sense,' he says.[1] 'There would be picket lines that we would act as legal observers on; there would be advice that we would give.' Indeed, it was through the Haldane Society that Starmer volunteered to be a legal observer at Wapping during the 54-week printworkers' dispute. As noted in the previous chapter, the strike came about as a result of Rupert Murdoch's decision to jettison the hot metal printing presses of Fleet Street and embrace the electronic revolution by building a modern printing plant in east London. From there, the four British newspaper titles which he owned at the time – *The Times*, the *Sunday Times*, *The Sun* and the *News of the World* – would be produced.

As this move placed thousands of printing jobs in jeopardy, the dispute became increasingly bitter and violent and led to clashes between protesters and the police, in which hundreds of arrests were made. The night of 24 January 1987 marked the first anniversary of the strike and was a particularly tense occasion, with bricks, bottles and iron bars being hurled at officers. Mounted units then charged at parts of the crowd. After a confrontation lasting for several hours, Wapping High Street was covered in debris, and it looked as though a battle had indeed taken place there. Starmer has claimed he was present that night, though in what capacity remains unclear. An independent group called the Wapping Legal Observers was formed with Haldane Society backing, after the print unions asked for help in monitoring and reporting on police activity and arrests. In a report it produced subsequently, however, which was written by the future QC Ben Emmerson, there was no mention of Starmer's name, leading to the possibility that he was there under his own steam.

Whatever the case, this was dangerous work which certainly showed Starmer's commitment to the cause, even if there was a certain paradox in his risking his safety in the name of people who were employed by newspapers which he probably did not read, whose editorial line he almost certainly opposed, and whose proprietor had a famously strong relationship with his bête noire, Margaret Thatcher. The ultimate defeat of the print unions in February 1987, two years after the miners were overcome, dealt a hammer blow to union power in Britain, but at least Starmer would in future be able to talk about Wapping with the authenticity of personal experience.

It is noteworthy that another lawyer who belonged to the Haldane Society at that time, Bill Bowring, claims that until the 1980s it was dominated by Communist Party lawyers. He adds: 'The initial leaders of the Haldane in the 1930s were Stalinists. They probably adopted the name Haldane – after Viscount Haldane, the first Labour Party Lord Chancellor – as camouflage.'[2] According to Bowring, who was chair of Haldane for several years while Starmer was secretary, several of the communist lawyers have gone on to join the ranks of today's legal establishment, leaving their political past quietly behind them.

Starmer's name first cropped up in the *Socialist Lawyer* in its second-ever issue, published in the spring of 1987, when he was halfway through Bar School and more than six months before he joined 1 Dr Johnson's Buildings as a pupil. It had been launched the previous year as a quarterly magazine and was edited by Nick Paul and Andrew Buchan, two youngish barristers who were themselves members of 1 Dr Johnson's Buildings. Starmer was listed alongside them as one of six members of its editorial committee. The others were Heather Williams, Alastair Smail and Beverley Lang. Other than Starmer, Smail was the only one who did not at that point have a seat in 1 Dr Johnson's Buildings. In fact, that set of chambers appears to have been the effective office of *Socialist Lawyer*. Anybody who wished to write for the magazine was asked to submit their ideas to its address and Lang, who is now a High Court judge, doubled up as its secretary and would take telephone calls concerning society business there.

Another member of 1 Dr Johnson's Buildings, Helena Kennedy, who was one of the first Labour peers appointed by Tony Blair in 1997, was listed as a vice-president of the Haldane Society at the time Starmer became involved. It will come as no surprise to anybody that networking has always been an essential ingredient of success for aspiring barristers. Whether or not Starmer had his eye on a pupillage at 1 Dr Johnson's Buildings in early 1987 – and whether he thought he might achieve that aim via the Haldane Society – is an open question. What is not in doubt is that he was mixing with a group of people who were already established there and who would be useful to him in the future.

He served in various roles on the magazine for more than five years, during which time it published articles by a range of lawyers, politicians and activists, including the barrister Marina Wheeler, who later married Boris Johnson; Tony Benn; and Peter Tatchell, the human rights campaigner. Starmer's first ever contributions to the magazine hardly ranked as earth-shattering. One was a discussion with two solicitors about the rights of tenants versus landlords; the other was a short piece on his pet subject: the need for trade union reform after two successive Thatcher administrations. His radical spirit was evident elsewhere, though. In the fourth issue, published in the winter of 1987, he reviewed a book titled *Immigration Law and Practice*, written by Ian Macdonald, in which he appeared to support the claim that immigration law is imbued by a 'racist undercurrent'. He wrote:

Ian Macdonald does not let the establishment off the hook by accepting the argument that any immigration law is bound to distinguish between 'us' and 'them', instead he points to the preferential treatment of EEC visitors and settlers in this country to show the racist undercurrent which permeates all immigration law, whether implemented by the Tories or Labour. It's not a question of numbers, it's a question of racism.

Then, in the winter of 1987, Starmer and Robin Oppenheim tried to overturn more than fifty years of history by suggesting that the Haldane Society should change its name, ditching 'Haldane' and instead calling itself either the National Association of Socialist Lawyers or the National Society of Socialist Lawyers. The justification for this idea was that the name Haldane apparently sounded like a 'London-orientated barristers' club'. In their manifesto, published in the *Socialist Lawyer*, the pair wrote that they considered broadening the society's membership to be vital because 'the context of the present hostile political climate, the inevitable attacks on civil liberties, jury trial, legal aid and the legal rights of trade unions will require us to turn ourselves outward and to build an effective national campaigning organisation'. This proposal was contested vigorously by many of Haldane's most senior figures, including John Platts-Mills, its president. As a former Labour MP with communist sympathies, Platts-Mills, by then in his eighties, can hardly be accused of having held small 'c' conservative opinions. Yet he and others wrote of their 'deep concern' at the Starmer–Oppenheim suggestion, on the basis that the name Haldane was 'an important part of our history' which 'is known throughout the British trade union movement and throughout the world as the name of Britain's organisation of socialist lawyers'.

In March 1988, a meeting was held at 1 Dr Johnson's Buildings to settle the question. Bill Bowring, who was there, remembers the occasion was 'really stormy with a lot of shouting'. He adds: 'Keir was the kind of Young Turk of the time, with quite a few supporters.' But not enough, it seems. His plan was voted down, and the name Haldane survives to this day. Bowring, though, says the episode is one indication, together with Starmer's proposals for Haldane's reform ('Haldane Forth') and his project for the 'modern prosecutor' while he was DPP, that Starmer is at heart 'a moderniser'.

By the fifth edition of *Socialist Lawyer*, in the spring of 1988, Starmer interviewed two other lawyers: his colleague Gavin Millar, and another barrister, Nick Blake. The premise of their discussion was the apparently inherent injustice of the judicial system. Starmer described the judiciary as 'notoriously white male and educated at Oxford or Cambridge', stating it is 'class-based and cannot be said to reflect the aspirations and anxieties of ordinary people in any way'. His opening question to Millar and Blake was: 'There is little dispute amongst socialists that the present judicial system needs changing. However, it seems that the left is not able to put forward a united and coherent alternative. What do you think are the most promising alternatives on offer?' Later, he asked them if they thought it was time for judges to be elected. If he wished to let Millar and Blake know that he was just as forward-thinking in his attitude as the next socialist lawyer, he went the right way about it. But of course, the 'radical' conversation that this trio enjoyed now appears somewhat hollow. All of them are white males who attended Oxbridge, though none of them thought fit to acknowledge this at the time. Furthermore, Starmer went on to become a QC, then DPP and to accept a knighthood; Blake is now Sir Nicholas Blake, a retired High Court judge; and Millar is a high-ranking QC.

It was in early 1988 that Starmer also joined the Haldane Society's executive committee. Bill Bowring was appointed at the same time. 'Keir's first activity in Haldane was as a member of the editorial team for *Socialist Lawyer*,' he says.

He joined Haldane shortly after I did, though for different reasons. I joined because [while a Labour Party councillor in Lambeth] I had deliberately broken the law and was being prosecuted by Margaret Thatcher for wilful misconduct. I was willingly taking the consequences. I wanted solidarity. Keir is someone who would never knowingly break the law under any circumstances.

This observation, Bowring believes, says much about his character. 'Keir's certainly not a Marxist,' he says.

> He has probably read some [Marxist] material. It's alleged that because he wrote for *Socialist Alternatives*, which was one of the fifty-seven varieties of Trotskyism called Pabloism, people say he was a Pabloite in his younger days, but I never heard him utter the words Pablo, Marx or Trotsky. I would put Keir down as a middle-of-the-road social democrat. I don't think Keir is in favour of an armed insurrection or anything like that. He would very strongly oppose it, because he's a law-and-order chap. Crucial to understanding Keir is that I think if there's a really bad law, one should break it, and of course one will then be punished. But he would have a really strong opposition to breaking a law under any circumstances.

By the autumn of 1988, Starmer had been appointed as the joint secretary of the society's executive committee along with Pam Brighton. Bowring was made its vice-chairman. Starmer had also taken on responsibility for the administration of another publication, *The Employment Law Bulletin*, which was described as 'a highly successful quarterly journal published by the Employment Law Committee of the Haldane Society' and which had a wide circulation among trade unions and labour lawyers. From the spring of 1989, he was the Haldane Society's sole secretary, shouldering ever more responsibility and, alongside his *Socialist Lawyer* duties, having to focus on the minutiae of the society's running. For example, if anybody wanted to bring a non-Haldane member to a committee meeting, they had to inform Starmer first. And he had to be notified of all proposals for the AGM. All this occupied much of his spare time, when he was not engaged as a barrister.

To have a cheerleader or mentor in the workplace is essential for almost any young, thrusting professional, and Starmer was no exception. That is why it was extremely useful to him that, by 1988, he had been taken under the wing of his senior colleague at 1 Dr Johnson's Buildings, Geoffrey Robertson. Robertson had recently been appointed a QC, and his own ambitions knew few bounds. Robertson is understood to have rated Starmer as a barrister in large part because he had solid qualifications, he was good at paperwork and he was happy to put in long hours at his desk. Starmer's reward for showing such devotion to his career was to be asked in late 1988 to accompany Robertson on a trip to the European Court of Human Rights at Strasbourg. This was to be Starmer's introduction to human rights law.

Things got off to an embarrassing start for the novice, however. A story circulated afterwards that when they landed at Strasbourg Airport, Robertson made it through customs successfully but Starmer did not. It transpired that he had lost his passport en route. With Starmer being threatened by the local gendarmerie with being locked up and returned to Gatwick Airport the next morning, Robertson had to telephone the British consul, who was persuaded to go to the airport and vouch for the hapless Starmer so that he could remain in the city for twenty-four hours. Miraculously, this ploy worked, and Starmer was able to witness Robertson acting for his client Mogens Hauschildt, a silver bullion dealer from Denmark who had been arrested for an alleged fraud but denied bail by the Danish authorities. Ultimately, Denmark lost the case – and Robertson therefore won it – and the country had to change its criminal justice procedures, as did some other European countries. Incidentally, *Hauschildt v Denmark* remains a leading authority when it comes to judicial bias, meaning that Starmer witnessed a little bit of legal history on that occasion.

Despite Starmer's work rate, he did allow himself some time off occasionally – as long as it allowed him to explore new left-wing ideas with like-minded people. Peter Tatchell recalls a trip they took together with others to a green-left summer camp in France in 1989. 'I first met Keir around 1987,' Tatchell says.[3]

> He was a fellow left-wing activist. He struck me as very intelligent, passionate and committed to a radical vision of what Britain could be. He was well to the left of Neil Kinnock, the then Labour leader, but what struck me was that he combined radicalism with pragmatism. His ideas were achievable and not far-fetched like some other people on the left. He was very much in the orbit of the emerging confluence between greens and socialists. He was quite in advance of Labour thinking at the time.

Tatchell remembers that whenever they met, they discussed a range of ideas which were not considered mainstream in Labour Party circles in the 1980s and early 1990s.

> Both he and I were already thinking about the potential of Europe-wide collaboration between socialist parties, trade unions and civil society groups to advance a progressive agenda. This went against the grain of traditional left-wing hostility towards what was then the EC. Keir was very strong on human rights. He also embraced new ideas on feminism, ecology and LGBT+ rights when some in the Labour Party – even on the left – were still quite hesitant.

Their joint interest in working with those who were involved in European politics was what took them on their Gallic exploit, yet there was little glamour about the trip on which they embarked. While some of Starmer's colleagues from chambers were jetting off to Greece or

Italy for a few weeks in the sun, he and Tatchell were among a group who travelled by coach to the Massif Central in order to attend a green socialist summer camp, which had been organised by the European Alternatives Youth Network. Starmer's girlfriend of the time, Angela O'Brien, did not go with them.

The journey began with the forty-strong delegation leaving Britain to visit Paris for the 200th anniversary of the Storming of the Bastille. They departed from Victoria station on the morning of 14 July and arrived in the French capital that evening for the celebrations. The next day, the group reboarded their coach and headed south, ending their journey when they reached the countryside close to the ancient village of La Couvertoirade, about an hour's drive north of Montpellier. The camp was held on farmland which belonged to a French left-wing activist. According to Tatchell, a couple of hundred activists from across Europe gathered there for seven days of radical lectures, debates and music.

'It was on the Larzac Plateau, a centre of Maquis resistance during the Second World War,' recalls Tatchell.

> We all camped out in tents in the fields and mucked in to cook meals and clean. Most of the people involved [from Britain] were from the *Socialist Alternatives* milieu, people like Ben Schoendorff and his then girlfriend, Flo Bertorelli. There were various people there, including the German Green MEP, Frank Schwalba-Hoth, plus some British Green activists, Dutch socialists and French radical leftists, all of us committed to left–green collaboration, Europe-wide co-ordination and a new kind of progressive politics.

So-called red–green parties were very much on the rise at the time, with several having sprung up in time to stand candidates in the 1989 European elections which had taken place the month before. They included the Dutch party GreenLeft, a political alliance comprising the Communist Party of the Netherlands, the Pacifist Socialist Party and two left-wing Christian parties, the Evangelical People's Party and the Political Party of Radicals. Unity List was the name of a similar socialist pick 'n' mix operation which had formed in Denmark.

Tatchell says he delivered several lectures during the conference:

> My talks at the summer camp were on building a Europe-wide red–green alliance and urging pan-European collaboration to push the EC in a more progressive direction on social justice, environmental and human rights issues. The overall focus was green socialist. Everybody there came from the green socialist milieu. There were daily talks, debates and musical performances. I can't remember if Keir played any music. He probably did, but I can't recall.

Nor does Tatchell have any memory of Starmer, who by this time was six weeks shy of his twenty-seventh birthday, taking to any of the platforms to make a speech. It seems that he preferred, somewhat characteristically, to stay under the radar, and adopted a more relaxed approach at this political festival. 'As well as the formal discussions, there were also lots of informal chats,' Tatchell says, throwing up the possibility that Starmer enjoyed talking one-to-one instead of addressing large crowds. English was the *lingua franca* at the event, allowing all those present to exchange ideas and information as they sought to advance their green and socialist agenda into all corners of Europe. 'People from France, Britain, Germany and other countries would link up and talk together over coffee or a beer,' Tatchell remembers. 'All the meals were communal. We prepared them together on a rota system, we ate them together and we washed up afterwards. It was a fantastic event. I was a bit sceptical when I was invited, but I was really glad I went.'

Tatchell adds that he and Starmer left the camp separately. He thinks Starmer caught the bus home, while he joined Schoendorff and Bertorelli to drive back to London by car. 'On the way back, we stopped off and met Pierre Juquin, a former member of the French Communist Party who had [by that point] broken with them.'

*　　*　　*

As well as his work as a barrister and his duties for the Haldane Society, Starmer also found time between 1987 and 1990 to take up a post as a legal officer for the National Council for Civil Liberties (NCCL), a civil liberties watchdog now known as Liberty. At the time he joined it, the NCCL was an organisation with a sordid recent past. Under the banner of promoting freedom, it had campaigned in the 1970s to liberalise the law on paedophilia and reduce the age of sexual consent to fourteen. In 1976, for example, the NCCL argued that 'childhood sexual experiences, willingly engaged in with an adult, result in no identifiable damage'. And in 1978, an organisation called the Paedophile Information Exchange (PIE) affiliated itself to the NCCL. As has been well documented, members of the PIE essentially tried to make paedophilia respectable by campaigning to lower the age of consent and resist controls on child pornography. Astonishingly, it was only in 1983 that the NCCL cut its ties with the PIE and its evil agenda. In holding a formal position within the NCCL, Starmer was following in the footsteps of other prominent Labour figures, including the future Cabinet ministers Patricia Hewitt and Harriet Harman, both of whom worked there in the 1970s, and in Harman's case in the early 1980s, too. Another future Labour MP, Diane Abbott, was also linked to the NCCL shortly before Starmer joined its ranks.

In the 1980s, the NCCL campaigned vigorously against various rights violations through the channels of the United Nations and the European Court of Human Rights in Strasbourg. By 1989, it viewed Margaret Thatcher as having decreed what its general secretary, Sarah Spencer, said was 'a peacetime state of emergency' through media censorship and extensive police powers. Spencer refused to co-operate with this book, saying somewhat bafflingly, 'If you attempt to imply that I have suggested [Starmer] either did, or did not, contribute [to the NCCL] then you will be misrepresenting what I have said.'[4]

Be that as it may, Starmer has been happy to state himself that he was linked to the group between 1987 and 1990. Records show that under Spencer's direction the NCCL also advocated introducing a Bill of Rights for Britain focused on civil rights. Harold Pinter, the playwright, was one of the NCCL's most prominent supporters. In February 1989, it changed its name to Liberty and embarked on a modernisation programme, shedding its intellectual image and adopting a more populist approach. Despite being apolitical, it was generally regarded as being on the libertarian left, lobbying to scrap the poll tax and proposals to introduce football ID cards.

Starmer's most public work for the NCCL and Liberty seems to have come at the very end of the 1980s. In June 1989, for example, he was linked to a battle against a clause in the Local Government and Housing Bill which sought to prevent officers who dealt with the public, earned more than £13,500 or worked in restricted areas from being politically active.[5] And in August 1989, he gave press interviews on behalf of Liberty in which he criticised proposals to introduce video identification parades.[6] That month, he also used his position as Liberty's legal officer to lambast the police for their attempt to crack down on an open-air acid house party in an area just outside Lambourn in Berkshire. After officers from Thames Valley Police set up roadblocks and confiscated electronic equipment to prevent the party from going ahead, Liberty chose to back the organisers in a court action. Starmer was quoted as saying that the police operation was 'outrageous and unlawful' and 'an incredible abuse of police powers'.[7] He is not thought to have been a regular attender of acid house parties, where taking proscribed drugs such as MDMA and LSD was not unusual, though one friend who prefers to remain anonymous says he was certainly not averse to 'smoking weed' at social occasions when he was a younger man.

*   *   *

By this point, Geoffrey Robertson was putting the finishing touches to his long-held ambition to shake up the legal establishment by abandoning 1 Dr Johnson's Buildings so he could set up a new 'post-modern' set of chambers. Since joining the Bar in the 1970s, Robertson had been uncomfortable with what he regarded as its outmoded quirks and had been ruminating on how to operate in a more contemporary environment. He wished to dispense with traditions such as having clerks who earned their money on commission and to appoint a practice manager on a salary instead. He also wanted to run an operation that welcomed a wider variety of people – women, ethnic minorities and those who did not come from middle-class backgrounds. Being physically situated away from the legal district was a priority for him. Robertson chose as the location of his new set some buildings in Doughty Street in Bloomsbury, far enough outside the confines of the Inns of Court but within walking distance of the High Court. The barristers bought the buildings collectively. All this was considered somewhat revolutionary at the time.

Starmer was one of twenty colleagues from 1 Dr Johnson's Buildings who decided to accompany Robertson on this adventure in July 1990. This breakaway move was said to be entirely amicable, with no hard feelings from those who remained at Dr Johnson's. Although Starmer was the youngest barrister on board this enterprise, he is remembered as having played a contributory role in its planning and negotiations and was said to be very excited by it. Among other figures to decamp to Bloomsbury were Helena Kennedy, Louis Blom-Cooper, Gavin Millar and Starmer's Oxford friend Anthony Metzer. During the first year of its existence, a further eight barristers from other chambers joined them. The new practice was founded upon what Robertson has called an 'imperishable commitment to the legal aid system',[8] with barristers split equally between civil and criminal practitioners. Robertson insisted that all barristers observe the so-called cab-rank rule, whereby they must accept any client whose case comes within their field of practice as long as they are available to do so. The only exception to this rule related to any case in which the death penalty would be upheld.

Colin Wells was one of the group that left 1 Dr Johnson's Buildings to join Doughty Street Chambers from its inception. 'We wanted to consolidate into a new, quite exciting radical set,' he recalls.

> *The Guardian* at the time called us the Young Turks, which was quite funny really, because we weren't that young. We were at the bottom, but the QCs were older. There was a group of us with a common interest in pursuing the human rights of individuals. We were all ages, from the bottom up.

Everybody contributed to the purchase of the building in Doughty Street, and the reputations of those involved apparently ensured the enterprise would be a success. 'It was very secure from the outset,' says Wells.

> Although we were a new set, there was strength in depth, so we knew that financially we were secure and we had good quality people. So,

for me as a junior of two or three years' call, it wasn't a risk at all; it was quite an exciting project. We didn't change the work we did; we carried on with the work we were doing, but it was a consolidation of ideas into one set.

Another Doughty Street figure says:

Doughty Street is a very good set because one of the problems about being a barrister is that an awful lot of barristers are pompous twerps. People like that were remarkably thin on the ground at Doughty Street, and Keir reflects that. He's just a thoroughly nice guy. He's a much more genial character than his persona in 2021 portrays. Usefully for him, there were always people at Doughty Street who were very closely involved in the Labour Party. They lived in north London and spent a lot of time discussing Labour politics. Everybody knew that. Some were Labour councillors. Their involvement varied. It is almost a question of who wasn't involved! I'm thinking of Robert Latham, Nick Toms, Helena Kennedy, Phillippa Kaufmann and Martin Westgate, to name a few.

The sense of modernisation at Liberty and also at his chambers seems to have rubbed off on Starmer. At the same time as Doughty Street Chambers was being set up, he and the executive committee of the Haldane Society were mulling over a series of proposals aimed at preparing the organisation for the new decade. In a trenchant piece for the *Socialist Lawyer* published in the autumn of 1990, Starmer wrote a rather bossy manifesto, stating that the society needed to raise its profile in the national left-wing press, citing titles including *The Guardian*. He also castigated other members in this document by stating, 'The Society is weak on policies. The Annual General Meeting is a farce.

Largely irrelevant and wordy resolutions are passed and then forgotten.' He called for more money to be pumped into *Socialist Lawyer* and suggested that a designated office worker be hired to handle all administrative matters. He also advocated a recruitment drive so that it would achieve a membership of at least 2,000 people. All this was rounded off with a warning that the society's finances were 'in an appalling state, perhaps worse now than ever before'. He then shared his idea to set up a charitable trust called the Haldane Educational Trust, which would finance all the society's educational research and publication work.

According to Bill Bowring, some of this worked – but not for long. 'He set out his plans to turn Haldane into something like [the pressure group] Liberty, with premises and a worker and an educational charitable trust, running professional development courses for money,' Bowring observes. 'We had premises in Took's Court and in Red Lion Square over Conway Hall. But it did not last more than a few years.'

As a footnote, it is worth adding that in February 2021 the Haldane Society seemingly attempted to humiliate Starmer by passing a motion at its AGM which stated, 'Sir Keir Starmer QC MP does not qualify for membership of the Haldane Society ... because he is demonstrably not a socialist.'[9] In a sense this was a futile gesture, on the basis that Starmer had ceased to play an active role in the organisation since 2008, when he resigned from its executive committee, and has had nothing formally to do with it since then. Not being able to expel him, the next best thing that those behind the motion could do was to state that he would 'not be permitted to rejoin the society unless and until his re-admittance is agreed by a future general meeting'. This would, of course, have required him to try to rejoin in the first place. However empty these words may seem, though, it must have stung Starmer to some degree to be subjected publicly to such treatment by a group to which he had devoted a considerable amount of his time over the years. The irony of a self-declared socialist being disowned for demonstrating insufficient socialism by a socialist group whose name he had tried to change thirty years earlier because it did not sound socialist enough cannot have been lost on him either.

CHAPTER 6

UPHOLDING THE RULE OF LAW

Two significant things happened to Keir Starmer towards the end of 1991 which confirmed that, on the cusp of turning thirty, he was making progress both personally and professionally. First, he and his girlfriend, Angela O'Brien, bought a flat in north London, thereby cementing their commitment to each other. The maisonette at 60 Ellington Street, a smart Victorian terrace close to Highbury & Islington Underground station, certainly represented a step up the ladder for them. Compared with their shared rental accommodation in Archway Road, and another flat at 32 North Road in Highgate where they had stayed more briefly, 60 Ellington Street was in a more fashionable part of town. Having secured a mortgage, they joined Britain's property-owning classes for the first time.

The second development that autumn concerned Starmer's decision to travel to Northern Ireland. His interest in the province can be traced back to two years earlier, in December 1989, when Kader Asmal, a senior lecturer in human rights law at Trinity College, Dublin, and president of the Irish Council for Civil Liberties, had delivered the D. N. Pritt Memorial Lecture for the Haldane Society. During his speech, Asmal criticised British lawyers for failing to hold the British state to account over what he regarded as its poor record in Northern Ireland. He said:

The list of abuses and catalogue of malpractices arising out of the current emergency which has now lasted twenty years may be well known, but whether they have made an impact on the consciousness of professional legal bodies – on your Bar council, your Law Society, your law schools or your voluntary associations – is doubtful.[1]

These words are said to have made a strong impression on Starmer. A few months later, in April 1990, he attended the Appeal Court hearing in London of the so-called Winchester Three, sitting in as a legal observer for the pressure group Liberty and also on behalf of the Haldane Society. This case concerned three young Irish people, John McCann, Finbar Cullen and Martina Shanahan. In 1988, they had each been found guilty at Winchester Crown Court of involvement in a plot the year before to murder the then Northern Ireland Secretary, Tom King. The trio, who had exercised their right to remain silent, were sentenced to twenty-five years in prison. Their convictions were overturned after serving just two years, however, because during the course of their original trial, the British government had announced its intention to abolish this legal principle in terrorist cases in Northern Ireland. King had spoken publicly in support of this move and made comments about terrorist suspects abusing the right to refuse to answer questions.

The Appeal Court ruled that King's words could have prejudiced the original trial of those suspected of planning to kill him. This was a highly controversial decision, and the group's release from prison was heavily criticised by some, including by the former Master of the Rolls Lord Denning. Starmer, however, was delighted. In the next edition of the *Socialist Lawyer*, published in the summer of 1990, he wrote triumphantly under the headline 'King Size Blunder':

Much work was done by the Haldane Society on the case of the

Winchester Three. *The Guardian* printed our letter shortly before the appeal and I observed the hearing of the appeal on behalf of the Society. The Court of Appeal found that statements made by Tom King during the trial in which he equated silence with guilt created a serious risk of prejudice to the fairness of the trial. The case is a glaring example of the miscarriages of justice that would result if the government's proposals to limit the right to silence were carried into force and vindicates the campaign to retain the right to silence of which the Society has been a long supporter.

Although he obviously felt it right that this principled position had won the day, it could be argued that he overplayed his hand. It is sobering to recall that on 30 July 1990 – around the time his words were published – another Conservative MP, Ian Gow, was murdered by an IRA bomb that was planted underneath his car outside his house in Sussex. Nobody has ever been convicted of Mr Gow's murder.

Over the course of the next eighteen months or so, Starmer assembled a delegation of lawyers and arranged for them to visit Belfast on a four-day fact-finding mission to investigate criminal justice in the province under the Emergency Powers, which were still in place. Under the umbrella of the Haldane Society, he and thirteen colleagues left London on 26 September 1991. It is no exaggeration to say that in making this trip, they ventured into a potentially deadly environment. Only the week before their arrival, a prominent Protestant businessman had been murdered by the IRA in Belfast. By a bizarre coincidence, he was called John Haldane. He was a father of four who had been dictating a letter to his secretary at his timber firm in the docks area when two men walked into his office and shot him three times at close range. Mr Haldane had been the sixty-first person to die violently that year in Northern Ireland. The IRA said he was killed because his company supplied materials to the security forces. Then, during Starmer's visit, a Catholic newsagent, Laurence Murchan, was murdered in the Falls Road area. The Loyalist Retaliation and Defence Group, a previously unknown organisation, claimed that Mr Murchan had stocked the IRA paper *Republican News* in his shop and said his killing was in retaliation for John Haldane's murder by the IRA. At the time, Mr Murchan was reported as being the 2,000th civilian to be killed in the conflict in Northern Ireland since 1969.

While there, Starmer's team observed the operation of the so-called Diplock Courts, in which criminal trials were held without a jury; they explored the effect of the removal of an arrestee's right to silence (a right which remained in place elsewhere in the United Kingdom); they scrutinised allegations of ill-treatment among those who had been detained by the Royal Ulster Constabulary; and they studied the Casement Park trials, which took place as a result of the deaths of British Army Corporals David Howes and Derek Wood in March 1988. Their deaths, also known as the Corporals Killings, were among the most dramatic and grisly of the Troubles.

There is no doubt that Starmer and his team used every hour available to them during their mission. In the context of their work, they met High Court and Appeal Court judges; they interviewed prisoners; they spoke to the Independent Police Complaints Commission and the Standing Advisory Commission on Human Rights; and they spent time gathering material from solicitors and academic researchers. Among those who accompanied Starmer were Phillippa Kaufmann, who is now a QC; Stephen Cragg, also now a QC; Nadine Finch, who went on to be an immigration judge; Stephanie Harrison, who is now a QC; and barrister and academic Bill Bowring.

In mid-1992, a report detailing their observations was published under the title 'Upholding the Rule of Law?' It concluded that the

Diplock Courts were 'failing to secure reliable convictions based on properly tested evidence' and should be abandoned. It also claimed that Catholic detainees were being subjected to interrogation techniques which amounted to physical and psychological torture. It further called for the right to silence to be reinstated. And, in a section devoted to the Casement Park trials, it alleged that the sentences of those found guilty of the murders of Corporal David Howes and Corporal Derek Wood were unsafe. 'It is plainly shown that these convictions cannot be sustained either on the basis of the evidence that came before the courts or the law which was applied,' the report stated. According to Bowring, who was then chair of Haldane and who wrote the introduction, the report was 'a collective effort', and it remains a project with which he is proud to be associated. 'It was a great team which went [to Northern Ireland],' he recollects.

In light of work for the Police Service of Northern Ireland which Starmer would take on later in his career, it is worth noting that the report's own authors acknowledged that their findings could be criticised on two levels. First, the group said it had no means of testing the testimonies it received, nor could it 'carry out empirical research over any period of time to determine whether the abuses reported to us were indeed taking place'. Second, and of more interest in relation to Starmer specifically, the Haldane Society had a clear policy at that time of supporting a united Ireland. 'We call for British withdrawal,' the report declared. 'We did not hide the fact we had such [a] policy.' This, therefore, cannot be classified as an impartial piece of work. Bill Bowring is cited as the person who wrote these words, which appeared in the introduction, but it seems highly unlikely that Starmer – the serious-minded convenor of the trip, which was co-funded by the Haldane Educational Trust, a body he was instrumental in setting up – did not know about them prior to the report's publication. This fuels questions about how neutral Starmer was, then and subsequently, on the Northern Irish question and gives pause for thought when it comes to assessing to what extent his own feelings about Northern Ireland have ever been scrutinised or understood. What is not in doubt, according to Bowring, was the effect that this delegation would have on his career. 'This experience was Keir's initiative,' remembers Bowring. 'He did all the spadework and had already done important work on terrorism and human rights. The mission gave him the contacts and experience which helped him to get so deeply involved in the peace process some years later.'

By the spring of 1992, Starmer the barrister was tackling the kinds of difficult and traumatic cases through which he would make his name as a representative for the hard-pressed and those who felt they had been hard done by. This sort of work may not have made him wealthy, but it certainly identified him as a lawyer who was driven by a desire to use his position to help others. For example, he was a junior to his head of chambers, Geoffrey Robertson, in a case which was highly inconvenient to the British and American governments. Robertson and Starmer represented the relatives of six privates from the 9th Royal Fusiliers Regiment who were among nine British soldiers killed by so-called 'friendly fire' during the Gulf War. The soldiers died, and eleven other men were injured, when an American A-10 aircraft fired on two British armoured personnel carriers on 26 February 1991. Robertson and Starmer were instructed by a young litigation solicitor called Mark Stephens, who is now a longstanding friend of Starmer. Unusually, the soldiers' families applied for a jury inquest into their deaths to make sure that public confidence in the case was not undermined. This request was granted by Nicholas Gardiner, the Oxford coroner, and the subsequent inquest determined that all nine soldiers had been killed unlawfully. One lawyer who remembers this case says it left a mark as far as Starmer is concerned. 'It had a powerful effect on Keir, who was very sympathetic to the bereaved parents,' says the lawyer. 'It also made him sceptical, both of the class system in the British Army and of the military alliance with the US.'

And in October 1992, he was a junior member of a team that tried to defend two murderers at the High Court who had been released on parole and then sent back to prison for leading an unsettled lifestyle. The men, Anthony Creamer and James Scholey, applied for a judicial review of decisions of the parole board not to recommend their release on licence, but this was denied by Lord Justice Rose. The judge appeared, however, to believe that Creamer and Scholey, who brought their action in an attempt to force the Home Office to disclose the unpublished reports on which its decisions were based, had a point. The refusal to show the pair the reports, Rose said in judgment, was 'a breach of natural justice'. He added: 'A prisoner's right to make representations is valueless unless he knows the case against him. Secret, unchallengeable reports, which may contain damaging inaccuracies and which result in continuing loss of liberty, are or should be anathema in a civilised, democratic society.'[2] Rose concluded that he was bound by legal precedent, meaning there was nothing he could do about his judgment.

This was exactly the sort of project in which Starmer appears to have relished being involved. With that said, it does throw up a rather more challenging question about certain beliefs he has held regarding imprisonment in general. One highly respected lawyer recalls with incredulity an occasion around this time when Starmer shared his views on this subject. According to this person, he certainly seemed keen to convert the idea of civil liberties for all into a practical reality. 'I remember sitting in the pub with him listening to him seriously say he doesn't believe in imprisonment for anything, ever,' reports the lawyer. 'We all say stupid things when we're young, but he wasn't that young. He was a practising barrister; he wasn't a teenager.'

Soon after Lord Justice Rose's decision, in December 1992, Starmer acted for another controversial client, the National Union of Mineworkers, whose president was Arthur Scargill. The case, which was heard at the High Court, challenged decisions made two months previously by British Coal and the then president of the Board of Trade, Michael Heseltine, to close thirty-one coal pits. The industrial relations specialist John Hendy QC, who now sits in the House of Lords as a Labour peer, led Starmer and another barrister, Jennifer Eady, who is now herself a judge. Mark Stephens was again the instructing solicitor. 'When you're a junior barrister, it's the icing on the cake to get brought into a case with a leader, particularly a big case that's in the newspapers and is going to set a legal precedent for the future,' says Hendy.[3]

> It was a massive case at the time. It was a very urgent case, and we worked on it over a period of weeks. [Starmer] would have been drafting the legal documents for the case, the pleadings, the skeleton argument and so on and working on the strategy of how we were going to argue the case, what legal arguments we were going to put together. He was a very bright, hard-working young barrister. He was very talented. Both of the juniors were. We had a great team.

The judicial review was successful for Hendy, Starmer and Eady. The closure of the pits was halted, essentially on the grounds that the British Coal Corporation had failed to consult with the unions. Indeed, the outcome has been of use to Hendy subsequently. 'I've used the judgment in the pit closures case many times since because it became one of the leading cases on what constitutes proper consultation. [Starmer] was innovative and committed. Both the juniors were very good. It was a pleasure to have a team like that.' He adds: 'The outcome of these difficult cases is completely unpredictable, so of course it's satisfying to win a case rather than lose one, but you put the same intensity in no matter what the outcome is. You don't know what the outcome's going to be when you start, of course.'

Unsurprisingly, not every brief Starmer took on as a relatively young barrister of just over five years' standing was as high-profile or as successful. In April 1993, he represented Elizabeth Marsh, who had produced a booklet claiming that a wonder drug could cure cancer and AIDS. She was being prosecuted by the Department of Health under the Medicines Act 1968, which makes it an offence to sell or produce any product that has not been through clinical trials. Marsh's booklet was sent with a covering letter to a gay pub in Camden, north London, asking for volunteers for clinical trials for the drug, which would be distributed free, although there would be an initial consultation charge of £95. Starmer argued that this did not amount to a commercial interest in the medicine, which the prosecution needed to show to prove Marsh's guilt. He said that even though Marsh had contracted for 300 copies of the booklet to be printed in November 1990, the Crown had produced no evidence to support the idea that she was responsible for its distribution. Furthermore, said Starmer, the booklet stated from the outset that it was merely a discussion document looking at possible cures for cancer.[4] As an explanation, it didn't stand up to scrutiny, and Marsh was jailed for six months.

It would be another case that crossed Starmer's desk soon after this one, also involving contentious literature, which would help to make his name, however. The action in question was a High Court libel trial involving two campaigners of modest financial means, Helen Steel and Dave Morris, and the hamburger chain McDonald's. Steel and Morris were environmental activists linked to a small protest group called London Greenpeace, which in the 1980s had begun producing leaflets titled 'What's wrong with McDonald's? Everything they don't want you to know'. The leaflets questioned the fast-food firm's practices in relation to animal cruelty and rainforest destruction, the nutritional value of its products, the exploitation of children in its advertising and employees' working conditions, among other things. In 1990, Steel, Morris and three London Greenpeace colleagues were served with a writ by McDonald's. A letter to them made clear that a court case would ensue unless they apologised. Of the five, Steel and Morris were the only ones who refused to comply with this order. They were entitled to two hours of legal aid, after which they were on their own and would have to defend themselves as so-called litigants-in-person.

This marked the beginning of what has become known colloquially as the 'McLibel' case. A total of twenty-eight pre-trial hearings were held before proceedings began in earnest in June 1994. As legal aid was not available for defamation actions, Steel and Morris had to represent themselves in court against some of the country's top libel lawyers led by Richard Rampton QC, who reputedly charged McDonald's £2,000 per day for his services. A solicitor friend of Steel's advised her to contact Starmer, believing that he might offer her and Morris some free advice. In fact, Starmer agreed to write their defence and to help draft the relevant documents without charge. Over the course of the trial, others helped Steel and Morris as well, including the aforementioned solicitor, Mark Stephens; representatives from the campaign group Liberty; and lawyers from the firm Richards Butler. Steel and Morris did not dispute handing out the leaflets, and McDonald's accepted that they did not write the material contained within them, but the company was determined to sue. Things got off to a dire start for the defendants when the High Court ruled that the case should be heard by a judge alone, as McDonald's wanted, and not, as is usual in libel, by a jury. Given that the burden fell on Steel and Morris to prove their case, the odds were well and truly stacked against them.

The McLibel trial was scheduled to last for twelve weeks. In fact, it was heard over 314 days, making it the longest-running libel trial in English legal history. A total of 170 witnesses gave evidence. Steel and Morris argued that the case was in essence about censorship, as McDonald's had previously used England's libel laws to quieten its critics. The pair cited at least fifty groups, including newspaper and television companies, which had been forced to apologise to the hamburger chain over the previous few years. Undoubtedly, it was a captivating contest, and Steel and Morris emerged from it as two brave individuals who were willing to take on a fight that others with substantial resources had ducked. When the judgment was handed down in June 1997, the judge, Mr Justice Bell, found largely in favour of McDonald's, though he also concluded that several of the points raised in the London Greenpeace leaflet were accurate, meaning the hamburger chain won only a partial victory.

Ultimately, McDonald's was awarded damages of £76,000, a sum of money which neither Steel nor Morris had and which they were open in saying they would not pay. It was a pyrrhic victory for McDonald's, however. Not only is the case thought to have cost the firm in the region of £10 million in legal fees, but it gained worldwide attention and enough negative press coverage for McDonald's to ensure that its executives shied away from ever chasing Steel and Morris for the money they owed. Indeed, the case is still universally regarded as a notorious corporate public relations failure. Shortly after the judgment, Jeremy Corbyn, then a back-bench MP, even used the result as the basis of a parliamentary Early Day Motion, in which he condemned England's libel laws.

Most profiles of Starmer that have been written since then have made a point of mentioning the McLibel case as a highlight of his legal career. It is certainly true that he played a significant role in it by helping the defendants on a pro bono basis. Some Doughty Street colleagues further recall that he extended to the pair not only the benefit of his professional wisdom but also the use of his chambers so that they could photocopy documents and access legal textbooks if need be. Yet one legal figure who knows Starmer believes that his role may have been misinterpreted by some members of the public, not to mention some journalists, insofar as Starmer did not actually defend Steel and Morris in court in the way that might be assumed by those who are unfamiliar with the law but have perhaps watched too many courtroom dramas on television. Neither was he the only lawyer involved. As Steel and Morris became known as 'DIY lawyers' during the trial, because they were doing a job normally undertaken by professional solicitors and barristers, it does not seem unreasonable to pursue this argument. 'The [McLibel] case isn't what it's purported to be,' says the person concerned.

> Keir didn't represent Helen Steel and Dave Morris. They used to go into his chambers and use the research facilities. Keir would occasionally draft documents for them because they were representing themselves. That's the whole point about that case – those two people represented themselves in a libel action that went on for about eighteen months. It was the longest libel action in English legal history. Keir did do the case in that he was like a litigation friend, but he didn't do any advocacy as far as I know.

This analysis is entirely accurate. Starmer did not appear at the High Court to cross-examine witnesses, nor did he appear as an advocate for Steel and Morris. In fact, he himself said in August 1996 that Steel and Morris had been legal novices when he first met them, but over the course of the trial they had learned enough about the law to be able to 'draft stuff on their own'. Such was their ability, he said that he thought they would make good lawyers themselves, and he even encouraged them to follow him into the profession. Moreover, it wasn't as though he wasn't busy with other matters at this stage of his career. In

March 1996, under the umbrella of the Haldane Society, he organised a 45-strong delegation to fly to South Africa to attend a conference arranged by the International Association of Democratic Lawyers at which Nelson Mandela gave an address. It attracted about 260 participants from thirty-three countries, though the British contingent was the largest. Among those on the trip with Starmer was Phillippa Kaufmann, his Doughty Street colleague who was, like him, a member of the Haldane Society's executive committee.

During the course of the McLibel hearings, Starmer also found the time to co-write, with Francesca Klug and Stuart Weir, a book called *The Three Pillars of Liberty*, which is described as an audit of British compliance with international human rights standards. In September 1996, he even drew attention to its publication by writing a letter to *The Times*. In it, he backed a call by Norma Major, wife of the then Prime Minister John Major, for the introduction of tougher privacy laws, which would bring the UK into line with other European nations. And he took on other work. In 1995–96, his clients included a Druid called King Arthur Pendragon, who was accused of trespassing while observing the summer solstice at Stonehenge. Defending him, Starmer was alarmed to discover that he would only swear an oath on his sword, Excalibur, forcing Starmer to research the law on oaths and then persuade Salisbury Magistrates' Court that this would be acceptable. It worked.

He also represented two people involved in what came to be regarded as a test case about the freedom to protest. Dr Margaret Jones, a university lecturer from Bristol, and a student in his mid-twenties called Richard Lloyd had taken part in a peaceful roadside demonstration, also at Stonehenge, in June 1995. They were the first two people to be charged with the new criminal offence of 'trespassory assembly' of twenty people or more, which had been brought in under the 1994 Criminal Justice and Public Order Act. Having been found guilty by

Salisbury magistrates, Starmer believed that this meant the police were legally entitled to use the new public order powers to ban peaceful demonstrations. He recognised it as a case which touched upon issues concerning fundamental public freedoms, which were perhaps under threat from wider law and order reforms introduced by the then Home Secretary, Michael Howard, who had signalled his intention to crack down on squatters, trespassers and protesters. When Jones and Lloyd appealed at Salisbury Crown Court in January 1996, Starmer represented them, arguing that the convictions could stand only if it were proved that his clients and others had exceeded their rights to be on the highway. He said there was a 'clear trend towards recognising peaceful, non-obstructive assembly as a reasonable and usual use of the highway', and said the evidence showed the appellants had been peaceful and non-obstructive. Michael Butt, for the Crown, claimed this submission was a 'thinly disguised' attack on the Criminal Justice Act and accused Starmer of wasting the court's time. Butt added that if Starmer was successful, a whole section of the Act banning assemblies within prohibited areas would be nullified. Starmer was successful – initially. The convictions were overturned that day, prompting the Crown Prosecution Service (CPS) to appeal to the High Court. There, in December 1996, Starmer tried to argue that if the CPS appeal was successful, it would mean that any group of twenty or more people gathered together on the highway could run the risk of breaking the law. It did not hold. The following month, it was ruled that there was no right in law for members of the public to hold a peaceful, non-obstructive assembly on the public highway. Despite this failure, Starmer had chalked up some more runs as a lawyer in whom a radical spirit burned. He was making a name for himself.

The High Court's finding in the McLibel case in June 1997 was not the end of that matter. Seven years later, in September 2004, Steel and

Morris went to the European Court of Human Rights in Strasbourg. On that occasion, Mark Stephens was their solicitor and Starmer represented them in person. He argued on their behalf that the British government had failed to meet the requirements under the Human Rights Convention to guarantee them a fair trial and to safeguard their right to freedom of speech. At the centre of the affair was the fact that no legal aid was available to Steel and Morris and that they were forced to represent themselves in court despite having no legal experience and no money to pay for so much as evidence transcripts. Starmer told the Strasbourg court that the 'inequality of arms' between a multi-national corporation and two largely unemployed and unrepresented campaigners could not have been greater. 'The result was that, without legal assistance, the case was under-prepared, unready for trial and was advanced by two inexperienced, untrained and exhausted individuals who were pushed to their physical and mental limits,' he said.

The seven judges hearing the case agreed that Steel and Morris had been denied their rights to free speech and to a fair hearing. In February 2005, the British government was ordered to pay them compensation of £24,000 plus £32,500 towards their legal costs. Afterwards, Starmer called the ruling a 'milestone for free speech'. He said, 'Until now, only the rich and famous have been able to defend themselves against libel writs. Now ordinary people can participate much more effectively in public debate without the fear of being bankrupted.' Some of his fees were awarded by the British government.

The entire saga, which had begun fifteen years previously, was made into a documentary, called *McLibel*, which was directed by Franny Armstrong with input from the left-wing filmmaker Ken Loach. An impeccably coiffed Starmer can be seen at various points of this film discussing developments in the case. The DVD of *McLibel* also features seven minutes of extra interviews given by Starmer which did not make the final cut. In one such scene, recorded in 2004, he talked about his recent appointment as a Queen's Counsel, commenting that his accepting this award was 'odd, since I often used to propose the abolition of the monarchy'. Years later, in February 2021, he came to regret his candour when the footage was rediscovered by some sections of the media and used against him at the very time the Labour Party was trying to be more patriotic in its attempt to win back voters.

There is another, rather more fascinating, aspect of the McLibel trial which in a sense haunts Starmer to this day, however. During proceedings at the High Court between 1994 and 1996, it came to light that McDonald's had placed some members of London Greenpeace under surveillance, using private investigators to monitor their activities and their personal lives. The sense of violation that this inspired in Helen Steel led her to question the true nature of a romantic relationship she had formed in the early 1990s with a man who called himself John Barker. They were involved with each other for a couple of years and had even lived together at one point, but by the time the McLibel trial began he had vanished, having written her a letter in which he claimed to have had a mental breakdown and moved to South Africa.

Understandably, Steel was devastated, and she began trying to find out more about this man, spurred on by a nagging feeling that he was not who he said he was. Her instincts were right. During the McLibel trial, her own detective work eventually confirmed that the name 'John Barker' was an alias. Just like the protagonist in Frederick Forsyth's book *The Day of the Jackal*, 'Barker' had assumed the identity of a dead child. He had lied to Steel about many aspects of his life. Steel eventually established that his real name was John Dines, and in 2010 she discovered that he was an undercover police officer who had been working for the Metropolitan Police's Special Demonstration Squad, which spied on political activists, including those linked to London Greenpeace.

In 2015, Steel, who was one of seven women who had been tricked into relationships of this nature, was awarded compensation by the Metropolitan Police, but, surprisingly, Starmer's stance on the issue subsequently does tend to suggest he has little sympathy with his former client's plight. In October 2020, he whipped his MPs to abstain on the government's Covert Human Intelligence Sources (Criminal Conduct) Bill, regulating the future conduct of secret operatives and whether they are allowed to commit crimes to obtain information in the course of their work. Guidelines have banned intimate relationships like the one Dines embarked upon with Steel, yet this piece of legislation, which gained royal assent in March 2021, has led to fears that it would make it harder for other women like Steel to unmask their own 'John Barker', the man who never was.

Some of Starmer's oldest political and legal friends have been surprised at what they consider to be his illiberal position. One of them was the aforementioned John Hendy, with whom he had worked on legal cases in the 1990s and who now sits in the House of Lords as a Labour peer. 'I was very disappointed that he instructed the Labour MPs and peers to abstain on the Overseas Operations Bill and on the Covert Human Intelligence Sources Bill,' says Hendy. 'I think that sends the wrong message. I think the Labour Party should stand up for human rights, and I think as a human rights lawyer he should have led that. I presume he thought it was more politically advantageous, which is not a position of principle, is it?'

In February 2021, there were calls from some activists for him to give evidence to a public inquiry into undercover policing, which was set up by the then Home Secretary Theresa May in 2015. They said that he should explain if he was involved in the cover-up of any officers' behaviour while he was DPP for England and Wales between 2008 and 2013.[5] What exactly Starmer knew about the existence and activities of 'spycops' long before he became DPP also demands a full public explanation which has not, so far, been forthcoming.

By the time the initial McLibel case had been wound up in June 1997, some significant changes had taken place in Starmer's personal life. His long-term girlfriend, Angela O'Brien, with whom he had lived in one capacity or another for the best part of a decade, had moved out of the flat they owned together in Islington. It is understood that Starmer remained there until it was sold in August 1997, for £170,000. By then he was almost thirty-five years old, and he had struck up a relationship with the aforementioned Phillippa Kaufmann. She was four years his junior, and having belonged to the same set since the early 1990s, they had become close over a long period of time. Kaufmann is a well thought of barrister and built her career through specialising in cases relating to prisoners' rights, mental health, inquests and actions against the police. One friend of the couple says O'Brien was rather hurt by the situation.

Another friend adds that by this point in his life, Starmer was devoted to playing football for his team, Homerton Academicals, when he was not watching his favourite team, Arsenal; but football did not prevent him from socialising more widely as well. Several people have claimed that he had 'other girlfriends' besides O'Brien and Kaufmann. Intriguingly, they note that he has always been careful about remaining on good terms with these women. 'He was quite clever at keeping in contact with former girlfriends, so they didn't do anything unpredictable,' says one friend. 'He'd always return their calls.' After he and Kaufmann went public with their relationship, they certainly didn't waste any time in taking things to the next stage, spending £262,500 on a four-bedroom house in Stoke Newington, north London, which they bought together in September 1997.

CHAPTER 7

DOUGHTY STREET

Throughout the 1990s, Doughty Street Chambers established itself as arguably the most forward-thinking and progressive set in London, committed to doing at least 10 per cent of its work pro bono. Initially, it occupied buildings at 10 and 11 Doughty Street, but by the end of the decade it had expanded, needing more space in order to accommodate its growing number of tenants. Its acquisitions included No. 54 in the same terrace. Next door, at No. 56, were the offices of *The Spectator* magazine. In July 1999, a new editor was appointed to the weekly title. This figure, made distinctive by his shock of blond hair, crumpled suit and plummy baritone voice, drew attention to himself in the street in a variety of ways, and there is no doubt that Starmer would have been aware of his presence. He was, of course, Boris Johnson. By an amusing quirk of fate, thirteen years after being students in Oxford at the same time, and a little more than twenty years before they faced each other across the despatch box in the House of Commons as Prime Minister and Leader of the Opposition, Johnson and Starmer became what might be called professional neighbours. They remained so for six years, until 2005.

When Johnson was made editor in 1999, he doubled up as the motoring correspondent of *GQ* magazine, and it is in that context rather than for his *Spectator* editorials that he is best remembered by some Doughty

Street barristers, who would see and hear him outside their window. 'I certainly knew Johnson was in the same street,' laughs one. 'These extraordinary cars that he had to review would turn up, and he'd be standing there trying to work out how to get into them.' Another Doughty Street member says he can recall almost colliding in his car with Johnson's 'badly ridden' bicycle 'more than once'. As well as staff who worked on *The Spectator*, a procession of the great and the good (and the not-so-good) of British journalism would file regularly into its offices at No. 56 Doughty Street to attend lunches put on by Johnson in the small dining room at the top of the building. Parties were also sometimes thrown on the premises. Starmer was not invited to these gatherings, yet he might have fitted in better at them than he would have assumed. *The Spectator* tended to reflect the libertarian views which its editor then held on sex, drugs, politics and life in general in a way that chimed with some of Starmer's own instincts – including in his attitude to the death penalty, one of the causes on which he has built his reputation.

Doughty Street's head of chambers, Geoffrey Robertson, has long believed that capital punishment is an outrage. By the time Starmer became a barrister, Robertson had spent years working on death-penalty cases, and he encouraged Starmer to develop his own interest in this area, tutoring him along the way. The reason they chose to devote time to this aspect of law is that, in a hangover from the days of the British Empire, the Judicial Committee of the Privy Council in London still hears death-penalty cases from various Commonwealth countries as well as UK overseas territories, Crown dependencies and military sovereign base areas. Although there appears to be an inherent contradiction in Britain, where the death penalty for murder was abolished in 1965, being the final arbiter on matters of life and death in corners of the globe where it once ruled, no replacement for this system has been agreed on. This gives British lawyers who are so inclined a genuine opportunity to defend those who face the death penalty. Another Doughty Street barrister with a longstanding interest in capital punishment cases, who is also credited as having been a mentor to Starmer, is Edward Fitzgerald. Blessed with a formidable intellect and great charisma, he is often spoken of within the Bar and across the judiciary as a legal giant of his generation. Rather appropriately, Fitzgerald is married to Rebecca Fraser, a granddaughter of the Earl of Longford, the late social reformer and Labour politician who spent much of his life backing unpopular causes.

Having talked to various lawyers while researching this book, it would be fair to say that Robertson and Fitzgerald are probably the two legal figures to whom Starmer owes most in a professional sense. The Labour peer Helena Kennedy was also his champion. It never does anybody any harm to have friends in high places, and Starmer is no exception. Yet the questions must be asked: why did this trio develop a soft spot for Starmer? And to what extent was their patronage warranted? Speaking on condition of anonymity, one person who knows Robertson and Fitzgerald says that they didn't just promote Starmer during his time at Doughty Street, they 'over-promoted' him by involving him in cases which enhanced his reputation, perhaps in the main because it suited them as much as it suited him. The upshot of this, in this person's opinion, was that Starmer 'began to believe the hype which went with his over-promotion'.

Robertson, Fitzgerald and Kennedy had all known Starmer since his days at 1 Dr Johnson's Buildings and found him to be competent and diligent. But was he in the top rank, as many newspaper profiles seem to suggest? This person says:

I don't know why, but they picked Keir as a shining star and gave him preferential treatment. He was the blue-eyed boy. Take Ed Fitzgerald.

He is a genuine human rights lawyer of the best kind, motivated by his Catholic beliefs, a really decent guy. He used Keir as a junior in lots of death-penalty cases. But I think you'd struggle to find one in which Keir appeared as the advocate, as opposed to junior counsel. He just used to sit behind Ed. All the puff about Keir's death-penalty work ignores the fact that he was mainly in trade for somebody else. I think they picked Keir because he could draft. He was a useful gopher. I also think Keir was politically manoeuvring. We all do that, figuring out how one case will generate more work. It's part of the prostitution of the Bar.

This may be a slightly harsh downgrading of Starmer's efforts in capital punishment cases in an overall sense, but the available court reports do suggest that it is broadly correct: Starmer tended to be the junior counsel rather than the advocate on his feet.

A second person with solid insights into Starmer's legal career agrees, saying:

Although Keir wrote books about miscarriages of justice, he did not do much jury advocacy, and this shows. He does not 'do' passion very well. He has no orator's ability to use emotion or humour. His real ability as an advocate came from his writing down of his case for judges – so-called skeleton arguments – which were so persuasive that they tipped them in his favour before the hearing. Then he would flesh them out with polite, often low-key arguments which were persuasive and not rhetorical. He never had to raise his voice or his hand to make a good point. In the High Court and the appeal courts, this is an important skill. Less so in the House of Commons, although I've noticed he has been working better in the House on showing his emotions and trying the odd joke.

Another figure who saw him in action as an advocate comments more bluntly:

> Fundamentally, he's dull as hell. His submissions were timid. He was reluctant to take a difficult point that might be very significant. He tended to go down the path of least resistance. It was compromise rather than confrontation. It was all derivative and regurgitated. It was an attempt to make a virtue out of blandness. I have a horrible feeling part of his success was based on the idea that he looks the part subliminally. That's one of the tricks of the light with Keir. He looks like a matinee idol with that coiffed hair, but in reality he's like the deputy manager of the local branch of Barclays Bank.

It is worth adding at this point that in August 2008, after twenty-one years at the Bar, it was calculated that although Starmer had appeared an impressive total of seventeen times before the House of Lords and in the European Court of Human Rights, he had for the most part done so as junior counsel, perhaps reflecting an acceptance on his part that his powers of oratory have never been as impressive as those of other barristers.[1]

Ken Macdonald, who preceded Starmer as DPP, first met him in the late 1980s, when they both worked as criminal barristers and moved in similar circles. Although they were never close friends, they did undertake a couple of cases together, and their paths crossed quite regularly. He broadly concurs that Starmer's abilities were chiefly to be found in the written rather than the spoken word. 'He's very forensic, clear, logical, rational and likes to take things in stages,' says Macdonald.[2]

> That's how he was as a lawyer. The thing about Keir in a case was he was always very thoroughly prepared. He always knew the facts. He

knew the law. And he would have a strategy. He would work out a case strategy in advance, and he would stick to it. I think what you see of him in politics is very similar to the way he was in law. He wasn't flamboyant. There were no great flights of oratory. There were no purple passages, none of that kind of stuff. It's a modern style of advocacy, actually. Giving great passionate speeches is a thing of the past. You have a much more conversational relationship with the court and the jury now. I'd say he was respected by judges because they thought he was smart and well-prepared and straight. He was never slippery. He didn't fall out with his opponents. He didn't push poor arguments. He didn't try to mislead a court about what the balance of the authorities was. He was very straight. He was clever and well-regarded as a barrister.

* * *

Many will wonder what the motivation is for taking on cases in which a barrister appears to be defending the indefensible, by representing a murderer, for example. Edward Fitzgerald has represented a range of hated and controversial figures, including the child killer Mary Bell; the Moors Murderer Myra Hindley; and convicted terrorist Abu Hamza. Starmer's own death-penalty work has involved clients who were convicted of some equally shocking crimes. The simple answer as to why lawyers like Fitzgerald and Starmer take on such causes is, as noted in Chapter 5, the so-called cab-rank rule. When Geoffrey Robertson established the set in 1990, he was (and remains) adamant that every barrister should follow this rule, meaning that they must represent any client – regardless of their identity or the nature of the case – if the instruction falls within their field of practice and as long as they have the requisite experience and availability to do so. There is also no doubt that barristers like Fitzgerald and Starmer believe in the right to a fair trial. 'It would be terrible if we stopped defending people because they're unpopular,' Fitzgerald once said, adding that 'the legal process is an attempt to civilise our emotions of revenge. Anything that's against lynch law seems to me to be a good thing.' These are sentiments which undoubtedly trumped any desire on Starmer's part to make large sums of money. Had he wanted to, he probably could have done so, however. 'He did a lot of pro bono work,' says Macdonald.

> He did a lot of death-penalty work. He did a lot of low-paid work. He was clever enough to be anything he wanted to be. He could have been a commercial silk earning millions a year, but he chose the public law, civil liberties, human rights route, which is less well paid. It's not badly paid but it's not the commercial chancery law division at all. There were people who were real stars in the area. People like Ed Fitzgerald. You wouldn't say that he was in that league, but he was a successful, well-regarded public law barrister and a well-respected public law silk.

An ex-Doughty Street barrister backs this up. 'I'm sure he earned a lot compared to the national average, but not in barrister's terms,' he says.

> I think he did a lot which was unpaid because he believed in the cause, as did a number of people at Doughty Street. It had a very different attitude to other chambers. Barristers don't work for nothing, of course. Even a badly paid Doughty Street barrister earns far more money than most people. It's a relative thing. It's probably that he could have earned a lot of money rather than that he didn't earn a lot.

As a self-employed barrister, Starmer was also free to take on as much work as he wished, meaning he could work for long periods without a holiday if it came to it. With the legal aid budget having risen to £2 billion by 2009, a cost met by taxpayers, there certainly would have been opportunities for a barrister like Starmer to have kept the financial side of his life ticking over.[3]

By the time the McLibel case had ended in 1997, Starmer had already embarked on some death-penalty projects. Some of this work required him to visit overseas territories. In order to practise abroad, he had to be admitted to a particular jurisdiction's Bar. One such application, to practise in Belize, ended in embarrassment for him. Records dating from October 1997 show that both he and Edward Fitzgerald were forced to appeal to the Supreme Court for an order to be enrolled as attorneys-at-law under the Legal Profession Act, as was necessary. Under this appeal, Fitzgerald was admitted; Starmer, however, was not. 'The case of Keir Starmer is different,' wrote the Supreme Court in its judgment. 'With an LL.B and a BCL from Oxford he clearly has received adequate training in law.' But, the judgment went on:

> With seven years of practice and appearances as junior in three appeals from Jamaica before the Judicial Committee it cannot be said that there is sufficient evidence of his competence to practise law in Belize. He has written a book on the legal protection of internationally recognised fundamental rights and freedoms, but this need not require any significant study and familiarity with Belize law. Accordingly, in the case of Mr Keir Starmer, I would dismiss his appeal.

It would be a further five years before he was admitted to the Bar of Belize, though in 1997 he was successfully admitted to the Bar of St Lucia and the Bar of St Vincent.

Alongside his own interest in natural justice, much of Starmer's death-penalty work came about as a result of his association with a

London-based campaigning group called the Death Penalty Project, which was set up by two lawyers, Saul Lehrfreund and Parvais Jabbar, and which offers free legal representation to those on death row. Through this, Starmer travelled widely. He played a part in advising a class action in Uganda in 2005 which ultimately overturned the death penalty there and, it is claimed, saved the lives of 417 people. He was also involved in obtaining a Privy Council ruling in 2006 that the mandatory death penalty in the Bahamas is unconstitutional. This was achieved when he defended two convicted murderers, Trono Davis and Forrester Bowe, who had been automatically sentenced to death for their crimes. (Separately to his original conviction, Bowe was part of a gang that allegedly murdered a prison guard called Dion Bowles during a prison break in January 2006, shortly before the Privy Council ruling. Bowe died of natural causes in prison in 2014.) Starmer also advised legal teams in Malawi which campaigned to end the automatic death penalty for all death row prisoners in that country. The success of this was evident when, in 2007, the High Court of Malawi declared that the death sentences on all prisoners on death row were unconstitutional.

Not every death-penalty case ended so well as far as Starmer was concerned, however. In December 2001, a BBC newsreader called Lynette Lithgow Pearson was killed in Trinidad at the age of fifty-one, along with her 83-year-old mother and her 59-year-old brother-in-law. All had their throats slit. Daniel Agard and Lester Pittman were convicted of this triple murder. In 2003, the Privy Council ruled that Trinidad's mandatory death penalty for murder convictions was unconstitutional, but, in July 2004, it reversed this ruling, leading Starmer, who had been closely involved in the case, to comment:

> The majority in the Privy Council have taken a step wholly inconsistent with that court's usual, enlightened, approach to human rights.

Those charged with implementing the criminal law in Trinidad and Barbados will now be forced to apply laws which are universally acknowledged to be inhuman. The constitutions of Trinidad and of Barbados were intended to be read so as to protect human rights, not to deny them. The ruling is bitterly disappointing both for those on death row and more generally for the development of the law in the Caribbean.[4]

When, on the eve of the Labour leadership election in March 2020, the *Sun on Sunday* revived details of Starmer's role in defending those convicted of this heinous crime, one Conservative MP, David Morris, opined: 'He shouldn't be interfering in Trinidad's criminal justice system or [that of] any other country for that matter.'[5] Those who share Morris's admittedly blunt view may be considered to be beyond the pale by some in left-wing legal circles, who no doubt regard Starmer's work in this field as brave and principled, but it is worth considering the viewpoints of the voters to whom Starmer must appeal if he is to return the Labour Party to power. After all, many of these voters probably do not have the time – even if they have the inclination – to debate points of law in foreign jurisdictions. Their priorities, quite naturally, are looking after their own families and making ends meet. To that end, some might argue that Morris speaks their language more fluently than does Starmer, in this regard at least.

Nonetheless, Starmer has continued to campaign against the death penalty. As recently as September 2018, he visited Taiwan for four days to lobby against it. His trip, which included meetings with senior Taiwanese politicians, was conducted with the support of the Foreign Office, a department which he got to know during some of the New Labour government's peak years, having served as a member of the Foreign Secretary's advisory panel on the death penalty between 2002 and 2008. This brought him into contact with those who held this post during those years: Jack Straw, Margaret Beckett and David Miliband.

During the 1990s and for most of the first decade of the twenty-first century, Starmer took on a wide range of work involving matters other than the death penalty. His growing reputation and his well-publicised commitment to human rights law guaranteed that his practice attracted more high-profile and professionally satisfying endeavours of its own volition. In January 2020, he produced a video to announce his intention to stand for the Labour leadership. A significant portion of the film included commentary about his legal career. This was hardly surprising given that he was a lawyer for much longer than he has been an MP, but there is no doubt that he sought to make political capital by emphasising the cases which he took on behalf of the underdog. From the printworkers at Wapping in 1987 to the National Union of Mineworkers in 1992, to the McLibel case of the mid-1990s, many of what were effectively his greatest legal hits were trumpeted in order to present the would-be leader in the most appealing light, as he declared, 'I have spent my life fighting for justice, standing up for the powerless and against the powerful.' Most candidates in his position would, of course, have done this as well, but it is interesting that some cases with which he has been associated – and which were Doughty Street's meat and drink as the 'go-to' chambers for this kind of work – were not mentioned in this film. To what extent their omission was deliberate is a matter for Starmer himself, though it is fair to say that many members of the public would not necessarily appreciate what the cab-rank rule is, nor, indeed, would every layman comprehend some of the more subtle legal arguments which help a lawyer to a build a case for the defence. Nevertheless, it is worth going over some of these overlooked cases to gain a greater understanding of what Starmer's legal experience at the 'pink end' of the Bar has entailed.

In 2000, he was part of a team headed by Edward Fitzgerald which represented Khalid Al-Fawwaz, a London-based Saudi dissident who was fighting extradition to America on charges relating to the 1998 bombing of the US embassies in Kenya and Tanzania in which 224 people died. Starmer and his colleagues argued – unsuccessfully – that Al-Fawwaz's actions in connection to the bombings did not constitute a prima facie case of conspiracy. Al-Fawwaz appealed, the protracted appeal process enabling him ultimately to stay in Britain until 2012. The cost of such a legal fight was vast. In September 2001, it was estimated by officials at the Lord Chancellor's department that Al-Fawwaz, who had claimed political asylum in Britain in 1994 but who remained a Saudi citizen, had received £1 million in legal aid by that point alone. In retrospect, it is no wonder that Starmer did not enlighten viewers of his campaign video of the principled stand he helped to create on behalf of Al-Fawwaz. Many – and probably most – British taxpayers would not approve of the generosity shown to this man and his lawyers. On top of his massive legal bill, though, Al-Fawwaz was later found to have run the London office of the terror group al-Qaeda and used Britain as a base for arranging interviews with Western media on behalf of its founder, Osama bin Laden. Al-Fawwaz is currently serving life in an American prison.

In January 2001, Starmer was part of a team that represented a group of armed prisoners who had escaped from HMP Whitemoor in Cambridgeshire in 1994. Prison officer John Kettleborough was shot in the ribs on the night of the escape. He survived. Years later, however, the escapees, including two former IRA prisoners, launched a legal battle for £50,000 each in damages over injuries sustained during the breakout. One of the IRA men was Gilbert 'Danny' McNamee, who had been jailed for the 1982 Hyde Park bombing. His conviction was later quashed. The other was Liam McCotter, who had been jailed in

June 1988 for conspiracy to cause explosions. Both claimed they were unlawfully assaulted while being recaptured. They were granted legal aid to launch the proceedings against the Home Office, together with Andrew Russell, an armed robber. The action cost taxpayers more than £500,000. Ultimately, McNamee was awarded £5,000 and Russell was awarded £2,500 in damages. McCotter's claim was dismissed.

In June 2002, Starmer defended a man who was to feature in a BBC 2 documentary called *The Hunt for Britain's Paedophiles*. The man, whose identity is unknown, had pleaded guilty the previous year to offences involving possession and distribution of pornographic pictures of children and had been placed under a three-year community rehabilitation order with a condition of treatment. This led to his face being shown on camera for about three minutes when the documentary was being made. Claiming his client would be at risk of physical attack if his face were broadcast in an identifiable form, Starmer made an emergency application to the High Court asking for the man's face to be obscured. Ultimately, this was rejected by Mr Justice Ouseley.

Another brief that was absent from Starmer's campaign video came in February 2003, when he represented five asylum seekers in a test case at the High Court. There, it was decided by Mr Justice Collins that the Labour government's new policy of denying refugees food and shelter if they did not make an asylum claim in Britain as soon as reasonably practicable, and preferably on arrival at a British airport, was illegal. David Blunkett was the Home Secretary who had introduced the new rule because of mounting concerns that Britain had become a soft touch for refugees, with at least 6,500 applications each month at an annual cost to taxpayers in welfare benefits alone of £1 billion. Blunkett was livid about the ruling at the time but was more sanguine when asked about it for the purposes of this book. 'This was where we'd tried to avoid people hanging about in the country, having a job and then claiming asylum,' Blunkett recalls.[6] 'It was to try and stop people who'd clearly not declared they were refugees when they first arrived.' When asked about Starmer's involvement in the case, Blunkett says:

> The old adage is they [barristers] are like a taxi queue. They take the case that is top of the queue. And they always stick to that, right or wrong. We lost because Andrew Collins, who was the judge, was on a mission to determine that the judiciary should be able to strike down government actions on immigration. I felt exactly the same as I felt on a number of occasions when I lost a judgment in the eight years I was in Cabinet. I was cheesed off that that's the way our system works.

At the time of the judgment, Starmer gave an interview to *The Times* in which he was asked to explain the wider implications of the case. He said:

> First, there is the development of the notion of dignity and humanity in our law. It doesn't matter whether the foundation of that notion is the European Convention on Human Rights or the common law, it is simply unacceptable in a civilised society to prevent a vulnerable group of individuals from working, to exclude them from the welfare benefits system and then to deprive them of a roof over their heads and of food. The other, wider, implication concerns the relationship between the government and the judiciary. Like many others, I was shocked at the personalised and ill-informed response of the government and some of the press to Mr Justice Collins's judgment.[7]

In 2003, Starmer also represented Colin Richards, an armed robber who had held up two post offices in Essex before murdering a policeman,

Acting Sgt Brian Bishop, at Frinton-on-Sea in August 1984. Richards was sentenced in 1985 on a tariff set at seventeen years which expired in September 2001. The Parole Board recommended him for release in November 2001, but he was not freed until August 2002, leading to him seeking compensation for the 'extra' period in which he was incarcerated. Ultimately, this was denied.

In March 2006, Starmer acted for Hilal al-Jedda, who held dual British and Iraqi nationality and who was suspected of recruiting terrorists to Iraq, where he was held in a British facility in Basra for eight months. He was also detained for helping a known terrorist travel to Iraq and conspiring with him to target coalition forces around Fallujah and Baghdad and was further thought to have conspired with an Islamist terror cell in the Gulf to smuggle detonation equipment into Iraq. In 2007, the House of Lords ruled his detention was lawful, but that ruling was later overturned by the European courts. It is noteworthy that in this case, Starmer was instructed by a firm called Public Interest Lawyers, which was run by a left-wing solicitor called Phil Shiner. Shiner made a fortune over a period of years by using legal aid to sue the Ministry of Defence over alleged misdeeds by British troops in Iraq. His reputation suffered lasting damage when he was struck off the roll of solicitors in 2017 after the Solicitors Regulation Authority found him guilty of professional misconduct of a 'criminal standard'. He had claimed falsely that British soldiers murdered and tortured hundreds of civilians during the Iraq War.

In 2006 and 2007, Starmer represented three people in separate cases whose identities were not revealed but whose profiles attracted the attention of British authorities at a time of heightened concern for national security. One was a Tunisian asylum seeker who had a control order imposed for his membership of the Tunisian Islamic Front. The second was an Islamist extremist who attempted to travel to Iraq to fight against coalition forces. The third was an immigration case involving an Algerian national who was a follower of the radical Egyptian cleric Abu Hamza at the Finsbury Park Mosque (the latter of whom is now serving life in an American prison after being found guilty of various terrorism charges). Starmer also wrote a piece for the *Socialist Lawyer* in April 2007 which appeared to criticise the proposed deportation from Britain of another radical cleric, Abu Qatada, noting that

the Special Immigration Appeals Commission ruled that it would be lawful, and no breach of Article 3 ECHR, for the government now to deport Abu Qatada to Jordan. Unsurprisingly, that decision was subject to immediate appeal. This flies in the face of the opinion of international human rights bodies and individuals worldwide.[8]

As well as these cases failing to make the final cut of Starmer's promotional video, most of them share another characteristic: namely an adherence to the Human Rights Act 1998. The aim of this Act, which came into force in October 2000, is to incorporate into UK law the rights contained in the European Court of Human Rights. Its introduction heralded a new legal landscape in which government departments strove to act in a way that was more progressive. One human rights lawyer says:

I know the Act has had an awful reputation since then and is thought of as the source of all our ills, but then and now it's a very sensible piece of legislation. It has a more objective approach to problems. Until the Act, if a client came to you with a problem, you'd often have to say, 'I know it's unfair, but that's what the law says.' After the Act came in, you could look at the law and, if it produced an unjust result, find a way of penetrating under the body of law to ask yourself questions which the convention demands, like what is the proper balance between the rights of an individual and the rights of society.

Another lawyer, who is in practice as a criminal QC, is more scornful of this entire area of law. 'To call yourself a "human rights lawyer" is absurd,' he says.

> Any defence lawyer involved with defending people or involved with ensuring the rules of natural justice are complied with is in effect a human rights lawyer. All of us are involved in human rights – the human right not to be falsely convicted. Does that make Doughty Street a particularly 'human rights' set of chambers? I don't think it's any more 'human rights' than any of the more traditional sets. It's an American idea, but I suppose it's very nice if you want to talk up your credentials when applying for a Labour seat.

When you consider that the Human Rights Act has led to some highly controversial outcomes, it is hard to disagree. These include the rights of prisoners to give sperm to their wives or girlfriends for artificial insemination being upheld in 2009; the Asylum and Immigration Tribunal in 2007 allowing Learco Chindamo, the teenage killer of London headmaster Philip Lawrence, to remain in Britain despite being born in Italy because 'he has a right to a family life in Britain'; and, in 2004, nine Afghans who hijacked a plane which landed at Stansted Airport in 2000 being allowed to remain in Britain so as not to breach their human rights.

These more extreme examples apart, the late 1990s was a time of change in terms of engaging with the problems that the strict application of the law could create, and human rights was a cause which Starmer took up with energy. It became his specialism. In 1998, he published a book titled *Signing Up for Human Rights: The United Kingdom and International Standards*. That year he also accepted a fellowship of the Human Rights Centre at Essex University. In 1999, he published another book, *European Human Rights Law*, which one lawyer says he 'churned out surprisingly quickly'. That year he also became a member of the council of the campaigning organisation Justice, which was run at that time by his Doughty Street colleague and longstanding friend, Helena Kennedy. (Incidentally, another board member was Sir Michael Tugendhat, a former High Court judge whose son, Tom, is a Tory MP and friendly acquaintance of Starmer.) In 2000, Starmer became chairman of the Human Rights Act Research Unit at King's College School of Law, London. He was also named the Liberty/Justice Human Rights Lawyer of the Year, being praised by the judges for his work in representing at the Privy Council convicted murderers awaiting execution. As the winner of the main individual prize, he was singled out for his detailed work on making human rights legislation accessible to lawyers and laypeople. There was no mention in the accompanying press reports that he had professional links to the bodies after whom the prize was named – Liberty and Justice – though perhaps there should have been.

In 2000, a new set of chambers was established in London. Called Matrix, it immediately attracted attention because Cherie Blair, wife of the then Prime Minister, Tony Blair, was among its twenty-two founding members. Matrix hit upon the idea of focusing its efforts on the new Human Rights Act, prompting many commentators to conclude, perhaps cynically, that those involved were simply cashing in as the new law made its presence felt. As *The Times* reported shortly after the new set's creation:

> Matrix, led by star-studded names, which include the QCs Cherie Booth and Ben Emmerson, the guru on the new Act, is the first

concrete spin-off in the profession to come from the forthcoming legislation. It is a clear sign that, despite the benefits the Act will bring – enabling people to pursue breaches of human rights in the English courts for the first time – it is also set to be a lawyers' bonanza.[9]

Emmerson, who is a year younger than Starmer, was a member of Doughty Street Chambers when he left for Matrix. His expertise on the Human Rights Act was apparently derived from the fact that he had advised on its drafting, having spent much of his career taking cases to the European Court of Human Rights at Strasbourg, of which Starmer had less experience. Indeed, such was Emmerson's knowledge in the field of human rights that in the late 1990s, he was asked by the Lord Chancellor's department to teach other lawyers, civil servants and even judges in England and Wales about the implications of the new Human Rights Act. Emmerson joined Matrix with another recruit from Doughty Street Chambers, Tim Owen.

Starmer and his girlfriend, Phillippa Kaufmann, were also invited to defect from Doughty Street and join Matrix at this point. One of their former colleagues remembers: 'When Matrix was set up, they were keen to pinch our people. Keir was tempted but didn't go. Those who did go were quite a big loss to Doughty Street.' Another explains: 'When Matrix Chambers came along, with Cherie Blair and other luminaries, they made a big pitch for Keir. They lured two of our silks, but Keir rejected their blandishments. He wanted, he said, to position himself with pioneers rather than opportunists.' Who can say if Starmer came to regret this principled decision, however? For although he chose to remain at Doughty Street with Kaufmann, the pair split up the following year, with Starmer cashing in his £140,000 share of their house in Hackney and moving into a property in Kentish Town, north London, which was owned by his friend from Reigate Grammar School, Mark Adams.

It is no exaggeration to say that in the 1990s and early 2000s, Starmer's personal life and professional life became more and more entwined in a way that other people might find somewhat suffocating. As described in Chapter 6, his relationship with Angela O'Brien had ended by 1997, and he subsequently took up with Kaufmann. After he and O'Brien had ceased to be an item, she struck up a relationship with one of Starmer's colleagues from Doughty Street Chambers, Hugh Barton, who was the same age and had the same kind of practice as Starmer. Around the time that Starmer and Kaufmann separated, O'Brien and Barton, who are married, moved to the north of England, where they still live happily. Then, even more awkwardly for Starmer, after he and Kaufmann had split, she began a relationship with *another* Doughty Street colleague of hers and Starmer's, Paul Brooks. Kaufmann and Brooks soon married and had two children. Many people would find it difficult enough that one ex-girlfriend had started seeing one of their colleagues, but for two exes to be involved with colleagues would be too much to bear. Yet Starmer seems to have coped. One person with knowledge of the situation says, 'I'm not sure why it ended between Keir and Phillippa Kaufmann, but there were no hard feelings as far as I know. Keir and Phillippa even continued to work on cases together.'

* * *

In March 2002, Starmer became a QC at the relatively early age of thirty-nine, joining the cadre of senior barristers who are considered the best in their field of practice. A few months later, he was mentioned in an *Observer* profile piece, headlined 'The new legal crusaders', which focused on a group of ambitious lawyers under the age of forty-five with a 'burning desire for justice' who 'defend dissidents and terror suspects'. This article is also noteworthy for the following sentence:

'Among them was Ben Emmerson, the dashing young advocate and colleague of Cherie Booth at the fashionable Matrix Chambers. Admirers say that if Colin Firth's human rights lawyer in the film *Bridget Jones's Diary* wasn't based on Emmerson, then it should have been.' These words solve a mystery which has portrayed Starmer in a very useful and flattering light for many years for absolutely no reason other than what appears to be sloppy journalism. Starmer was always happy not to disabuse people of the notion that *he* was the inspiration for Mark Darcy, who was created by Helen Fielding, the author of *Bridget Jones's Diary*. As we shall see, the fact is that he never was.

What appears to have happened is that in April 2012, a decade after the *Observer* article was published, a *Sunday Times* journalist called Camilla Long went to interview Starmer. 'Just before my interview with Keir Starmer, the Director of Public Prosecutions (DPP), someone tells me that the chisel-jawed former human rights lawyer was the inspiration for Mr Darcy in *Bridget Jones*,' Long wrote at the time. 'I am not sure if this is true – but I can confirm he is every bit as awkward and tongue-tied as the fictional character.'

From that point on, other journalists decided that it *was* true, and the myth held. Starmer never denied it, no doubt relishing the touch of glamour it gave him, though it does appear that he allowed his vanity to get the better of him. For example, in January 2020, during the Labour leadership contest, when ITV News asked him if the Darcy character was based on him, he answered: 'Everybody asks me this question when they should be asking [Fielding] the question because she knows the answer and I don't. It's a rumour that's been doing the rounds for some years, but I honestly don't know the answer to it.' In the end, it was Fielding herself who explained the truth on *Desert Island Discs* in July 2020, making clear that Starmer played no part in her thinking up Mark Darcy.

While this may seem to be a trivial matter, one friend of Starmer says it is in fact rather revealing. The Starmer whom this person knows apparently paid attention when members of the opposite sex said he was good-looking. 'What's interesting is he knows full well he wasn't the model for Mark Darcy because he's never met Helen Fielding and has nothing to do with her,' says the friend. 'His answers were always designed to suggest it was true, but he knew it was bollocks.' The irony of all this is that in 2019, Hollywood actor Ralph Fiennes, who is a friend of Colin Firth, played Ben Emmerson – whose mention in *The Observer* in 2002 had kicked off the various Mark Darcy rumours – in the film *Official Secrets*. Emmerson was depicted in this thriller for the work he did in support of the GCHQ whistleblower Katharine Gun.

Becoming a QC in 2002 marked a new phase in Starmer's life. As he was not in a serious relationship with anybody at the time, he was able to throw himself into work and take advantage of his enhanced professional standing. When he won his silk status – so called because of the silk gowns QCs wear – he was one of 111 barristers to do so. In those days, the Lord Chancellor's department picked the new silks under a system apparently based on merit, meaning that Starmer was ultimately anointed by the Lord Chancellor at the time, Lord Irvine of Lairg, who had been Tony Blair's pupil master in the 1970s. According to *The Times*, which carried a report about the new elevations, the Law Society, the solicitors' professional body, had attacked the QC system as a 'cartel that sustains a market in high fees', though this had little effect. The newspaper also revealed that the highest paid of the new QCs declared earnings of £705,000 a year, while the lowest paid re-ported a salary of £64,000, with the average salary of the new QCs being £268,688. Starmer would almost certainly have been earning a very healthy six-figure salary by this stage, even if it was not as high as £705,000.

A few years previously, he had worked as a junior on an appeal case which had given him some valuable insights into the post-Belfast Agreement situation in Northern Ireland. This work would, in turn, make him the ideal candidate for his first big publicly funded role, which he took up in 2003. In 1999, Starmer was part of a team that defended Private Lee Clegg, a paratrooper who had been convicted in 1993 of the 1990 murder of Karen Reilly. She was the eighteen-year-old backseat passenger in a stolen car which raced through an army checkpoint in Belfast at high speed. Clegg had opened fire on the joyriders with other members of his patrol. The driver, Martin Peake, aged seventeen, had also died. The case became a cause célèbre when Clegg was given a life sentence for Miss Reilly's murder and four years for attempting to wound with intent Mr Peake. Clegg appealed several times and was released on licence in 1995 by the then Northern Ireland Secretary, Sir Patrick Mayhew. This decision infuriated Republicans and Miss Reilly's family, who felt Clegg was shown leniency because he was a soldier. Widespread rioting in Republican areas across the province ensued. After his release, Clegg rejoined the army and launched a further set of appeals which led to the murder conviction being overturned in 1998. A retrial was held in March 1999 after new forensic evidence suggested one bullet entered the side of the car. At the retrial, Clegg was cleared of murder, but a conviction for 'attempting to wound' the driver, Martin Peake, was upheld. This led to another appeal where the lesser conviction was also quashed in January 2000.

According to Starmer's friend Mark Stephens, a solicitor who had instructed Starmer on many cases, some London lawyers threatened to stop giving him work because of his involvement in the Clegg case. 'He was heavily criticised at the time by the unthinking left of the legal village in London,' Stephens has recalled. 'Whereas Keir could see that [Clegg] had rights that were being infringed, and it didn't actually matter who was infringing rights – if you had rights that were taken away then you ought to do something about it. They didn't get that, and Keir did.'[10] It is said that Starmer spent the best part of three months working on the case and would sometimes go to the British garrison to play football with the squaddies. He liked Northern Ireland in spite of its complications and liked to think he understood it. All this would later work in his favour.

Policing in Northern Ireland has long been a contentious issue. Under the terms of the Belfast Agreement of 1998, an independent commission was established under the former governor of Hong Kong, Chris Patten, which made a series of recommendations including the abolition of the existing police force, the Royal Ulster Constabulary. It was renamed the Police Service of Northern Ireland (PSNI) in 2001 and the PSNI Board was established that year. It is an independent public body made up of ten political and nine independent members whose job is to hold the PSNI to account on behalf of all communities in the province. In May 2002, the board held a meeting at which it was agreed that in order to monitor police compliance with the Human Rights Act, a human rights adviser would have to be hired. This paid position was never advertised. Instead, candidates with the requisite expertise were invited to an interview in January 2003. A three-year contract, which might be extended, was on the table for the right person. Starmer got the job, his experience as a human rights lawyer and his work as a consultant to the Association of Chief Police Officers apparently being the chief reasons that he was chosen.

Initially, he was required to spend a day or two per month in Northern Ireland. He reported to Trevor Reaney, then the chief executive of the Northern Ireland Policing Board. He was the sole human rights adviser to the board, though from 2004 another lawyer, Jane Gordon, was hired as his assistant. Ian Paisley Jr, the son of the founder of the

Democratic Unionist Party, the Rev. Ian Paisley, was at the time the member of the Northern Ireland Assembly for North Antrim. He was also a member of the PSNI Board who worked closely with Starmer. Paisley says:

> When Keir Starmer came on, we knew we had a job to do that was seen to be fair, seen to be impartial, that was able to appeal across the communities so we could say the PSNI is a perfectly legitimate force, and it's perfectly legitimate to serve us. We needed a defence line that allowed us to say, 'We acknowledge human rights issues, that's why we do this, this is how we police' and so on. We saw his role as providing the support to allow us to make the case about the human rights record of the police, so we could say here's our defence line, and he helped us provide that.[11]

The job entailed Starmer attending a monthly meeting, giving briefings to the board, preparing board members for interviews and providing human rights training support on matters over which they had to hold the police to account. Paisley says:

> If the police did something and there was a question about it, we would know these were the probe lines we would have to go down to get satisfactory answers. We would hold the police to account by being a good critical friend and making sure they had growing community support.

Although the role was primarily a desk job, the police did take Starmer on patrol to give an insight into some of the issues they faced and to show the line that must be negotiated between the divided loyalist and nationalist communities. 'Every action has to be authorised by Gold or

Silver Command and consistent with human rights regulations,' says Paisley.

> People like him, pushing a pen, looking at these things from the safety and comfort of an office is very different from being on the ground. I've seen it from all sides, and you get a real sense that it's a difficult and nail-biting job for those in command because of the split-second decisions they have to take.

Starmer has spoken of one close shave he experienced while he occupied this post. The Orange Order marches held on 12 July every year to mark the victory of William of Orange over James II at the Battle of the Boyne in 1690 attract large crowds and have in the past led to sectarian violence. 'I was on the ground sometimes outside the Ardoyne shopfronts in North Belfast on 12 July when the parades were happening, there were all sorts of things happening on the ground,' he recalled. 'We were there with our clipboards observing what was going on and suddenly golf balls were being thrown and there were petrol bombs and I was thrown in the back of a police van for safety.'[12]

Situations like this cemented his awareness that a balance had to be struck in Northern Ireland. For this reason, Starmer was apparently scrupulous about keeping his counsel at all times and never talked about politics in Westminster or elsewhere. 'I only ever engaged with him professionally,' says Paisley.

> I had no social life with him. There was no after-work drinks party. I found him to be a consummate professional. I can't say he put a foot wrong in his engagement with us. He didn't engage in social chit-chat or show any inquisitiveness. He just did the job, which was perhaps unusual given the length of time he was there.

Asked whether he was well liked, Paisley is happy to confirm that he was. 'He was professional and reassuring in terms of how he did the job. I never heard a word of criticism about him from other colleagues of other parties or from independent members. So he kept his nose very clean and was scrupulous about that.' Paisley added that he had no knowledge of the Haldane Society trip to Northern Ireland which Starmer had led in 1991, referred to in Chapter 6. As previously mentioned, its subsequent report, 'Upholding the Rule of Law?', stated in its introduction: 'We call for British withdrawal [from Northern Ireland].' It remains unclear whether those who appointed Starmer knew about it either when they appointed him or at any point during the four years he held the PSNI Board job.

Yet his legacy is secure, as far as Paisley is concerned:

In terms of hard policing and the force of hard policing, he gave us the tools and the arguments and the defence lines to allow us to say that water cannon are necessary or plastic bullets are allowed. They are still permissible today, as shown in the riots of April 2021. And all police officers in Northern Ireland carry a gun. The argument for retaining this was defended. I would say his lasting legacy is that you can have all of these accoutrements to policing provided they meet human rights guidelines efficiently, and he provided the board with the arguments to do that and the legal cover to do it. If the police had been using them without cover, I can imagine the board would have faced inquiries every day.

It was at this time that Starmer embarked on a new relationship with Victoria Alexander, a London-based solicitor eleven years his junior. She is the daughter of a Jewish accountant, Bernard Alexander, whose family came from Poland, and a Yorkshire-born doctor, Barbara Moyes, who converted to Judaism. She grew up in north London and went to the fee-paying Channing School for Girls in Highgate, where she is understood to have taken politics at A-Level and to have been left-leaning as a teenager. She qualified as a solicitor in 2001 and worked for the London firm Hodge Jones & Allen before later retraining in occupational health, in which capacity she now works in the NHS. She and Starmer met in 2005, apparently when she was preparing case files for him before he went into court. Starmer has recalled:

> The bundles of documents in front of me had to be 100 per cent accurate. I phoned up to check and said: 'This schedule, is it any good? Is it absolutely accurate?' She quite indignantly, quite rightly, said: 'Absolutely.' She says she then put the phone down and said: 'Who the fuck does he think he is?'[13]

This encounter led to their first date at the Lord Stanley pub off the Camden Road in north London. They married in May 2007 on the Fennes Estate in Essex and started their honeymoon in Belfast before touring the whole island of Ireland. Aged forty-four, it is true to say that Starmer was fairly long in the tooth to be embarking on his first marriage, perhaps reflecting the rather complicated love life he had had up until this point. One who knows the couple says that they have a tight circle of friends in north London, many of whom are left-wing lawyers, but of Victoria they say: 'It's not clear if she realised when she married Keir that she was going to become a politician's wife.'

The couple began their married life in the four-bedroom terraced house in Kentish Town, which Starmer had acquired with a mortgage for £650,000 in April 2004. They still live there today. In the seventeen years since he bought it, the house has more than doubled in value, with neighbouring properties routinely selling for £1.5 million. A few months after he made that purchase, he also bought a house with his sister, Katherine, in Oxted for £410,000. Land and property are only worth what people are prepared to pay for them, as is well known, yet it is worth pointing out that for the first six years that Starmer was an MP, his portfolio was theoretically worth significantly more than the value of his share in these two houses alone. The reason for this is that in 1996, he also bought a field situated behind the house in which he grew up in Tanhouse Road, on the outskirts of Oxted. At the time of publication, he was still registered as its owner, according to Land Registry records. In May 2020, the *Mail on Sunday* published a story about this parcel of land, which covers almost eight acres, having been tipped off about it by a neighbour. A spokesman for Starmer claimed to the newspaper that the purchase had been made for his mother so that she could keep donkeys there. To that end, a small summer house was built in or near the field, from where she was able to observe the donkeys after being confined to a wheelchair. Starmer's mother died in 2015. The following year his father, Rodney, obtained retrospective planning permission for the summer house. (Neighbours who contributed to this book say that Rodney effectively moved into the summer house after being widowed. Sadly, while he was in hospital in 2018, it burned down in a fire which also killed his pet dog.)

The *Mail on Sunday* pointed out in May 2020 that because of the perceived pressure to build more houses in the south-east of England, this land could be worth up to £1.5 million per acre if planning permission to build a substantial number of houses on it were secured. In such a situation, Starmer's holding would be worth more than £10 million – on paper, at least – making it an extremely canny investment. One Surrey-based land agent who was willing for the purposes of this book to give his assessment of the value of Starmer's undeveloped greenbelt land says that it is worth about £10,000 per acre, or just under £80,000 in its current state. What is surprising is that when Starmer's entry in the House of Commons Register of Members' Financial Interests is examined, there is no mention of this landholding. Until June 2021, he did acknowledge in the register that he was the 'co-owner of [a] house in Surrey, inhabited by family members', this being the house in which his sister lived. The house was sold in the spring of 2021. It is not clear if Starmer's investment was returned to him. Yet parliamentary rules state categorically that, with the exception of their main residence, an MP should declare ownership of 'any land or property if the MP's port-folio has a value over £100,000'.[14] Aside from his residence in London, Starmer's portfolio comprising his sister's house and his separate land-holding clearly exceeded the £100,000 threshold. As a Westminster insider says:

> MPs are expected to register their additional assets on top of their normal living arrangements so that people can see if there is a po-tential conflict of interests. It is important for people to know this so they can judge an MP's political decisions. The advice of officials to an MP would always be to make a declaration if they are in any doubt about whether they should do so.

Breaching parliamentary rules of this nature is not always considered to be a serious offence and usually requires an MP to apologise publicly if they are found to have erred, sometimes by making a statement to the House. In Starmer's case, however, the events of April 2021 bring his failure to declare to the parliamentary authorities over the past six years his ownership of this land in Surrey into much sharper focus. At a session of Prime Minister's Questions held on 28 April, he took Boris Johnson to task over the matter of who had initially funded the refur-bishment of the flat in which Johnson lives with Carrie Symonds and their young son, Wilfred, above 11 Downing Street. Johnson's former adviser, Dominic Cummings, had claimed publicly a few days before that Johnson had told him in 2020 of a plan to 'have [Conservative Party] donors secretly pay for the renovation' – an idea which Cummings had apparently warned Johnson was 'unethical, foolish, possibly illegal, and almost certainly broke the rules on proper disclosure of political donations'. Inevitably, a torrent of press speculation about the affair, which was dubbed 'cash for curtains', ensued. This helped to trigger official inquiries into Johnson from the Electoral Commission and the Parliamentary Commissioner for Standards. Material of this kind is manna from heaven for any Leader of the Opposition, and Starmer tried to capitalise on the opportunity. He labelled Johnson 'Major Sleaze' and accused his government of being 'mired in sleaze, cronyism and scandal'. If it was his intention to raise Johnson's temper, he succeeded, as an increasingly angry exchange between the two men took place across the despatch box.

Starmer also used this occasion to quote to Johnson the various ethical standards to which those working in the public sector are expected to adhere. Known as the Seven Principles of Public Life, they are: selflessness, integrity, objectivity, accountability, openness, honesty and leadership. These principles were first set out by Lord Nolan in 1995, and they are included in a range of codes of conduct across the public realm. Yet on the basis of Starmer's own failure to declare his ownership of potentially valuable land in Surrey, it is clear that he has failed to follow some of the Nolan Principles. It is hard to avoid wondering who advises Starmer when it comes to such a clear-cut case of the pot calling the kettle black.

As for the land itself, it is striking that it appears to remain in his ownership despite his late parents' house having been sold in 2020 and their donkeys therefore being long gone. Starmer's decision to hang on to the land has allowed the idea to form in the minds of some of those living in Tanhouse Road that he or somebody close to him does intend to develop it one day. One Tanhouse Road resident says, 'Rodney Starmer used to brag that he was worth millions because of the land's value. We found it a bit odd.' It is certainly odd for Rodney Starmer to have made this claim, if he truly did so, given that he never owned the land. As it is Keir Starmer who owns this land, however, it is certainly the case that *he* is currently sitting on what could one day be a handsome fortune.

In April 2008, there was a management shake-up at Doughty Street Chambers, which led to Starmer becoming joint head of chambers with Geoffrey Robertson. By then, it had ninety barristers and Robertson needed somebody with whom he could share the organisational burden. Peter Thornton, who left to become Chief Coroner of England and Wales, had done the job previously, and Starmer replaced him unopposed. In the event, he would not be in this post for long, however. Having always wanted to be more than just a barrister, he soon had his sights set on an altogether different role, which just happened to be one of the biggest jobs in the public sector.

CHAPTER 8

'CREDIBLE AND TRUE'

In February 2009, a businesswoman called Penelope Edwards placed an advertisement in the Encounters section of the *Sunday Times* which read: 'Amazonian professional, forty-one, intelligent, gorgeous, vivacious, enjoys swimming, travel, driving fast, seeks spontaneous, caring, well-spoken professional for loving relationship.' Perhaps surprisingly, Ms Edwards was not inundated with responses to this message from other lonely hearts, but within a couple of months one reaction did catch her eye. It was from a man who described himself as a 'successful barrister, fit, very spontaneous, looking for relationship'. She texted her phone number to the respondent and before long he rang her, introducing himself as Keir Starmer of the Crown Prosecution Service. They arranged a date. Not having heard of Starmer before, Ms Edwards hunted for a photograph of him online and considered him to be good-looking. As DPP, the third highest-ranking public prosecutor in England and Wales, he was also clearly very successful. When he showed up as agreed at a car park in Windsor on 19 April bearing a bouquet of flowers and a bottle of pink champagne, nothing seemed untoward, and they enjoyed lunch together by the Thames.

The relationship progressed rapidly over a very short space of time and might have become serious but for one thing: this man was not Starmer at all. He was, in fact, a Northamptonshire hairdresser turned serial conman called Paul Bint who had at that time more than 150 convictions to his name, having passed himself off previously as a banker, an aristocrat, a police officer, a ballet dancer and a property tycoon. Worse still for Ms Edwards, it later transpired that at the same time as he was seeing her, he had tricked another woman, Vivienne Walsh, into believing he was a criminal barrister called Jonathan Rees. His deception came to light when he told a taxi driver he could not pay a £60 fare because his wallet had been stolen. He asked that the bill should be sent to his place of work. When no money was forthcoming, the furious driver went to the offices of the DPP to complain and had to be placated by the secretary of the real Starmer, who is the same age as Bint. From that point, the charade quickly disintegrated, and the wheels of justice began to turn swiftly. In November 2009, Bint was jailed for three years at Southwark Crown Court after being found guilty of fraud and theft.

Starmer has dined out on this rather surreal story ever since, often quipping publicly that when Bint was arrested, the question arose of whether he should be prosecuted. Starmer, being the DPP, realised immediately that he could not be party to this decision, though his sense of humour did prompt him to ask jokingly whether Bint was pleading guilty, whether he was still claiming to be Starmer, and, if acquitted, where he – Starmer – would stand from a legal point of view. 'During the trial it was put to one of the women [Bint] had an affair with that he didn't look particularly like me,' Starmer also laughed on *Desert Island Discs*. 'To which, if I'm right in recalling, she said: "Well, everybody can have an off day."'[1] It is certainly true that Bint resembles Starmer only faintly.

Some people have expressed surprise that Starmer should have been appointed to the exalted post of DPP. On paper, the man who was known for challenging government decisions on the grounds of human rights was not necessarily the natural choice to take on the responsibility of bringing to court most criminal prosecutions in England and Wales. So how did he come to take on this role, in which he was effectively ceasing to be a poacher and becoming a gamekeeper? Before answering this question, it is important to establish what the CPS is and what the responsibilities of the DPP are.

Until 1986, when the CPS was created, criminal prosecutions in England and Wales were brought by individual police forces or county solicitors. Its establishment meant that the business of prosecuting crime fell to regional CPS offices, each of which was split into specialist divisions, such as counter-terrorism, fraud, serious organised crime and so on. The CPS does not have the power to investigate crime. Instead, it considers evidence that has been gathered by police and other agencies and determines whether a suspect should face criminal charges. When deciding whether somebody should go to court or not, crown prosecutors must consider if there is sufficient evidence to provide a realistic prospect of a conviction and whether or not a prosecution is in the public interest.

Alongside this gatekeeping function, it has responsibility for preparing cases, for prosecuting them before a court and for reviewing them if new evidence comes to light. As the head of the CPS, the DPP is the third most senior public prosecutor in England and Wales after the Attorney General and the Solicitor General. The relationship between the DPP and the government is one of superintendence, meaning that the Attorney General answers for the DPP in Parliament but the DPP's decision-making is independent of the Attorney General. The Attorney General does have some powers of intervention, but they should be used only *in extremis*. The DPP is ultimately in charge of between 6,000 and 7,000 members of CPS staff working in offices around the country, who oversee an estimated 800,000 prosecutions every year, making the job as bureaucratic as it is legal. The DPP can also have some influence over the development of criminal justice policy, acting in concert with the Home Secretary and the Justice Secretary.

Starmer's route to this role began on 18 May 2008, when an advertisement seeking a new DPP appeared in the Appointments section of the *Sunday Times*. The same advert was subsequently placed in *The Times* and *The Lawyer*. Prospective candidates were given three weeks to apply. They had to supply a covering letter and a CV and complete a diversity form, and then submit to a round of interviews. Ken Macdonald was the incumbent DPP at this point, having been appointed in 2003. He was the first person to take on the job under Tony Blair's Labour government, and it is generally accepted that in doing so, he broke the mould. Until his elevation, the DPP had always been a career prosecutor. Macdonald, a longstanding criminal barrister, was best known as a defence lawyer. It was said that the Labour government had wanted to take a new approach to criminal justice when he was appointed, triggering accusations from some quarters of political interference. Whatever the truth of that matter, Macdonald effectively cleared the path for Starmer – or indeed anybody else with limited prosecutorial experience – to succeed him. At the time that Starmer applied to be DPP, Labour was still in power, this time with Gordon Brown in Downing Street, and appointing another defence specialist would certainly be less controversial than it had been five years previously.

Details released under the Freedom of Information Act confirm that eighteen people applied to become DPP in 2008. One person with knowledge of the process says that the field was 'weak' and Starmer was quickly identified as being the pick of a poor crop. The £195,000 salary, which is relatively low by the standards of what can be earned by Britain's top legal minds, is one possible reason why the post did not attract higher-calibre individuals. Another is the fact that those who become DPP know that in taking on this job they are effectively bringing down the curtain on their career as a lawyer. One of Starmer's former colleagues says:

It's not a job you take if you've got a good practice and you're enjoying yourself at the Bar. There's always a pay-off if you become DPP. Everybody knows it's a public service, but it's a miserable thing to do. So afterwards you either become a High Court judge or get a peerage. Keir would have got a peerage if he hadn't wanted to become Prime Minister. There was talk he might become Labour's shadow Lord Chancellor after he'd done his term as DPP, which would have put him in the Lords, but it was clear he didn't want that because he wanted to become Prime Minister, so he had to be in the Commons.

It is now obvious that in accepting the job, Starmer knew it was a stepping-stone to Westminster.

Having sifted through the covering letters and CVs, the interview team invited all eighteen candidates to attend a technical interview. They were then whittled down to the four best contenders. One withdrew, leaving the remaining three to be evaluated by an occupational psychologist and to undertake a mock media interview. They then attended a final formal interview, with a selection panel comprising the then Attorney General Baroness Scotland; senior judge Sir Brian Leveson; the then permanent secretary to the Ministry of Justice Sir Sumantra Chakrabarti; and a fourth figure called Philip

Oliver. Starmer was announced as the new DPP in July 2008, and he began the job three months later, shortly after celebrating his forty-sixth birthday. Recently married (his wife had by this point ceased to be a lawyer) and with his first child, Toby, only a few months old, this was the domestic backdrop to what was surely the most challenging and demanding work he had ever done to that point. His daughter, Lara, was born in November 2010, almost midway through his five-year contract as DPP, no doubt making further demands on his time and energy. Perhaps the only real perks of the job were that he had a car, a chauffeur and a generous pension.

'I don't know if anyone else encouraged him to apply for the post, but I was pleased when he expressed an interest in doing it because I thought he'd do it well,' says his predecessor Ken Macdonald, who now sits in the House of Lords as a crossbencher.[2]

> It is highly burdensome. It's quite a powerful position; there's a lot of accountability to ministers, to the Prime Minister, to the government, to the public. All of that weighs on you to an extent. Apart from that, it's about running quite a large organisation of several thousand lawyers, who aren't the easiest people to manage. Running public organisations is frustrating at times. There are quite a lot of issues of morality and competence to deal with. You tend to get the blame when anything goes wrong. Some prosecutor could be sitting in Manchester making some stupid decision which two days later is on the front page of the *Daily Mail*, and you get the blame for it. That can be quite frustrating. You have to be able to take all of that. You have to develop a thick skin.

It says something about Starmer's cautious instincts that he opted to spend his first few months as DPP travelling the country to review the way the CPS functions. This certainly suggests that he entered this very prominent position in public life well aware of its potential pitfalls and concerned not to put a foot wrong. One figure who has followed Starmer's career closely has a rather more cynical interpretation of what he thought this might achieve, however:

> As soon as Keir was appointed, he immediately set about announcing he would visit every CPS area in the country on a listening tour, which struck me as a useless waste of time because that was not a systemised way of obtaining information, it was a way of trying to make himself seem popular. Ken Macdonald was loved by the CPS staff and no doubt Keir wanted to emulate that, but what a massive effort and what a massive waste of resources when he should have been checking the systems in a way that would enable issues to be brought to his attention – issues that needed his attention. You're not there to go around doing a roadshow. I thought that was odd.

This is, of course, just one point of view, but Ken Macdonald also acknowledges that Starmer adopted what might be described as a rather technical approach to the job. 'Keir was certainly interested in policy,' he observes.

> Keir's very interested in process. I think you can see that in his political life. He's very interested in how things work and how to make them work better, so he was much more focused as DPP than I was on the processes of decision-making: how were people making decisions; how can we get them to make decisions better? You tend to have one great theme as DPP. Mine was to try and get the CPS lawyers into court arguing their own cases rather than using independent barristers the whole time, because I thought that would make it

a more exciting job and we'd be able to recruit better people. His was developing what he called 'core standards', so he was trying to work out what are the core standards that we should be applying in various stages of our work, and how can we guarantee that those standards are met. So his approach to the job was quite process-driven. It was similar to the way he did his cases – process-driven and careful and taking it stage by stage. I think you see that in his approach to politics quite clearly.

It wasn't just CPS staff whom Starmer wanted to get to know. Nazir Afzal, who worked as a director of the CPS in London in 2008, recalls Starmer asking him to go on a meet-and-greet-style outing shortly after he took on the DPP role. This was part of a strategy to make the CPS better known to the public. It eventually became clear to Afzal that the event to which he was invited had been organised by somebody who was already very well known to Starmer – and who had nothing to do with his work. For the purposes of this book, Afzal shared unpublished excerpts of an interview which he gave to a journalist in March 2021. He says:

Within a couple of weeks of [Starmer] arriving in 2008, I got a call from him [Starmer] saying, 'Come with me, we need to go to this school and talk to them about the CPS.' I thought, 'Fine.' There was me geared up to go to this school in north London and expecting to talk to A-Level students about constitutional law or separation of powers and finding myself in a primary school with forty six- and seven-year-olds. The conversation was all about whether I sat in a police car, what's a good guy and what's a bad guy. Literally, it was at that level. But it was enriching to hear that conversation and the teachers were there. It was only afterwards that I learned

[Starmer's] sister-in-law was a teacher at that school. She facilitated the engagement.[3]

There was a more serious side to the listening tour, however. Afzal adds:

I remember we spent most of 2009 travelling up and down the country. He was very keen to visit prosecution divisions and police colleagues everywhere. I remember arriving at Carlisle station visiting the police in Cumbria, for example, or in parts of Wales or wherever it may be. He did get around and every time he met with a prosecution team, he was keen not just to meet them; he would meet with the senior police team and also ask us to invite senior members of the community – victims' groups and local charities. And so, the conversation wasn't just focused on how we as prosecutors might do better; it was about what the relationship with the police was and what the relationship with the community was and where the gaps were. It might have been strange for him given he'd spent all his life in defence work and not prosecution work, but he rapidly understood that our work would be improved substantially by better engagement with the police and that clearly happened.

Starmer's record as DPP is a matter of public debate. For every lawyer or politician who would commend him for his time in the office, there is another who would point to an issue which raises questions about his decisions or those of the CPS. His instruction to CPS staff in 2009 to consider the Human Rights Act before they try to prosecute, for example, was regarded by many Conservative MPs as problematic because of the inherent risk in allowing criminals to escape justice on what could be a technicality.[4]

What cannot be disputed, however, is that the DPP must assume responsibility for the heaviest cases, and in this regard Starmer's five years in the job now appear to have covered a fairly momentous period, with a large range of complicated and very high-profile matters crossing his desk between 2008 and 2013, including the London riots of 2011 and the fallout from the highly contentious death of the newspaper vendor Ian Tomlinson. 'The case load is very interesting because you pick which cases you want to lead in and which cases you want to make decisions in,' says Ken Macdonald. 'So if you're a criminal lawyer that's a fantastic position to be in in terms of professional satisfaction.'

Be that as it may, Starmer also occupied the post during a change of government from Labour to the Tory-led coalition which was in situ from 2010. It put in place a round of sharp public expenditure cuts following the world financial crisis of 2008. The CPS was not immune. During Starmer's tenure, the CPS's budget was cut by 27 per cent, with the inevitable consequence that staff numbers were cut radically as well. None of this would have made his job any easier and might go some way to explaining why in March 2012, for example, it was revealed by the CPS's official inspectors that 63,000 criminal cases a year – or 7 per cent of the total – were wrongly dropped or unjustifiably brought to trial.

Dominic Grieve was the Attorney General from May 2010, meaning that he and Starmer worked closely together for most of the time Starmer was in post. He says their different political views had no impact on the way Starmer approached the job. 'The relationship of the Attorney General and the DPP is quite a complicated one,' says Grieve.[5]

The question, probably for both of us, was whether this was a re-lationship that was going to work well. And I quickly became very impressed by him in terms of his professionalism, and we had a very good working relationship. Bear in mind that it was a time of very considerable challenges, the biggest one of which was that the Crown Prosecution Service was being asked to make significant and substantial cuts, as everybody else was, following the formation of the coalition government. And he did that, in my judgement, show-ing considerable leadership and very considerable effectiveness, because we were obviously both worried that it would diminish the efficiency of the CPS. It was asked to carry out reforms that were going to have quite a profound impact on the morale of those people working within it, because it required the closure of offices; their amalgamation; changes to the way the work was carried out. And he carried that out with great efficiency.

Grieve says he and Starmer would meet on a monthly basis to discuss these cuts, giving Starmer valuable insights into the workings of White-hall and government, which he would not have had if he had been a back-bench opposition politician, for example. This suggests that he had an eye on the future. 'We'd also talk sometimes, of course, about other things, about casework and things of that sort,' Grieve recalls.

But the truth was that the biggest challenge he was facing was this substantial paring down of the CPS without curbing its effectiveness. And while I think it can be said that we were all very lucky that it took place against a background of diminishing crime – or at least, put it this way, it wasn't rising, which it has done since – neverthe-less, even when you take that into consideration, I think it was a considerable achievement on his part, and it was carried out with pragmatic realism.

Starmer also made it his business to meet journalists and other opinion formers from time to time. One such person recalls: 'Over lunch he was personable, charming, nice, easy to talk to, he had no side, and he was just straight. He wasn't like some people, who are terribly guarded. I wouldn't say he was suspicious of journalists. He didn't have that in-built hostility towards journalists. He was likeable.' This person adds:

> As DPP, I would say he had a mixed record. Some people think he did a great job, but he was very governed by consensus and commit-tee and doing the right thing. He's very correct, and he was like that during the whole of his tenure. He had these round-table events, he had journalists in to talk about social media and so on. But he wasn't an old-style person; he was guided by what he thought was right. He was very much doing the right thing by getting everyone on board. He was a bit of a bureaucrat.

Given the volume of cases which are prosecuted by the CPS each year, it would obviously not be possible to examine every one of them, but it is worth mentioning a few of the better-known ones to illustrate their sheer range. For example, no sooner was Starmer in the job than he had to grapple with the highly emotive subject of assisted suicide. He chose not to prosecute the parents of a 23-year-old man called Daniel James who was paralysed while playing rugby and who subsequently visited a suicide clinic in Switzerland. Although the Jameses had taken their son to the clinic where he died in September 2008, Starmer said that there was no public interest reason to take the matter to court. This prompted him within months to introduce new guidelines ulti-mately indicating how families, doctors and nurses could escape crim-inal charges in similar situations. Inevitably, there was condemnation from opponents of euthanasia, and this was echoed by politicians who expressed worries that the DPP, a paid public official, had exceeded his authority by usurping the role of Parliament in fashioning the law as he saw fit. It is hard to imagine a public official having to engage with a more complex and ultimately personal question, and no politician, surely, would have envied him this task.

Another delicate matter Starmer dealt with early on involved the Conservative MP and shadow Immigration Minister Damian Green, who was arrested at his house in November 2008 as part of a police inquiry into Home Office leaks. Starmer was apparently given ten minutes' notice of this action. It emerged that Green was passed information which was considered embarrassing to the government about immigration and crime by a junior Home Office employee, Christopher Galley, some of which was given to a newspaper. In April 2009, a £5 million police investigation into the matter collapsed after the CPS decided there was insufficient evidence to prosecute either man because the information given to Green on the government's immigration policy was not secret and did not affect national security or put lives at risk. Bearing in mind this happened under a Labour government, Starmer did at least eventually demonstrate the kind of independent view that the office of DPP demanded, even if serious questions were asked on civil liberties grounds about why a serving politician in a country with a supposedly free press had been arrested in the first place.

Parliament appeared on Starmer's radar for a second time in 2009, when the *Daily Telegraph* obtained evidence that dozens of MPs had misused their expenses allowances to the tune of hundreds of thousands of pounds. In 2010, four Labour MPs and two Conservative peers were jailed for fraud. The CPS's decision to prosecute these men regardless of their political affiliation proved that Starmer was able to keep his own political views in check, as would be expected. Indeed, he has even boasted of this aspect of his time as DPP while he has been the Leader of the Opposition. In April 2021, the Conservative Party was confronted with what potentially amounted to a lobbying scandal as a result of David Cameron's association with the Australian businessman Lex Greensill. When Starmer tackled Boris Johnson about the Greensill affair at a session of Prime Minister's Questions, Johnson mounted a defence of his government's general position on lobbying by pointing out that Starmer was being advised by the architect of New Labour, Lord Mandelson, the owner of a business called Global Counsel Ltd, which has long been rumoured to work with clients who operate in authoritarian states such as China and Russia. Starmer hit back, telling the House of Commons: 'I remind the Prime Minister, I not only prosecuted shoplifters; I prosecuted MPs over the MPs' expenses scandal, so I stand on my record.'

As DPP, Starmer also earned himself a footnote in the Stephen Lawrence affair after personally applying to the Court of Appeal in 2010 for the original acquittal of one of those who had long been suspected of murdering Mr Lawrence in 1993, Gary Dobson, to be quashed. This meant that Dobson and another man, David Norris, could be tried again for the same crime after new forensic evidence had come to light. The case duly went to court, and in January 2012, Dobson and Norris were convicted of murder.

The following month, February 2012, Starmer tackled another high-profile case involving a politician, when he decided there was sufficient evidence to charge the Liberal Democrat Cabinet minister Chris Huhne and his ex-wife, Vicky Pryce, with perverting the course of justice. They had been under investigation for several months in relation to which one of them had been driving a car when it was caught speeding in 2003. Both were jailed in the spring of 2013.

Inevitably, however, there are cases dating from Starmer's stint as DPP which he would no doubt rather forget. In September 2010, he had to apologise to a woman for 'failings' in the trial of a man who was accused of sexually assaulting her. The woman, who was awarded £16,000 in damages, was wrongly blamed by a member of the CPS for the collapse of the case against her alleged attacker. And in December 2011, a police corruption trial collapsed, leaving taxpayers with a bill for an estimated £10 million. The officers had been accused of framing three innocent men for the 1988 murder of Lynette White, but during their trial it was established that potentially vital prosecution files had gone missing, forcing the judge to abandon the case. Such blunders no doubt rankle to this day the man who prides himself on being the master of his brief.

Another memorable case which ended badly for the CPS has been dubbed the 'Twitter Joke Trial'. In January 2010, Paul Chambers, twenty-eight, was intending to travel from England to Northern Ireland when he learned that Robin Hood Airport in South Yorkshire had been forced to cancel flights due to bad weather. Fearing delay, Chambers wrote on Twitter to his 600 followers: 'Crap! Robin Hood Airport is closed. You've got a week and a bit to get your shit together otherwise I am blowing the airport sky high!!' A week later, an off-duty manager at the airport found the message and reported it to airport security, who recorded it as 'not credible' as a threat. Nonetheless, protocol meant the police had to be informed, and Chambers was arrested at his office by anti-terror officers. He was charged with sending a 'menacing' message under the Communications Act 2003 and found guilty at Doncaster Magistrates' Court. He spent two years trying to appeal his conviction, during which he was locked in what has been described as a Kafkaesque nightmare.

As the case generated wider attention, comedians including Stephen Fry, Graham Linehan and Al Murray backed Chambers. Eventually, his conviction was overturned at the High Court in July 2012, raising serious questions from politicians and members of the public about why the case was ever taken so seriously. One figure with knowledge of this case claims that Starmer 'gave consent' and 'authorised the resistance of the appeal' through the CPS at the time. This case did force Starmer, in June 2013, to issue guidelines for the CPS on when to take legal action against those who breach UK communications laws on social media. He warned that a 'high threshold' should be applied by prosecutors when assessing social media communications, because of their volume and to prevent the legal system being deluged. In this, senior legal figures generally believe that he drew a sensible line in tackling what is theoretically an endless problem.

*   *   *

Two even more prominent cases with which Starmer is associated are worth examining more deeply on the basis that they help to inform us about his character and his success in the DPP post. The cases in question are the police operations known as Operation Elveden and Operation Midland.

Starmer was in post when the first prosecutions arising from the News International phone-hacking scandal involving the *News of the World* eventually began. Given that phone hacking involved hundreds of victims, because it went to the heart of Rupert Murdoch's media empire and as a result of it having been indefensible, this impropriety will obviously be remembered for many years to come. Yet the phone-hacking scandal itself led directly to another matter involving journalists, which can now be seen as a somewhat hysterical overreaction to the mood of the time and which did immense damage to all parties concerned. It related to allegations of inappropriate payments to police officers and other public officials. The police investigation which looked into this was given the codename Operation Elveden. It was launched on 19 June 2011 after officers ordered News International to hand over confidential emails containing details of the payments. This case remains a running sore to many in journalistic circles and beyond, and in light of Starmer's role in its outcome, it certainly warrants scrutiny.

Between July 2011 and September 2013, thirty journalists from News International (which became known as News UK from June 2013) and the Mirror Group (which changed its name in 2018 to Reach plc) were arrested or charged under Operation Elveden. After Starmer stepped down as DPP in late 2013, four more journalists were arrested, making a total of thirty-four journalists who were arrested or charged under its banner. Most of the thirty-four individuals who were caught up in this tangled story worked for *The Sun*. It is worth stating from the outset that Starmer had previously been happy to court this newspaper, presumably because he knew it was the most widely read in Britain. In fact, according to one well-placed source, he even had a private lunch with its then editor, Rebekah Brooks, shortly after he was appointed DPP in 2008 and long before Operation Elveden was conceived. At that time, *The Sun* still supported the Labour Party, though this alliance ground to a dramatic halt in September 2009, when the newspaper announced that it had switched to backing the Tories. The end of this relationship was revealed under the brutal front-page headline: 'Labour's Lost It'. Pouring petrol on the fire, this declaration was made during the Labour Party conference. Gordon Brown was said to be furious at what amounted to a very public humiliation for him. It has been alleged that he even telephoned Rupert Murdoch, with whom he had previously had a cordial relationship, and threatened him by saying, 'You are trying to destroy me and my party. I will destroy you and your company.'[6]

It does not compromise this account to reveal at this point that, ultimately, not one of the thirty-four journalists arrested or charged under the guise of Operation Elveden has a conviction on their record. Yet the alarming truth is that many of them spent years on bail; they were put through gruelling court trials; they were unable to work; and in some cases, their careers were ruined. At least two are known to have attempted suicide because of the stress they endured. The experience of a *Sun* reporter called Vince Soodin was not untypical and is worth recounting to give a sense of the type of treatment that was meted out. Soodin was arrested in a dawn raid in August 2012 for having written a story two years previously about a fox attacking a three-year-old at a school in Brighton. A police officer using a fake name had tipped off *The Sun* about this. Soodin was assigned the story and the tipster – whom Soodin never met – was paid £500. At 6 a.m. on 7 August 2012, eight police officers knocked on Soodin's door, went into his property, seized his belongings and those of his girlfriend, went through their clothes, underwear, diaries and any other item they deemed relevant, and then drove Soodin to a police station, where he was put in a cell. Later, he was questioned, released and re-questioned twice more. In August 2013, he was charged under an obscure thirteenth-century common law of conspiracy to commit misconduct in public office. He was suspended from his job and in September 2014 tried – like other Operation Elveden journalists – at the Old Bailey, a court usually reserved for the most serious crimes. The jury was hung.

The following year, he returned for a retrial but was told that the case against him had been abandoned and he could leave without a stain on his character. This was a result of the then Lord Chief Justice, Lord Thomas, quashing the conviction of another News UK journalist, Lucy Panton, shortly before. Defending press freedom and citing case law, Lord Thomas said that the trial judge in Panton's case, Charles Wide, had misdirected the jury by failing to tell them of the high threshold required for a conviction. Thomas also pointed out that jurors had to be satisfied that the defendants' conduct had harmed the public interest. Lord Thomas said, 'This is without doubt a difficult area of the criminal law. An ancient common law offence is being used in circumstances where it has rarely before been applied.' It appeared that the CPS had failed to make prosecution counsel and the trial judge aware of the latest developments in case law on misconduct. Lord Thomas added, 'The judge was entitled to far more help by the prosecution than he was given.'[7] Soodin's agony was over, but it is astonishing to think that he was held on bail for 989 days. Many others suffered a similar ordeal.

It remains very difficult to understand why Starmer, who was ultimately at the helm of attempting to convict Soodin and twenty-nine others, should seemingly have been unaware for so long of the case law that Lord Thomas cited. The stories written by the journalists who were arrested concerned matters which fell squarely into the public interest. They included details of how British forces suffered kit shortages while at war, and of the authorities' soft treatment of the child killer Jon Venables after he was returned to prison for downloading child abuse images. It is somewhat ironic that the man who apparently expended considerable amounts of energy fighting for the rights of striking print-workers in the 1980s should, a quarter of a century later, have considered it appropriate to prosecute journalists working for the same company on what turned out to be a highly questionable basis. It is also strange that his much-vaunted liberal instincts seemed to evaporate when it came to dealing with these journalists, and that he was prepared to put in peril the important relationship between the state and the press.

On top of all this, the heavy-handed investigations and trials which sprang from Operation Elveden cost taxpayers something in the region of £20 million. The only justification for the exercise that the CPS can rely upon is that some of the journalists' public sector sources were eventually jailed. Perhaps the most notable is Bettina Jordan-Barber, a Ministry of Defence strategist who in 2015 pleaded guilty to conspiring to commit misconduct in public office after accepting £100,000 for assisting *The Sun* with a total of sixty-nine stories between 2004 and 2012. She was sentenced to twelve months in prison.

On 30 October 2016, three years after he had stepped down as DPP, Starmer was quizzed by the journalist Robert Peston about his responsibility for Operation Elveden during an edition of the television programme *Peston on Sunday*. He did not take the opportunity to apologise, instead claiming, somewhat disingenuously given that they were for the most part arrested and charged when he was DPP: 'Well, most of the prosecutions took place when I ceased to be DPP; I'm not the DPP, I didn't handle those cases and it's really not for me to comment on them.' He also said: 'I obviously have not had anything to do with those cases for three years now, so I'm not in a position to comment one way or the other.'

In January 2020, as mentioned in the previous chapter, Starmer released a campaign video as part of his bid for the Labour leadership which made much of his role in prosecuting journalists. In this short film, Rebekah Brooks, who has been the chief executive of News UK since 2011 and who was arrested under Operation Elveden, featured twice in library footage; Rupert Murdoch, the owner of *The Sun*, featured once as a voiceover intoned that Starmer had 'stood up to the powerful'. Was it mere political convenience that meant Starmer was prepared to leave it at that? Vince Soodin and countless others may be decent journalists, but in most people's eyes they would not be described as 'powerful'. Including images of Brooks and Murdoch in this film without their blessing was a curious decision on Starmer's part anyway. Not only is the position of DPP supposed to be non-political, raising questions about why Starmer was using his work as DPP for political purposes, but Brooks was never found guilty of any offence in relation to any matter connected with her work as a journalist.

It says much about Starmer that, subsequent to all this, he has tried to mend his fences with *The Sun*. According to several well-placed sources, after he became Labour Party leader, he even telephoned Victoria Newton, *The Sun*'s editor since February 2020, in an attempt to find some sort of modus vivendi so that both parties could move on. Given the events described, it is hardly surprising that Ms Newton was decidedly lukewarm when it came to responding to his overtures.

Intriguingly, one source who has examined the Operation Elveden affair in detail believes there may have been a political dimension to the decision to prosecute so many *Sun* journalists. This source says:

Gordon Brown was livid about *The Sun* turning its back on him and his well-known fury may have influenced the process of investigating the hacking. It wasn't against the law for these journalists to publish this information – even if they had to pay for it. The only law that was broken, if it was broken at all, was by the public officials for leaking confidential information. Even that may have only been a breach of employment conditions. It's a very grey area. I think that what Starmer did would have been the subject in any other circumstances of a furore. Say it happened to someone on the *Telegraph* or *Times*, for instance, I don't think this would have been buried in recent history in the way it has. Because it was *The Sun* and because of the association between it and its sister title, the *News of the World*, where the phone hacking took place, *Sun* journalists were tarred with the same brush. They are the unmentionables. These reporters were hung out to dry. I think Starmer is unfit for public office.

This account is given some credence by Tom Newton Dunn, who was political editor of *The Sun* throughout the phone-hacking saga. In May 2021, following the death aged seventy-seven of his former *Sun* colleague John Kay, Newton Dunn wrote that he believed political pressure was to blame for the pursuit of those journalists who were later found innocent. In his column in the *Evening Standard*, he wrote that Kay, who was charged under Operation Elveden and eventually cleared, had died a 'broken man' because of the toll it took on him. He further noted that Ed Miliband, who was the Labour Party leader when the scandal reached its height, devoted a considerable amount of his time to the wider matter of News International's practices. Newton Dunn opined: 'When the phone hacking scandal broke in 2011 ... Miliband threw the kitchen sink at trying to bring down Rupert Murdoch's News International. Starmer – who was Miliband's protégé – came under pressure to investigate and prosecute News International journalists for pretty much anything.'[8]

*   *   *

It was another of Rupert Murdoch's newspapers, *The Times*, that first brought to national attention while Starmer was DPP the appalling matter of the sexual exploitation of young girls in the north of England. This outrage came to light as a result of the sterling work of a reporter called Andrew Norfolk. From 2010, he began looking into evidence suggesting that gangs of mainly Asian Muslim men groomed and abused white teenage girls. It was a story he worked on for years, but some of his earliest reports concerning the town of Rochdale caught the eye of the aforementioned Nazir Afzal, himself a Muslim, who had been appointed the CPS's chief prosecutor for the north-west in the summer of 2011. In fact, Greater Manchester Police had heard about grooming in Rochdale when a teenage girl made a complaint in 2008. Her case was taken seriously, but in 2009 the CPS decided not to charge the accused men. Afzal overturned this decision shortly after he took up his post, later revealing that the original decision not to prosecute was based on the victim's perceived lack of credibility. Bluntly, it had been assumed that a jury would not believe her. There is no doubt that Afzal deserves credit for going against the grain in the way he did, yet, as we shall see, it could be argued that this single decision by him had profound, if unintended, consequences.

'It might have been strange for [Starmer] given he'd spent all his life in defence work and not prosecution work,' says Afzal.

> But he rapidly understood that our work would be improved substantially by better engagement with the police and that clearly happened, and I think the best example of that was a little bit later when I was dealing with so-called grooming gangs and child sexual abuse in 2011 or thereabouts. We knew how impactful that work was, how the public were seeing what was happening or what was not happening, and once I'd prosecuted the Rochdale case in early 2012, then the world was looking down at authorities and saying, 'What are you going to do about this?'

Afzal says that from this point Starmer encouraged him to review similar cases that might have been dropped by CPS and to pursue the wider scandal of child sexual exploitation. To that end, he appointed Afzal to be his national lead on the subject. A panel consisting of Starmer, Afzal, various chief constables and other chief prosecutors invited police officers and police prosecutors from around the country to refer other past cases that were of concern to them. 'When we talked about the child abuse cases, [Starmer] was absolutely apoplectic about

why children had been let down the way they'd been let down,' Afzal
adds. 'Not just by us, but by every agency. And literally that became his
priority for the whole of 2013. He let me do the media and so on, but
internally he was absolutely determined to bring the change.'

It is relevant to say, however, that these sexual exploitation allegations were not the only ones to have cropped up during this time. In
2007 and 2008, Surrey Police and Sussex Police conducted separate
interviews with four women who told them of various unpalatable experiences they had suffered at the hands of the television personality
Jimmy Savile in the 1970s. This led to Savile being questioned under
caution – but not arrested – by police on 1 October 2009, exactly
eleven months after Starmer became DPP. During his interview, Savile
was asked about the three Surrey allegations, but the claim dealt with
by Sussex Police was not mentioned. In summary, Savile told police
that the allegations were invented and that he believed that the complainants were after his money.

Later that month, the CPS lawyer reviewing the case determined
that there was insufficient evidence to charge Savile with any criminal
offence. One reason given was that it was perceived that none of the
complainants was 'prepared to support any police action', making any
prosecution very difficult. When the full horror of Savile's crimes came
to light in 2012, almost a year after his death, Starmer asked his legal
adviser, Alison Levitt QC, to launch an inquiry to establish if the CPS
had been right not to charge him during his lifetime. In her report,
Levitt criticised the approach of the CPS. She wrote: 'On the face of
it, the allegations made were both serious and credible; the prosecutor should have recognised this and sought to "build" a prosecution.'
She said that the police treated the victims and the accounts they gave
'with a degree of caution which was neither justified nor required'. She
added: 'Having spoken to the victims I have been driven to conclude

that had the police and prosecutors taken a different approach a prosecution might have been possible.' In January 2013, Starmer issued a
public apology and said this was a 'watershed moment' in which the
'approach of the police and prosecutors to credibility in sexual assault
cases has to change'.

By the time Starmer had completed his term as DPP in the autumn
of 2013, the waves created by the Savile scandal led to sexual abuse
as a phenomenon being pushed somewhere near to the top of the
news agenda and staying there. While it may be true that he was not
personally responsible for the CPS's decision in 2009 not to prosecute
Savile, there is no doubt that this failure occurred on his watch and
was therefore, ultimately, his responsibility. This was the background
to his acceptance of an invitation in December 2013 to chair a taskforce
advising the Labour Party on transforming the rights of victims in the
criminal justice system. (The proposals it eventually produced were to
have been introduced by then Labour leader Ed Miliband had he won
the 2015 election; but as Miliband never became Prime Minister, this
work resulted in Starmer sponsoring the Victims of Crime Bill instead,
a Private Member's Bill which he introduced to Parliament in October
2015.)

When it was announced in 2013 that Starmer had taken on this job,
he gave an interview to *The Guardian* in which he said:

Our criminal justice system is riddled with assumptions about how
victims behave and most of them are misplaced. My main concern
is that the more vulnerable you are as a victim or a witness the less
able the criminal law is to protect you. We saw this as we unpicked
the child sexual abuse cases – both the Rochdale grooming cases but
also the [Jimmy] Savile cases. Victims did not have the confidence
to come forward; when they did come forward they had all sorts of

assumptions made about how they were going to behave. Then there was the journey through the courtroom itself.[9]

It was clear that under Starmer's plans, the rights and feelings of victims were to be put first, and he gave media interviews and made speeches throughout 2014 to promote this ideology. The Met Police chief at that time, Bernard Hogan-Howe, would later reveal that Scotland Yard's policy of immediately believing every allegation of sex abuse made by victims was founded on a report written in 2014 by the Chief Inspector of Constabulary, Tom Winsor, which stated: 'The presumption that a victim should always be believed should be institutionalised.' Winsor is said to have been influenced by Starmer's policy. So, too, was Starmer's successor as DPP, Alison Saunders. However well-intentioned all this was, it did not take into account the twisted mind of a man called Carl Beech.

In October 2014, the Metropolitan Police opened a triple-murder and historical sexual abuse investigation which they called Operation Midland. It was launched after a series of alarming accusations made by a man who was given the nom de plume 'Nick'. He claimed that he and others were the victims of what became known as the 'VIP paedophile scandal', in which members of the establishment had raped, tortured and murdered children in the 1970s and 1980s. 'Nick' – whose real name was in fact Carl Beech – told police that he had been physically and sexually abused at parties attended by various prominent individuals in London and elsewhere. He named the former Prime Minister Sir Edward Heath; the former army chief Lord Bramall; former MPs Harvey Proctor and Lord Janner; former Home Secretary Lord Brittan; former head of MI6 Maurice Oldfield; and former head of MI5 Michael Hanley as being among the perpetrators of these supposed crimes. Beech also said he had witnessed Mr Proctor murdering two children, one of whom he identified as Martin Allen, who disappeared in London aged fifteen in

The Starmers' family home, 23 Tanhouse Road in Oxted. It was bought with a mortgage in 1963, shortly after Starmer's birth, and his parents lived there for more than fifty years. He still owns a seven-acre field behind the property which could, with planning permission, be worth millions of pounds.

© Bagshaw & Hardy

Starmer attended Reigate Grammar School from 1974 until 1981. Via Margaret Thatcher's reforms as Education Secretary, it charged fees from 1976. Starmer having passed the 11-plus meant his parents did not have to pay. Despite his ambivalent attitude to private education, he still supports the school in various ways.

© Ian Capper, CC BY-SA 2.0

Music was prominent in Starmer's life as a schoolboy. He played the flute, piano and recorder and studied at the Junior Guildhall School of Music in London. He was also a member of various orchestras including this one, pictured, which performed at the Lord Mayor's Show in London in 1980.

Starmer captained the 1st XI football team in his final year at school. Their performances were mixed, but sports teacher Graham Best says Starmer was skilful and 'a good leader both on and off the field'. Starmer still plays football now, aged almost sixty. He is also an Arsenal season ticket holder.

Churchtown Farm Field Studies Centre

Education and Leisure Opportunities for all disabled people

During his year off between school and university, Starmer demonstrated admirable altruism by working with disabled children and adults at Churchtown Farm in Cornwall for several months. Staff member David Griffith remembers he was good at entertaining clients with quizzes and music.

Starmer, pictured with friends from the University of Leeds, which he attended between 1982 and 1985. Some there knew him as the 'King of Middle-Class Radicals'. © ITV

Class of 1985. Starmer, on the far right in the fourth row, did not know the difference between a solicitor and a barrister when he arrived to study law at Leeds. His relationship with one tutor, Clive Walker, is thought to have been pivotal to his professional legal career.

Starmer, pictured in the third row from the front, eight places from the left, as a freshman of St Edmund Hall, Oxford. He did the BCL course in 1985–86. One friend at Oxford was the future Labour Cabinet minister David Miliband.

The first issue of *Socialist Alternatives*. The periodical was at the centre of Starmer's life from 1986 to 1987. Contributor Richard Barbrook says Starmer was 'the guy who got the magazine done'. Drugs were apparently smoked at editorial meetings, though Starmer is not thought to have indulged.

Peter Tatchell at the socialist summer camp he and Starmer attended together in France in July 1989. Tatchell says Starmer was 'well to the left of Neil Kinnock' and 'very much in the orbit of the emerging confluence between greens and socialists'. Courtesy of Peter Tatchell

ABOVE Phillippa Kaufmann, with whom Starmer lived from 1997 to 2001. His love life has certainly been complicated, with two ex-girlfriends marrying colleagues of his from Doughty Street Chambers. © PA Images / Alamy Stock Photo

LEFT Starmer was made a Queen's Counsel in 2002 aged thirty-nine. In 2004 he said taking silk was 'odd, since I often used to propose the abolition of the monarchy'. © Avalon.Red

LEFT Starmer with his wife, Victoria, and his parents, Josephine and Rodney, on his wedding day in 2007. His relationship with his father was distant, but he adored his mother.

ABOVE Starmer was the Director of Public Prosecutions from 2008 to 2013. Decisions he took in this post made him enemies who maintain he ruined their lives, including the former Tory MP Harvey Proctor.

© Lewis Whyld / WPA Pool / Getty Images

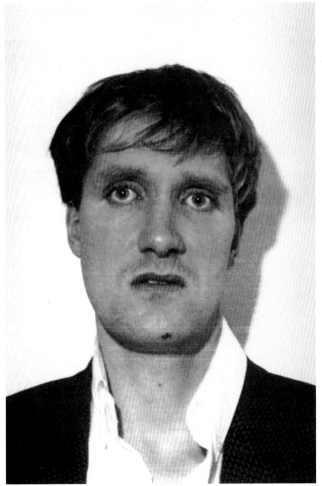

LEFT Paul Bint, the conman who pretended to be Starmer by describing himself as a 'successful barrister, fit, very spontaneous, looking for relationship'. He seduced several women and was jailed in 2009.

© PA Images / Alamy Stock Photo

Starmer, pictured with his wife, Victoria, after being elected to the House of Commons for the first time in 2015. It has been observed that he does not routinely wear a wedding ring, though he did on this occasion. © Nigel Howard / *Evening Standard* / eyevine

Starmer served as Brexit Secretary in Jeremy Corbyn's Cabinet for more than three years. Behind the scenes, they had an uneasy relationship. Some in Labour circles blame Starmer's anti-Brexit stance for Labour's catastrophic 2019 electoral defeat.

Starmer was the only man in Labour's main leadership contest in 2020. Many members wanted a woman to lead the party, but he was the clear favourite throughout. He used every opportunity to canvass. One observer claims he even lobbied MPs at Frank Dobson's funeral.

Starmer and his deputy leader, Angela Rayner, 'taking a knee' in June 2020 in solidarity with the organisation Black Lives Matter. He also signed up for 'unconscious bias' training. The question is, what do so-called Red Wall voters think of these statements?

November 1979. Beech even gave police a penknife, which Mr Proctor had purportedly threatened him with, and told officers: 'I hope there will be enough evidence to see [Proctor] in court.'

Infamously, on 18 December 2014, Detective Superintendent Kenny McDonald told the BBC that 'Nick' had been interviewed at length by 'experienced detectives' from the child abuse command and an investigator from the murder command. 'They and I believe what Nick is saying to be credible and to be true … so yes, we do believe what Nick is saying,' McDonald stated.

Operation Midland now ranks as one of the biggest police scandals of recent years. The Met spent £2.5 million investigating Beech's claims before turning its inquiries onto this alleged whistleblower himself. After indecent images were found on electronic devices he owned, it transpired that he was in fact a paedophile. He was also a fantasist. Operation Midland was closed in 2016 without any arrests having been made. In 2019, Beech was convicted of twelve counts of perverting the course of justice and jailed for eighteen years. In light of the trouble to which Starmer went to advance the idea that all victims must be believed, the fallout from this extraordinary case continues to haunt him as much as it does the Met. In March 2021, six former Home Secretaries wrote to *The Times* urging the incumbent Home Secretary Priti Patel to open an investigation into Operation Midland, specifically in relation to the procedure by which search warrants are issued. Lord Baker of Dorking, Lord Clarke of Nottingham, Lord Howard of Lympne, Jack Straw, Lord Blunkett and Lord Reid of Cardowan said that they are 'acutely conscious of the need to maintain public confidence in the police'. They added that they agree with Sir Richard Henriques, the retired High Court judge who reviewed Operation Midland, that 'confidence in the police and the Independent Office for Police Conduct has been seriously damaged'. When Starmer was asked about this on

LBC on 22 March 2021, he acknowledged that the operation went 'very, very wrong' and said there needs to be some 'basic accountability', but he seemed sceptical of the idea that there should be an inquiry. Others, plainly, would disagree.

Among them is the criminal barrister Daniel Janner QC, son of the late Lord Janner, who was falsely accused by Beech. Mr Janner has known Starmer since the 1990s via their legal careers. Though he would not claim to know him well, he certainly has strong feelings about what he regards as the complicated situation that Starmer had a hand in creating. 'We're both benchers of Middle Temple as it happens,' says Janner.[10]

I've known him for many years. We took silk on the same day. I wouldn't say he's a friend but a work colleague. There's absolutely no doubt that the genesis of the false allegation industry which reached its height with the Carl Beech trial emanated from the approach of Keir Starmer in relation to his determination that all victims are to be believed. He denies he had that policy. But Harvey Proctor has gone into some detail showing how this *was* his view. He made speeches which show he shifted the way police approach victims. And the shift was this approach that all victims are to be believed. If you go from that stance, you will find it leads to fantasists and those who are chasing money. My issue is it put the police in a very difficult position because it was coming from the prosecuting authority down through the police, and what on earth are they meant to do? And it leads to the madness we had with Carl Beech. He made false allegations against many, including my father, who was meant to have allegedly raped him in the Carlton Club. Then you get an appalling DPP who wasn't up to the job, Alison Saunders, who comes in and carries that policy forward. It was a Starmer policy.

In the case of Lord Janner, nine High Court cases were brought against him. When the Janner family made it clear that they would not pay any compensation to any alleged victims, 'the entire lot collapsed like a pack of cards', says Daniel Janner. He adds:

> If there was anything in it, the lawyers would have disputed it. It emanated from Keir Starmer, and it shows a complete lack of judgement. That's what's disturbing about it. There were nine separate claims against my father and then his estate when he died, and the entire lot were either dismissed or withdrawn. So of course I feel angry and resentful about it, but this is serious stuff. My impression of [Starmer] as DPP in respect of this policy is that he not only lacks judgement but it has an appalling knock-on effect, and he's very rigid. The rigidity of his approach led unquestionably to the unravelling of Operation Midland.

So strongly did Janner feel about Starmer's lack of suitability to remain in public life that he wrote to *The Times* in January 2020 urging Starmer to pull out of the leadership race on the grounds that the prospect of him becoming opposition leader was 'unacceptable in a just society'.

The former Tory MP Harvey Proctor, who was also falsely accused by Beech, remains deeply aggrieved by Operation Midland as well. He, too, blames Starmer personally for his plight. 'Starmer began his political career which was based on a "believe the victim" policy', Proctor claims.[11]

> As DPP he was concerned with the insufficient number of convictions for rape and sexual abuse which were detrimental to his reputation and his role as DPP and on his potential future political career. He made it clear as DPP, and subsequently as a politician, that 'victims' should be believed and supported. He placed them at the heart of

the criminal justice system. He was the head of the CPS when it took a decision not to prosecute Jimmy Savile for historical child sexual abuse in 2009. By way of attempted redemption, he gave speech upon speech to promote the 'believe the victim' strategy. It was such pressure and 'political' challenges that in November 2014 led Tom Winsor of Her Majesty's Inspectorate of Constabulary to instruct the Metropolitan Police Service and all police constabularies that [the view that] 'a victim should always be believed' should be institutionalised. Starmer initiated the undermining of centuries of British justice that people should be judged innocent until proven guilty. We will never know the full extent of the suffering Starmer has caused to others.

His policy reached its zenith in Operation Midland with many but not all being led to question Starmer's stance. The direct impact on my life of this wrong-headed policy was to lose me my job, my reputation and my home. There continues to be unresolved family difficulties and the irreparable loss of friendships. Emotionally and financially, I am not in the same position I used to be. I was falsely accused of serial child murders and sexual child abuse and the torture of children. My home and my office were illegally searched by eighteen Met Police officers. I now know the search was illegal as the Met Police misled district judge Howard Riddle into granting the search warrants. Riddle himself has confirmed that he was misled, and distinguished former High Court judge Sir Richard Henriques has backed up this claim. Such alleged criminality requires proper investigation. The consequence for me was that effectively I felt my life had been extinguished. Sir Keir has not apologised to me or taken any personal responsibility. He has not communicated with me in any way. I believe Sir Keir Starmer is not fit to be Prime Minister. He is not fit to be a Leader of H. M. Opposition and he should not grace the benches of the House of Commons.

Ironically, it is now clear, of course, that the House of Commons was the very institution on which Starmer had his eye at the point he stood down as DPP in October 2013. By then, he had earned the unbending respect of the sitting Attorney General, Dominic Grieve, with whom he'd had to work closely. In summary, Grieve remembers Starmer as 'a good manager' who was 'helped also by some senior [CPS] staff who were very good as well'. Of the tougher cases which Starmer prosecuted, Grieve is equally supportive. 'Inevitably, there were some prosecutorial decisions which he had to make at times, and sometimes they required input from me, where they were what I would call rather finely balanced issues,' he says.

> We could have quite vigorous discussions about the matters around it. But they were always professionally conducted, and I was always impressed with his reasoning and I was always prepared to back him because part of the attorney's job is to make sure that the DPP gets proper backing when he has to make controversial decisions. The fact that I might have made a different decision, although I think there were very, very few such circumstances, is not the issue because he is there ultimately as an independent decision-maker. And I can say there was never any occasion where I felt that I ought to be intervening to override something which had been done. I'm sure that some of the decisions were quite complicated and difficult. Yes, some of them attracted some controversy, but they were always very well-reasoned. And when there might be an issue about them and we talked it through, it was always very helpful because of the clarity of his own thinking about why he was deciding to do something.

CHAPTER 9

'ONE OF THE STARMERS
SHOULD BE AN MP'

Keir Starmer is often described as being an intensely ambitious man, yet it is arguable that this trait is at least in part a consequence of the hopes and dreams of other members of his family, which were foisted upon him. As we have seen, his parents longed for him to do well at school and then to study a subject at university that would lead him directly to a profession. Yet by – supposedly – naming their eldest son after Keir Hardie, the first Labour Party leader, they were not just making a political statement; they were also acknowledging a desire that had existed within the wider Starmer clan for many years. The evidence for this comes from a letter written in December 2014 by Starmer's father, Rodney. One of the recipients of this round robin letter was kind enough to share it for the purposes of this book. After the main body of the typed text, under the heading 'PS… Stop Press…' Rodney Starmer expressed to friends his delight that his son had just been elected as Labour's prospective parliamentary candidate in the safe Labour seat of Holborn & St Pancras. He then wrote:

Keir lives, works and the children go to school in the constituency. We are very pleased and wish him well. My dad, Bert, said many years ago that one of the Starmers should be an MP. He thought it would be my brother Dennis but that was not to be. Bert was the only Radical in his generation of Starmers.

Who can say why Starmer's grandfather, a mechanic, seemed so fixed upon a Starmer making it to the House of Commons? What is easier to imagine is that Keir Starmer himself was aware of Bert's dream. After all, if Rodney Starmer was prepared to share this anecdote with friends, he must have told his son about it sometime beforehand.

Starmer returned to private practice as a barrister in late 2013, after his five-year contract as DPP had concluded, but it was obvious that he did not intend to confine himself solely to the law for much longer. Indeed, he was open to discussing a future in politics with friends and acquaintances. One journalist recalls having such a conversation with him around this time. 'I think he must have a sense of destiny,' they say.

I remember having lunch with him when he was shortly to leave the job of DPP, or had just left it. He was talking about what he was going to do next, and he said he was considering politics. It looked as though Labour were destined for the wilderness for some time. He said, 'Maybe I'll look for a seat to contest,' and I said, 'Labour will be in the wilderness for years. I wouldn't do that. Why not just go to the House of Lords and be active there? At least that's safer and you'll get in,' and he said, 'I think I'm going to do it. I want to be properly in it, on the frontline.'

This certainly feeds into the idea that Starmer had planned for some time to forge a path to Westminster. What was very much to his advantage was the fact that, under the Fixed-Term Parliaments Act 2011, everybody knew that the next general election would be held in May 2015, giving him a date he could work towards.

Starmer's acceptance of his friend Ed Miliband's invitation in late 2013 to chair a Labour Party taskforce on victims' rights, as referred to in Chapter 8, all but made public his intention to move into politics. Yet before he could do so, there was another, more pressing, matter to tackle. As Starmer well knew, it is customary for retiring male DPPs to be honoured with a knighthood, but he had to decide whether he would go against his progressive instincts by accepting a title which he would keep for the rest of his life, and which would allow his wife to be addressed as 'Lady Starmer' to boot. He had already joined the ranks of the establishment by becoming DPP, but would there be any consequences for him politically if he cemented this status with a knighthood? What would his Labour-supporting parents and friends say? One who knows him well says he certainly wrestled with the problem. 'Keir has always been cautious,' says the friend.

> Some advised him not to take a knighthood, for the sake of his Labour career, but of course he did. They all do – even Republicans and left-wingers, who are told it's expected of them when for example they become judges. He prefers not to use it, but it probably provides a certain reassurance to Middle England.

The Cabinet Office has refused to confirm who nominated Starmer for his knighthood. All it did reveal under Freedom of Information laws was that the State Committee considered his nomination and that its members in 2013 comprised Dame Mary Marsh, Baroness Bottomley, Dame Suzi Leather, Elizabeth McMeikan, Dr Diana Walford, Dr Suzy Walton, Sir Paul Jenkins and Sir Bob Kerslake. Having been vetted and cleared, he would have been advised about a month before it became public that he was to be honoured 'for services to law and criminal justice'. The statement announcing this was published in the 2014 New Year

Honours list, which was released to the press on 30 December 2013, and the investiture took place at Buckingham Palace on 12 February 2014. He asked his parents to join him at the palace, where he was knighted by the Prince of Wales, and his father later wrote to tell friends about the occasion. Explaining that they set off for London at 6 a.m. for the 10 a.m. ceremony, they were accompanied in their car by a Great Dane called Chip, which they had taken in as a rescue dog the previous year.

> At BP [Buckingham Palace] the car was inspected underneath, that was fine, a police officer looked in and saw Chip. Is that a lioness, he asked, you cannot take her with you. We produced our invitation, saying we were not going back. The police constable went to see his sergeant, he said no but I will see the inspector. The inspector arrived and asked if he could stroke Chip. I opened the rear window, the inspector stroked Chip who then set about licking the inspector's face. He was a dog lover and then produced a sheet of paper, indicating a Special Dispensation for Chip. The young lady minder asked for car keys and said she would look after Chip for us! The service we received at the palace was superb, especially for Jo in her wheelchair.

Rodney Starmer described himself and his wife as 'the proudest parents there', having seen their son kneeling before Prince Charles. He even wrote a short account of Keir's career, culminating with the knighthood, which was published in the newsletter of the Barn Theatre in Oxted, one of his favourite haunts, in 2014. Keir has always maintained that his relationship with his father was distant, and this belief is backed up by Bruce Reed, the theatre's chairman. Reed says, 'It's interesting, because it was many years before any of us knew of the existence of Keir Starmer. It wasn't until he became Director of Public Prosecutions [in 2008] that Rod said, "Hasn't my boy done well?" I thought, "Boy? What boy is this?!"¹ This suggests that, like many men of his generation, Rodney Starmer perhaps had some difficulty showing his emotions, leading to a less fulfilled relationship between father and son than either side wanted. It also gives credence to the notion that Keir felt that being recognised at Buckingham Palace might be more important to his parents than it was to him. That would explain why he has always been somewhat reticent about using the title. In 2015, he told his local newspaper: 'I've never liked titles. When I was DPP, everyone called me director and I said, "Please don't call me director, call me Keir Starmer." It's a very similar battle now.'² Similarly, the parliamentary authorities only refer to him as plain 'Keir Starmer' in all official communications, at his request. Of course, accepting an honour and then refusing to use it does leave him open to accusations of what Boris Johnson has called 'cakeism', that is to say, having your cake and eating it. It also puts him in direct contrast to other big Labour Party figures. For example, Tony Benn, a politician whom Starmer is known to admire, famously renounced his hereditary peerage in 1963, albeit so that he could take his seat in the House of Commons, whereas Starmer actively collected his title.

Bill Bowring, who worked closely with Starmer at the Haldane Society in the 1980s and 1990s, believes that Starmer might not be as resistant to joining the establishment as he would have people believe. Bowring comments:

I don't think he would have been shocked if you'd told him in 1990 that he would one day be a QC, a former DPP and a knight. I think one of Keir's faults, which has come out from time to time, is his wanting to insist how working-class he is, when he's absolutely plainly not. I mean, if you're a QC and former DPP, you've left your working-class roots far behind. That's a weakness of his, to go on about it. He's become very middle-class. I think he finds the aristocratic end of the Tory Party very disagreeable. I think he thinks being Sir Keir Starmer QC is really as far as he wants to go in the establishment. But he is establishment; of course he is.[3]

Just before his inclusion in the New Year Honours list was announced, the idea surfaced that he was sizing up his local parliamentary seat in north London, Holborn & St Pancras. Encompassing most of the London Borough of Camden, it has long been considered one of the safest Labour seats in the country and, given its proximity to Westminster, is highly desirable from a practical point of view. It contains pockets of poverty as well as of prosperity and stretches from Covent Garden in the south to Hampstead Heath in the north, and from Primrose Hill in the west to Islington in the east. It had been held by the former Labour Cabinet minister Frank Dobson since its creation in 1983. Dobson's majority at the 2010 election had been a rock-solid 9,942. A week before Christmas in 2013, the *Daily Telegraph*'s diary column noted:

> Frank Dobson may be seventy-three but the old Labour Dread-
> nought hasn't made any comments about how long he intends
> to remain in situ as the MP for Holborn & St Pancras. Still, Keir
> Starmer, the former Director of Public Prosecutions, appears to have
> his eyes on the prize. The QC has taken what is a popular stand in
> the area opposing the HS2 rail link, and, last week, he joined Tom
> Watson, the Labour Party election 'mastermind', at a fundraiser in
> Kentish Town. Helpful photographs of him have also appeared in the
> local paper with the area's Labour councillors.

This speculation may not have been welcomed by Starmer, but it was perfectly true. He had been quietly cultivating the seat, and in this he had the support of Dobson himself. A close friend of the late MP says, 'I remember talking to Frank about Keir. Frank was always very keen that Keir should succeed him. He had known him for quite a while, he really liked him, he thought he was impressive, and he never thought anyone but Keir should take over the seat from him.' Starmer also enjoyed the backing of the then Labour leader Ed Miliband, who happened to live in the constituency and who moved in the same circles as Starmer. He, too, had privately given Starmer his blessing. As noted in Chapter 8, Miliband was determined to hold Rupert Murdoch and his newspaper empire to account over the phone-hacking scandal, and some even believe Starmer's decision as DPP to sanction the prosecution of journalists from Murdoch's stable pleased Miliband so much that he was even happier to support his political ambitions.

The rumours that Starmer was limbering up to launch a bid for the seat were aired in other national titles, and by June 2014 the 'Heathman' column in one of the constituency's papers, *Hampstead and Highgate Express*, began to list the number of local events Starmer had appeared at despite Dobson still officially being the MP. 'The 51-year-old [Starmer] would neither rule himself in or out of any future Labour parliamentary race when Heathman spotted him at a presentation evening for pupils at William Ellis School in Highgate Road last Thursday,' the paper reported.

> Sir Keir … lives in Kentish Town with his wife and two children and has been popping up increasingly for public appearances of late. On Friday, he is due to speak to children at Holy Trinity Primary School, in Trinity Walk, Hampstead, for their afternoon assembly. Last month, he was sighted at the local election count at Somers Town Community Sports Centre and was then spotted in the chamber of Camden Town Hall for the new council's ceremonial annual meeting on June 11.

Starmer further sought to boost his credentials as a community-minded man by taking a position in June 2014 with the London-based charity Kids Company. It was run by Camila Batmanghelidjh, who once claimed to be a 'psychiatrist', and its chairman of trustees was the BBC executive Alan Yentob. Since the early 2000s, it had been astonishingly successful in persuading central government departments to give it more than £42 million of public money, allegedly to help deprived inner-city children. Thanks to its well-oiled PR machine, it was also feted by rock stars and celebrities, becoming a fashionable and very well-supported cause in the process. Yet getting involved with Kids Company was arguably an ill-judged decision on Starmer's part, however well-intentioned. He presents himself to the public as a forensically minded barrister, but it is clear that he did not undertake sufficient due diligence before hopping on board this enterprise. The fact that he has never discussed his association with the charity publicly all but proves he knows this.

On 24 June 2014, Starmer took to Twitter to announce that he felt it a 'privilege' to be asked by Batmanghelidjh to become chairman of a child protection taskforce operating under the umbrella of an initiative called 'See the Child. Change the System'. It was billed by the charity as 'a Kids Company campaign to rethink children's social care and mental health services'. At the point Starmer took up this post, the coalition government run by David Cameron and Nick Clegg was in its twilight, and there was a genuine belief among some senior employees at Kids Company that the then Labour leader, Ed Miliband, would become Prime Minister after the next general election in May 2015. As Starmer had strong links to Miliband, securing him for this role was considered a coup for Kids Company, as it would potentially provide a direct line of communication to Downing Street. Since Kids Company said it needed £1.5 million to start work on 'See the Child. Change the System', Starmer's worth to the charity was obvious.

Although a press conference was held to announce that Starmer had joined this Kids Company project, nothing of any consequence happened for several months in relation to it. Then, in February 2015, questions began to be asked about Kids Company itself, starting with an article in *The Spectator*. The magazine pointed out that the charity had made a series of claims which were so far-fetched as to be unbelievable, including in its own annual reports, which stated that the number of people it helped in 2010 was 16,500, a figure which had more than doubled to an astonishing 36,000 the next year. *The Spectator* raised concerns about Kids Company's spending habits, its accountability, its transparency and about what appeared to be an unusually cosy relationship between Batmanghelidjh and the then Prime Minister, David Cameron.[4] Other media outlets took an interest in the story, matters escalated, and by the summer of 2015, the charity was forced to close down amid a raft of accusations about its apparently serial misuse of public money and allegations concerning sexual abuse, which were later dropped. Starmer's initiative had quietly sunk without trace by this point, meaning that he escaped from involvement in the fallout of one of Britain's best-known charities dissolving into a scandal that made headline news for weeks. No doubt he counted himself lucky that 'See the Child. Change the System' never got off the ground properly under his stewardship. This was one failure of his with which he could be pleased.

*   *   *

In mid-July 2014, Frank Dobson finally announced at a constituency meeting his intention to stand down at the next general election, thereby firing the starting gun for the competition to succeed him and represent one of Labour's strongholds in the capital. Starmer's campaign was already under way but had been forced to operate in the shadows until this point. Out of respect for Dobson and the integrity of a contest, which had to be seen to be open and fair, he had necessarily but covertly begun to assemble the support and financial backing he would need to mount a credible campaign. Dobson's statement removed this cloak of secrecy and allowed him to become an even more visible figure in the constituency. Bill Bowring recalls that Starmer left no stone unturned in his quest to become an MP. Even though Bowring had not had much to do with Starmer for several years, he received a call and was invited to help. 'He lobbied me and others relentlessly at the time he was going for Frank Dobson's seat,' remembers Bowring.

> He was on to me for anyone I knew who could possibly be lobbied to vote for him in the local Labour Party. I know people in St Pancras, people in particular who were on the Haldane executive who live in the constituency, and he was very keen that I should ask them if they'd be supporting him, which was fair enough. I strongly suspect they did.

Within a couple of weeks, Starmer was able to confirm that he was ready to put his name forward to stand as a parliamentary candidate, as long as Labour did not run an all-woman shortlist. Although the area had never had a female MP before, it now appears as though Starmer knew by this point that a shortlist excluding men was not on the cards. Apart from anything else, he would hardly want to lose credibility so early in his career as an aspiring politician by announcing he was entering a competition which it would be impossible for him to win. He told the *Camden New Journal* on 31 July:

> It would be an honour for anyone to succeed Frank Dobson. It will

now be for the party to agree the process and timetable but if it is an open shortlist I intend to seek selection from members of Holborn & St Pancras, my home for over fifteen years. Our constituency needs an MP who will continue Frank's principled campaigning, fight to get the Tories out of power and be able to influence a future Labour government. I believe I can bring my experience as a human rights lawyer, DPP and campaigner to do that. I am only too aware of the impact that politics has on the daily lives of all of us.

As a result of his jostling and networking efforts, he was able to inform the paper that he had already received 'strong support' for his candidacy from local party members and others, including the former chairman of the Equality and Human Rights Commission (EHRC), Trevor Phillips; the Labour peer Helena Kennedy (whom he had known for twenty years by this point); another Labour peer, Joan Bakewell; and the former Labour Cabinet minister Tessa Jowell. 'I am also grateful to have trade union support from Aslef,' he added. Given that King's Cross, St Pancras and Euston railway stations are all in the constituency, securing Aslef's support was certainly important.

Starmer was not the only person who was interested in succeeding Dobson, of course, and it would not be accurate to surmise that Ed Miliband's tacit approval of his candidacy made it a foregone conclusion that he would do so. For example, Sarah Hayward, then the leader of Camden Council, also signalled her intention to stand. Soon, others expressed an interest in joining the race, though Hayward was always regarded as Starmer's principal threat. As summer turned to autumn, however, one undeniable fact which pointed to Starmer having received some preferential treatment did dawn on his competitors. It became clear that Labour high command was in no hurry to find Dobson's replacement. Even in September – two months after Dobson had said he would quit – party chiefs were suggesting it might be November before the lucky man or woman would be named. Local journalist Richard Osley, deputy editor of the *Camden New Journal*, noted in his blog on 9 September that

> when [Labour] regional director Alan Olive came to speak to the constituency party tonight, to explain how it would all pan out, a motion was brought and carried demanding that the process is begun immediately. It was a little stand, but not much more – because it is the National Executive Committee which holds the power over the timetable, and it has shown little interest in speeding this one through.

What lay behind this relaxed attitude? One explanation that has never been denied relates to the Labour Party's own rules. These state that nobody can be selected as a prospective parliamentary candidate until they have been a party member for a minimum of a full calendar year. As DPP, Starmer was meant to be politically neutral and was therefore not allowed to belong to a political party. For this reason, he had only been able to rejoin the Labour Party after having ceased to be DPP on 1 November 2013. Mutterings were soon heard that the selection contest was being delayed solely for Starmer's benefit. These grumbles were arguably borne out by the protracted timetable eventually decided upon. The contest would not open in earnest until 29 October, with all candidates needing to submit their papers by 10 November and the final selection taking place on 13 December. If these arrangements really were part of a fix that was weighted in Starmer's favour, it says much about the Labour Party at that time that they were put in place for a man who had no formal political experience whatsoever.

In 2014, there were about 1,200 local party members who would be eligible to vote in the contest. Ultimately, Starmer had to appeal to them. He was brilliantly placed to do so, thanks to having cultivated a public image as a high-profile barrister and then as DPP. Securing an interview with the *Evening Standard* was, for example, far easier for him than it would have been for his rivals. Indeed, in early September, he invited a *Standard* reporter to Doughty Street for a wide-ranging chat about his political aspirations, in which he trotted out familiar, though as already established somewhat dubious lines. For example, he said: 'I had a very traditional Labour background ... My dad worked in a factory all his life.'[5]

Despite being willing to charm anybody and everybody who might be of use to him in his quest for a seat in Westminster, he was not above putting some people's noses out of joint. One barrister, Jon Holbrook, says that Starmer accepted an invitation to speak at the Battle of Ideas law debate being held in London on 18 October. Almost four weeks before the debate was to be held, on 23 September, Starmer wrote to Holbrook pulling out of the event, citing professional duties. 'I am really sorry,' he wrote to Holbrook, 'but a case of mine has been moved and now starts on Monday 20 October, and the only time the client can meet to go through some critical evidence is Saturday 18 October. Alas I will have to withdraw from the battle of ideas event.'

Holbrook takes up the story: 'I had no problem with him doing so – we were not, for example, paying him – save that he chose not to tell us the real reason when making his excuses,' he says.

He claimed [his absence] was due to a professional legal commit-ment meaning that he had 'to go through some critical evidence' on that Saturday. Surprise, surprise on the morning of Saturday 18 Oct-ober he tweeted how great it was to have met Sadiq Khan at the TUC march that was taking place that day. It always struck me as the actions of a weak man. If he had simply said to us, as organisers,

'I'm sorry, I now realise that, particularly as an aspiring Labour MP, I need to attend the TUC march and rally' I would have entirely understood.[6]

On 12 October, those who had declared were invited to a warm-up event in Camden Town to address branch members from four wards in the constituency on a subject of their choice. Starmer chose to speak about 'Why Labour needs a values-based approach to 2015', a topic which, in retrospect, was not guaranteed to set anybody's pulse racing. On 29 October, however, he raised his game significantly by publishing a glossy leaflet featuring more than 100 prominent people who had come out to back him. They included Doreen Lawrence, the mother of murdered teenager Stephen Lawrence; Fiona Millar, journalist and partner of Tony Blair's former spin doctor, Alastair Campbell; and Ken Livingstone, the former Mayor of London. The former Foreign Secretary, David Miliband, was also happy to be named as an endorser on the leaflet. He and his younger brother, Ed, had notoriously fallen out after both of them had a tilt at the Labour leadership four years previously, yet by gaining the elder Miliband's support, Starmer was seen to be above this unseemly sibling rivalry. Robert Latham, a wealthy Doughty Street barrister who has turned out to be pivotal when it comes to bankrolling Starmer's political aspirations, was also on the list, as was Labour Party worker Ben Nunn, who became Starmer's director of communications when he assumed the leadership in 2020. There is no doubt that Starmer put his rivals in the shade with this leaflet and the number of backers he had secured, but not everybody approved of it. Indeed, one party member even complained to the *Camden New Journal* that its mere existence confirmed Starmer and his team had been working the seat long before anybody else and 'surely before Frank Dobson had even announced he was going'.

By the time nominations closed, twenty-four people had put their names forward, illustrating a clear competition in those wishing to represent this plum constituency. Each submitted a personal statement. Starmer's, in which he called himself 'a national voice for local people', made great play of his familiarity with the constituency but contained at least two arguable assertions. 'I am local,' he wrote. 'I have lived in Kentish Town for fifteen years and worked in Holborn for twenty-five years.' This was somewhat misleading. As far as records show, he had lived in Kentish Town since his relationship with Phillippa Kaufmann had broken down just twelve or thirteen years previously; and although he had worked in Doughty Street, which is in Holborn, from 1990 until 2008, thereafter he was based at the CPS office in Petty France, in Westminster, until 2013, raising questions about where the 'twenty-five years' figure came from. Nobody seemed to pick up on this at the time. The rest of the one-page statement covered his family, his legal career, his work on Labour's criminal justice strategy and his ambition to serve as a constituency MP.

On 18 November, the first of the neighbourhood branch meetings took place, where nominations were made for the final selection contest. Every branch had to nominate two candidates, at least one of whom had to be a woman. Branches were able to add a third name if an ethnic minority candidate had not been chosen in the first two votes. More nomination meetings in other branches followed. Starmer did well, as predicted, sailing through to the final round of candidates, who were interviewed by a ten-member committee of senior Holborn & St Pancras Labour Party figures and then whittled down to a shortlist of five to compete in a final hustings on Saturday 13 December. Alongside Starmer and Sarah Hayward were hospital consultant Dr Patrick French; former Camden Council leader and human rights lawyer Raj Chada; and West Hampstead councillor Angela Pober.

On the eve of that final meeting, Starmer received the endorsement of an elder statesman of the Labour Party in the form of Neil Kinnock, who praised his 'courage, integrity and principles'. It was further proof of Starmer's single-mindedness that he was able to wheel out such a big gun at this late stage. A few days later, at St Pancras Church, all thoughts of spending the afternoon Christmas shopping or watching Arsenal play at home were put aside by hundreds of party members, who queued round the block to be able to have their say in selecting the person who they knew, barring a freak result, would almost certainly be their next MP. By this point, more than 200 postal votes had been cast, yet each candidate still had to perform well in front of the membership in order to secure a majority of the rest.

The aforementioned Richard Osley, who was present, noted in his blog:

> When his turn came to speak at the final hustings, Sir Keir talked about his family: his six-year-old son who was desperate for this selection campaign to end, and a deeply personal story about the NHS. He talked about how immigration should be celebrated in an answer to one question, and fudged another about his thoughts on the coalition.

In Osley's opinion, Starmer did not speak as well as another candidate, Raj Chada, but by then it was probably too late anyway. Having as an MP a figure with a profile as high as Starmer's was seemingly enough to satisfy the appetites of most people present. Frank Dobson, who was officiating, announced after just one round of voting that Starmer had scored a sizeable majority of votes, though the exact number has never been made public. After making a short victory speech, in which he urged everybody present not to hold an inquest into which candidate each had voted for, he repaired to the bar of the Premier Inn in the Euston Road for a celebratory drink before hosting his closest friends and advisers at home. Amusingly, one aide contacted Osley that night and asked him – not for the first time – to stop using Starmer's knighthood when writing about him, presumably because of fears it might alienate voters. Osley took the view that this request simply meant he was duty-bound to use the title more often when writing about Starmer in the *Camden New Journal*.

After Holborn & St Pancras Labour members had had their say, ending the party's suspiciously long five-month wait to select a candidate to succeed Dobson, there was not an enormous amount of time left for Starmer to 'nurse' the constituency before the election. Just before he was selected, he claimed to dislike the type of campaigning which focused on his personality, telling the *Hampstead and Highgate Express*: 'I want to get on with the real job of winning the next election. I don't find the self-promotion of this process a comfortable experience.'[7] Despite this professed reservation, he still found the time to give interviews to the national press. Within a week of his nomination, he told *The Guardian* why he had chosen politics over the law, predicting that

> 2015 is going to be a defining election. If I'm right, then the next ten years are going to be really tough and – this isn't meant to sound arrogant – but I think if I do have skills and experience that might help, I don't really think I can walk away from it.[8]

The *Sunday Times* was also invited to Doughty Street Chambers for a chat with the aspiring MP a few days after he was named as the candidate.

If Starmer hoped such exposure would encourage others to take an interest in him, he was not disappointed. Michael Crick, then political correspondent for *Channel 4 News*, decided it might be beneficial to get to know him a little better. 'I invited Starmer out to lunch not long after he was selected and a few months before the 2015 election,' Crick remembers.[9]

> I took him to Osteria Dell' Angolo, a wonderful Italian restaurant opposite the Home Office. It was very pleasant; he was friendly. We discussed mutual Oxford friends, and I tried to work out where he stood politically, but he didn't give much away; you couldn't pin him down. But in everything he said, he was trying to learn about how Westminster worked and looking to the long-term future. It was clear he wasn't going to be an anonymous backbencher. He wasn't thrusting or pushy, though – it was all quite pleasant. He reminded me of the Tony Blair of the early 1980s, a north London barrister-type trimming to fit in with his party. I've written about quite a few ambitious politicians in my time – Heseltine, Archer, Farage – and I left the lunch thinking, 'This is one of the most ambitious politicians I've ever met.'

Having inherited a constituency that was his to lose, there were no serious obstacles in Starmer's way as election day loomed. Still, he campaigned hard in the seat, sometimes with Frank Dobson's help, no doubt spurred on by the fact the leader of the Green Party, Natalie Bennett, posed a potential threat, as did the Conservative candidate, Will Blair. It was only when his mother died less than two weeks before polling day that his progress was interrupted. A large funeral attended by almost 150 people was held. Josephine Starmer was seventy-five years old and, despite her crippling illness, had overcome the odds to lead a much fuller life than any medical professional had ever believed possible. What was no doubt a personal tragedy to Starmer was that his mother did not live to see him win a parliamentary seat and enter the Commons.

CHAPTER 10

CORE GROUP PLUS

On 7 May 2015, Starmer was elected the Member of Parliament for Holborn & St Pancras with nearly 53 per cent of the vote and a majority of 17,048 – an increase in the Labour haul of more than 7,000 since the previous election in 2010. At the age of fifty-two, he had made it to Westminster at the first attempt. Bert Starmer's wish had finally been granted.

Nevertheless, the new member was disappointed. In defiance of most polls and to the surprise of David Cameron himself, the Conservatives swept to victory with an overall majority for the first time since 1992. As in other similar seats, left-leaning voters punished the Liberal Democrats for going into coalition with the Tories, boosting Labour's local support and giving Starmer what he called the 'delusion' that his party was on course to win.[1] 'In those final weeks on my patch, it looked as if we were getting better results, so the exit poll was crushing,' he later said.

The new MP had hardly had time to get his feet under his new desk in Parliament's Portcullis House when a clamour arose for him to take a further giant leap in his political career. The comment pages of *The Guardian*, often considered Labour's house journal, began to feature serious discussion of the idea that Starmer should stand in the contest to replace Ed Miliband, who had announced his resignation as Labour leader the morning after the party's drubbing.

'Who better than the new MP Keir Starmer, former Director of Public Prosecutions and human rights lawyer, to help stop the UK joining Belarus outside the European Court of Human Rights?' asked veteran columnist Polly Toynbee. Lord Myners, who had been a minister in Gordon Brown's government, said he was underwhelmed by the current contenders – former frontbenchers Andy Burnham, Yvette Cooper, Liz Kendall and Mary Creagh, and a left-wing perennial backbencher called Jeremy Corbyn – and that he 'would like to see someone really quite radical. I would like to see Keir Starmer, who has only been a Member of Parliament for a week, but he's got a real background, he's done a proper job.' Could the party really consider such a new candidate? 'Many people would say no. But goodness me, wouldn't that electrify the campaign?'[2]

A grassroots movement also sprang into being. Under the rather cumbersome title 'Sir Keir Starmer QC KCB for Labour Leader', a group of online devotees set up a Facebook page urging their hero to put himself forward, attracting hundreds of followers within a few days. The fact that Starmer had not responded to the group's tweets and emails did not discourage them. 'Silence speaks volumes,' said Narice Bernard, a disenchanted Labour supporter who helped found the campaign. 'He hasn't said he'll stand, but he hasn't said he won't. It's clear that when someone goes into politics at his stage of life they do so for a very good reason – they want to make a difference.' The crusade was not factional, Bernard stressed. 'I suspect he is from the left of the party, but it's not about left and right, it's about leadership.'

Starmer put a stop to the speculation after a few days, tweeting 'V flattered by #keirforleader initiative and thanks for so many supportive messages but Labour needs s/one with more political experience.' He also responded directly to the group's entreaties, writing to Bernard on 4 June:

Thank you for your email urging me to stand for the Labour leadership. I am genuinely touched by the suggestion and appreciate your support. However, having only just entered Parliament, I have decided not to put my name forward. We need an open and honest debate in the Labour Party about our future and our core purpose. I will endeavour to make my voice heard in that debate.[3]

The new MP had taken so long to reply that the group concluded that he was seriously considering the move. 'It was an extraordinarily long time,' says Bernard. 'I think it was about ten days. Some of us became quite optimistic. I think he must have been taking soundings.'

This theory appears to have amounted to more than mere wishful thinking on the part of his fans. Michael Crick was intrigued by the idea that he might be a candidate and texted Starmer to ask if he would stand. 'He could have texted back straight away and said, "Don't be silly" or "No way," but it was two or three days before I got a reply to say he wasn't,' Crick recalls.[4] 'So I suspect he did at least think about it, if only briefly.'

Having decided against a run on his own account, Starmer had to choose among the real candidates to lead the party. He backed Burnham, a former Health Secretary, who was initially the bookies' favourite to succeed Miliband. Once considered a Blairite, Burnham was regarded as being in the centre-left mainstream of the party. His leadership manifesto pledged to restore the 50 per cent tax rate on high earners that had been abolished by the Tories, to renationalise the railways and to raise the minimum wage. However, he said he would scrap Labour's commitment to a mansion tax, describing the idea as 'the politics of envy'. Burnham believed Labour had lost because 'a sense has built up that we aren't in favour of people getting on. That is toxic. We need to get back to communicating simple policies that will make a real difference to people.'[5]

Candidates needed the support of at least thirty-five MPs to make it onto the ballot, and Burnham received sixty-eight nominations, more than any of his rivals. This counted for nothing with the Labour membership, who four months later elected Corbyn with 251,417 votes, nearly 60 per cent of the total and more than three times as many as second-placed Burnham.

*   *   *

However preposterous, the experience of being touted for the leadership within days of his election underlined how high expectations were for Starmer by the time he arrived in Parliament. This would also have created considerable pressure, since an impressive record in another field was no guarantee of political success: Archie Norman and Sebastian Coe, for example, returned to their respective arenas of business and sport after brief, non-stellar spells in Westminster.

In his former role, Starmer had been within the orbit of the political world. He had worked closely with ministers, given evidence to parliamentary committees and become a public figure in his own right, making decisions on controversial issues at the heart of national debate. Even so, politicians who dealt with him in his legal role admit to being astonished that he made the move into full-time politics.

Some also wondered how readily he would adapt. Dominic Grieve says that when he first saw the new MP in the Commons, 'We greeted each other as friends because he's someone whom I'd come to respect very much in his professional capacity. I was pleased to see him there.'[6] At the same time, however,

I wondered how much he would enjoy politics and take to it, because he's quite an austere man, and Parliament is not a very austere place.

And an outsider coming in to the House of Commons and looking at the general antics of their colleagues – some people take to it like a duck to water, and other people don't, which made me wonder what he would make of it.

In his early months in Parliament, Starmer eased the transition by sticking to familiar policy territory. In his maiden speech on 28 May, during a debate on home affairs and justice, he used the presence of four surviving Magna Carta manuscripts in the British Museum, located in his constituency, as a hook to attack government plans to replace the Human Rights Act with a British Bill of Rights:

> As we now celebrate the 800th anniversary of Magna Carta, let us affirm the principle that human rights apply to everyone equally. Any proposed British Bill of Rights inconsistent with that principle will not be worth the paper it is written on and will face widespread opposition, not least from me on behalf of my constituents in Holborn & St Pancras.

Following tradition, Starmer also paid tribute to his long-serving predecessor. 'Although I doubt I will clock up thirty-six years, I intend to follow in Frank Dobson's footsteps – albeit my jokes are likely to seem tame when compared with his, and I might give the beard a miss.' (Dobson's jokes were indeed notorious. The late former Conservative minister Alan Clark recorded in his *Diaries* that they were 'so filthy that really they're unusable, even at a rugger club dinner'.)

Michael Gove, then Lord Chancellor and Justice Secretary, acknowledged Starmer's contribution when he wound up the debate. 'I hope there will be many other opportunities for us to hear him, when we may perhaps have occasion to tease out the wisdom behind his remarks,' he said, referring to the tradition whereby maiden speeches are heard without interruption. Gove continued:

> I very much enjoyed his speech, both the analysis of the strengths and deficiencies of Magna Carta and the passion he showed in defence of human rights as a way of safeguarding the interests of his constituents, many of whom are among the poorest in our capital and our country. They will have an effective advocate in him.

Starmer continued the theme, speaking on issues including the Crown Prosecution Service, the government's powers of surveillance and data collection, and the rights of victims of crime. During questions to the Attorney General, he prefaced a question on victims' rights by declaring an interest as a barrister and a former DPP. 'I think he must win the prize for the most impressive declaration of interest so far this morning,' replied the Attorney General, Jeremy Wright. 'He comes at the issue from a uniquely knowledgeable perspective, and we are grateful to have him here.'

In July he began a short stint on the Commons Home Affairs Select Committee, chaired by Labour MP Keith Vaz. Only four meetings were held during his membership: hearings on the migration crisis at Calais and the prevalence of new psychoactive substances, and sessions with Metropolitan Police Commissioner Bernard Hogan-Howe and Home Secretary Theresa May. He asked Hogan-Howe about body-worn police cameras, expressing the hope that they would soon be used by all London police officers carrying out operations in public. Given the opportunity to grill May, he chose the perhaps obscure topic of Ofcom's role in dealing with broadcasters disseminating extremist content – and in particular, the balance between the need to tackle extremism and the broadcasters' right to freedom of expression under Article 10 of the Human Rights Act.

One major departure from Starmer's preference for criminal justice matters was HS2, the proposed new high-speed railway linking London with Birmingham and the north of England, terminating at Euston station. The building works would mean years of disruption for Starmer's constituents, 17,000 of whom lived within 300 metres of the planned construction work, and the demolition of hundreds of homes. In a debate in September 2015, he described the impact on local residents, businesses and the environment of work that could last twenty years:

> A child born next year in my constituency will grow up and leave home knowing nothing but construction work. A pensioner beginning retirement at seventy next year will live out their entire retirement knowing nothing but construction work around them. It is no wonder that at every meeting and everywhere I go in my constituency, anxiety is etched on the faces of everybody who talks to me about HS2 ... I was elected to represent the people of Holborn & St Pancras. It is my privilege to do so; it is also my duty. I speak for each and every one of my constituents when I say that I will stand with them and fight with them to resist the wholly unacceptable damage that HS2 will bring to our communities.[7]

The Bill was passed, but Starmer voted against, defying the Labour whip for the first and so far only time.

Early in the new parliament, MPs were faced with the ticklish question of how much they ought to be paid. After the expenses scandal of 2009, whose worst offenders Starmer had prosecuted as DPP, the matter was put into the hands of the Independent Parliamentary Standards Authority (IPSA), which recommended in June 2015 that MPs' salaries should rise from £67,060 to £74,000 – an increase of 10 per cent at a time when pay remained frozen in much of the public sector. Some MPs voiced opposition to the proposal, including Starmer's constituency neighbours Tulip Siddiq in Hampstead & Kilburn and Catherine West in Hornsey & Wood Green, but Starmer declined to do so. He said he accepted that any increase was hard to justify in the prevailing economic climate, but 'having overseen the prosecution of a number of MPs for expenses fraud, I firmly believe that any decision should be taken by IPSA, an independent body, without lobbying by MPs one way or the other'.[8]

The IPSA proposal was implemented, taking Starmer's salary from one third of what he had earned as DPP to just under three eighths. He did not have to make do with that, however. According to the Register of Members' Interests, between the 2015 and 2017 elections, Starmer earned a further £45,490.62 for legal work on top of his parliamentary duties, plus an extra £1,609.22 for six articles in *The Guardian*.

His clients included the Government of Gibraltar, who paid £9,480 for twenty hours' work in December 2015, leading to speculation that he had advised the territory on how to 'nobble' Brexit as the UK prepared for its referendum. Starmer was unable to deny this, maintaining that 'legal advice is confidential and privileged', but Gibraltar itself later spared his blushes by issuing a statement that 'his advice was sought in relation to non-political matters affecting prosecutions and procedures relating thereto. Both instances were entirely unrelated to the UK or Gibraltar's membership of or exit from the European Union.' Another customer was the prestigious law firm Mishcon de Reya, whose in-house learning and thought-leadership academy he advised for six hours a month from June to September 2016, for a monthly fee of £4,500.

Though many would see such earnings as a substantial top-up to what they might consider an already handsome salary – especially in the Holborn & St Pancras constituency, which includes some of the most deprived areas in the country – they do not put Starmer in the top tier of highly paid MPs. A survey by the *Daily Mirror* found thirteen MPs had outside earnings into six figures in 2016 alone, with nine earning more from part-time jobs than the Prime Minister's salary of £150,000. However, most on the list were Tories: Starmer's non-parliamentary work made him one of the highest earners on the Labour benches.

*　　*　　*

That summer's leadership campaign was not the only event that would signal the direction the Labour Party was taking. After eight years in the job, Boris Johnson was to stand down as Mayor of London at the following year's election. The clear favourite to be selected as Labour's candidate was the Blairite Tessa Jowell, who, as Culture Secretary, had led the city's successful bid to host the 2012 Olympics. Starmer, however, backed Sadiq Khan, the MP for Tooting and former Transport Minister, who was considered well to the left of Jowell. The two men knew each other well, Khan having been a solicitor specialising in human rights law before entering politics. 'Sadiq made his name rooting out injustice and righting wrongs,' wrote Starmer in the *New Statesman*. 'He was never afraid to take on powerful vested interests in the government, the police or the prison service. This is precisely what we need in a mayor.'

However, one Labour strategist close to the eventual winner also sees a telling degree of political acuity in Starmer's choice. 'It was a foregone conclusion that Tessa Jowell was going to win the mayoralty for Labour because the era of the soft left and the left in the Labour Party was over,' they say.

> The party was supposedly about to take a hard turn to the right. And yet his political rune-reading was astute enough, even in those early days before the Corbyn phenomenon took off, to sense that Sadiq would gather the momentum to make it all the way. That's a sensitivity to political currents and a willingness to engage with the left that was an important early indicator of just what a canny operator this guy was.

Five years later, Khan would return the favour.

*   *   *

As Parliament prepared to return in September, Corbyn assembled his first shadow Cabinet. As well as left-wingers like John McDonnell and Diane Abbott, appointed shadow Chancellor and shadow International Development Secretary respectively, the team included more moderate figures such as Hilary Benn and Lucy Powell, who led on foreign affairs and education. When more junior front-bench appointments were announced a few days later, Starmer was named as a shadow minister in Labour's home affairs team, leading on security, immigration and asylum.

Inevitably in the competitive world of politics, there was a degree of envy at Starmer's rapid promotion. 'There is always resentment for people who end up on the front bench from others who don't,' observes a colleague. 'What they said was, he's just an automaton lawyer, he hasn't done the hard yards. But actually, that was a mistake; he was very political. He understands politics inside out.'

According to Burnham, now the shadow Home Secretary and effectively Starmer's boss, the new spokesman had not displayed any of the self-importance that might have come with his former status. 'The fact he was a former DPP and came to work in my shadow Home Office team with no airs and graces says a lot about Keir Starmer,' he said later.[9]

One of Starmer's first actions was to introduce a new law on the rights of victims of crime. This was an issue on which he had long campaigned, as mentioned in Chapter 8. The way victims were treated ought to lead to a 'pause in the oft-repeated mantra that we have the best criminal justice system in the world', the former DPP had written in 2014.[10] His Ten-Minute Rule Bill – under which MPs can make the case for new legislation in a speech lasting up to ten minutes – included measures giving victims the right to appeal against a decision to stop a criminal investigation and establishing a duty to report suspected child abuse in regulated professions like healthcare and teaching.

Despite attracting cross-party support, the proposal went the way of most Private Members' Bills and failed to attract enough backing to make progress in Parliament. Many of its provisions were attached as amendments to the government's own Policing and Crime Bill the following year, but protocol meant that despite his expertise in the subject, Starmer was barred from speaking in the debate since he was by then shadowing a different department. ('That's the rules,' he said. 'I'm not grumbling.')

Otherwise, Starmer's nine months in the shadow home affairs post were dominated by three issues, each of which had previously been difficult territory for Labour. The first of these was the Investigatory Powers Bill, known to its critics as the 'snoopers' charter', which would govern the security services' ability to access private communications, including internet records. Alert to the risk of seeming to hamper the fight against crime and terrorism, Starmer went out of his way to strike a constructive note. He welcomed the Bill as a necessary step given advances in communications technology but emphasised the need to balance public safety with concerns about personal privacy and abuse of power.

'I spent five years prosecuting some of the most dangerous terrorists in this country, so it would be quite difficult for people to pin the charge of being soft on terrorism on me,' Starmer said.[11] 'The public do want to be properly protected, and that is my position and the party's position. It's a case of getting the balance right, and that doesn't mean we simply yield to everything the security services, law enforcement or the government says it wants.' On the other hand he noted, 'If there's not a new act, the security services will continue to use powers exposed by Edward Snowden [the former CIA operative who leaked details of government surveillance programmes] but without the safeguards that we now think are appropriate. You need the powers, but they've got to be properly administered.'

As DPP, he told the Commons, he had worked with the security services on cases 'that involved some of the most serious and grotesque crimes, and I shared the anxiety of tracking down individuals before they committed unspeakable crimes. For me, that has always made a compelling case for retaining some communications and personal data.'[12]

While proposals for bulk data collection certainly amounted to an intrusion of privacy, he said in a BBC interview:

The question is whether it can be justified. Privacy is a right, it's a really important right, but it's not an absolute right. The question is, is any invasion necessary, and is it proportionate? ... I've seen this from both sides of the argument. I spent twenty years as a human rights lawyer, taking on cases for people who had had their human rights invaded. I then spent five years as Director of Public Prosecutions working with the security and intelligence services. We do need these powers but there must be the right safeguards.[13]

Labour abstained at the Bill's second reading stage in March 2016, arguing that the proposals did not offer tough enough safeguards against unwarranted intrusion. By the third reading in June, however, the government had offered significant concessions – for which Starmer received a good deal of the credit – including greater privacy protections, stronger judicial oversight, a commitment that interception warrants could not be issued because of legitimate trade union activity and an independent review of the use of bulk data. Now Labour officially backed the legislation, to the consternation of civil rights campaigners and some in the party.

Two Labour MPs were conspicuous by their absence at the vote. One was Corbyn, the party leader. The other was Diane Abbott, who went on to condemn the new law as a 'serious erosion of our rights and liberties' after she succeeded Burnham as shadow Home Secretary later in the year. 'I tried to raise these points in the course of the final debates,' she said, implicitly criticising Burnham and Starmer for their approach.[14]

The second big issue to confront Starmer in his new role was the mounting crisis as huge numbers of refugees crossed the Mediterranean, especially from Syria, in the hope of a new life in Europe. While still a backbencher, Starmer had criticised the government for failing to uphold Britain's 'long and proud tradition of helping those most in need'. Along with neighbouring constituency MPs West and Siddiq, he wrote to the PM calling for more of the migrants who had found their way to Europe to be housed in Britain. 'Just 1,000 Syrians, at the very most, will be granted asylum under our schemes – a fraction of the tens of thousands whom Germany and others have helped,' they wrote. 'We must also take our fair share of those affected by this crisis.'

As Labour's spokesman, he backed ministers' refusal to accept a mandatory quota of migrants under the EU's scheme. But while he welcomed the government's move to accept 4,000 refugees a year over the course of the parliament, he was not satisfied. '4,000 refugees represents less than 0.5 per cent of the refugees entering the EU this year,' he complained. 'That is not good enough.' While it would be for the government to decide on the right number, Starmer noted: 'It has been suggested that if every city or county in Britain took just ten refugee families, we would be able to help perhaps 10,000 individuals.'

Starmer implied that Britain itself had some responsibility for the situation that had prompted millions to leave their homes. 'Following the decision to extend our military action in Iraq to Syria we now have an even greater moral responsibility to provide a fair and humane response to those fleeing persecution in both countries,' he asserted. 'Yet by limiting our response to just 20,000 Syrian refugees over the next five years, the government has failed this test of moral responsibility. More should be done, and quickly.'[15]

In January 2016, Starmer visited camps in Calais and Dunkirk where migrants had gathered in anticipation of what they hoped would be an onward journey to England. He described the 'truly appalling' conditions in a debate shortly afterwards. The Dunkirk camp was

> basically a forest in which there is a swamp. On the ground is mud, water, urine and everything else that one would expect to find mixed in when there are no toilets or running water. In the middle of that, on any piece of semi-firm soil, are pitched flimsy tents. I do not think that anybody could go in any capacity to those camps and not come back a changed person.

The plight of refugees and the treatment of asylum seekers in Britain became a regular theme of Starmer's interventions at the despatch box. He rejected the argument that welcoming more migrants in Britain would create a 'pull factor' by encouraging more to make the hazardous journey; opposed plans to remove state support from young migrants in the UK when they turned eighteen if their asylum application was rejected; and pressed the government to change its stance of refusing to take asylum seekers who had already reached European countries. He supported the successful Dubs Amendment – named after its proposer, Labour peer Lord Dubs – under which the government would transfer 480 unaccompanied asylum-seeking children from Europe.

Though he later commended programmes for settling asylum seekers in the UK and praised the minister responsible for refugees, Richard Harrington, for his work, he concluded:

In twenty years' time chapters in history books will be written about this moment in world history, in European history and in our own history, and I have concerns that – on reflection and looking back – our response will be judged as reluctant and limited, and in comparison with others not fair and not proportionate.[16]

Sincere as it no doubt was, the position Starmer expounded on refugees and asylum seekers was the one that might traditionally have been expected from Labour: generous, and in the eyes of many voters perhaps too generous. Critics of the party's policy asked in what sense people seeking to enter the UK could still be said to be fleeing persecution if they were already in France; where extra asylum seekers were to be housed given Britain's well-known shortage of social housing; and why those like the shadow minister who were pushing to receive more migrants never seemed to be offering their own spare rooms for the purpose.

Nevertheless, Starmer's long-held position on asylum did not make it any easier for him to pursue another of his objectives: to change perceptions of Labour on the broader question of immigration. The issue had become a major concern for voters in Labour's later years in government and was widely held to have contributed to the party's defeat in 2010. While the Conservative-led coalition government had failed to meet its target of bringing annual net migration below 100,000 – not least because of the EU's freedom of movement policy, which, as long as the UK remained a member, made it impossible to restrict migration into the UK from the twenty-seven other member states – Labour still lagged behind the Tories in public trust on the issue.

At the beginning of 2016, Starmer launched a three-month listening tour of the UK in order to help construct a new approach. 'Many Labour voters and supporters are worried about migration and their concerns must be our concerns,' he said. On his travels he would be 'listening to the arguments and seeing for myself both the advantages and the challenges that migration brings in different places.' Starmer accepted that his party had sometimes tried to avoid the issue. 'I do accept that many in the Labour Party have not really wanted to have the difficult conversations with people about immigration,' he said in Oldham, an early stop on his expedition. 'What Labour can't do is start with the assumption that there are some views we don't want to hear or are somehow not legitimate.'

Given Starmer's strong support for EU membership and the commitment to free movement that came with it, it is unclear how radically he would have been prepared to shift Labour's position. Either way, the exercise ultimately bore no fruit in terms of policy, for two main reasons. First, the immigration question was soon engulfed by the Brexit referendum campaign, in which the debate over free movement would play a major part.

The second reason was that responsibility for the policy passed to Abbott, who, as with the Investigatory Powers Bill, once again took rather a different view from Starmer and Burnham. She dismissed the idea that Labour should adopt a firmer stance on the issue in response to public opinion, writing later that year that 'Labour cannot outdo UKIP or this government on immigration. It should not try. It should pursue its own principled immigration policies which recognises [*sic*] the large benefits of immigration along with some costs.'[17] In any case, it seems unlikely that any dramatic policy overhaul would have been sanctioned by Corbyn, who had said during the leadership campaign that Britain should celebrate its high levels of migration and described Labour's 2015 manifesto commitment to control immigration as 'appalling'.

*   *   *

Two further contentious issues confronted Starmer in his first year as an MP. In September 2015, he found himself in the minority in his own party, as well as in Parliament as a whole, when he voted to legalise assisted suicide. Under the Assisted Dying Bill, on which all MPs were given a free vote with no instructions from party whips, people with less than six months to live would have had the option of being pre-scribed a lethal dose of drugs, provided each case was approved by two doctors and a High Court judge.

During the debate Starmer recounted at length, and to the frustra-tion of some fellow MPs, how and why he had drawn up the existing guidelines during his time as DPP. These stated that the criminal law should rarely, if ever, be used against those who assisted loved ones to die at their request, provided the patient had reached a voluntary, clear, settled and informed decision, but that no such stipulation could be made for doctors and nurses under existing legislation. We had therefore 'arrived at a position where compassionate amateur assistance from nearest and dearest is accepted, but professional medical assistance is not unless you have the means of physical assistance to get to Dignitas', he told Parliament. 'That, to my mind, is an injustice we have trapped within our current arrangements.' Despite Starmer's arguments, the Bill was defeated by 330 votes to 118.

The other controversial issue was that of whether to approve the government's plan for airstrikes against ISIL in Syria in December 2015. The day-long Commons debate included the unusual spectacle of two frontbenchers from the same party making an impassioned contribution on opposite sides of the debate. While Corbyn criticised what he described as 'an ill-thought-out rush to war' and said that 'only a negotiated political and diplomatic endeavour' would bring an end to the Syrian crisis, shadow Foreign Secretary Hilary Benn won a rare standing ovation on both sides of the House for his speech declaring, 'We are here faced by fascists ... What we know about fascists is that they need to be defeated.' This, he said, was why socialists had joined the fight against Franco in the 1930s and the entire House had stood against Hitler and Mussolini. 'My view is that we must now confront this evil. It is now time for us to do our bit in Syria. And that is why I ask my colleagues to vote for the motion tonight.'

Starmer steered between the two poles. 'I am not a pacifist and I would back a lawful, coherent and compelling case for the use of military force by the UK against ISIS,' he wrote shortly before the debate. But although he believed there was a sufficient legal basis for the action, 'I am driven to the conclusion that the strategy outlined by the Prime Minister is flawed.'[18] In the debate, he said:

I am not against airstrikes per se, and I accept that it is difficult to see how territory can be taken from Daesh [as ISIL/ISIS were also known] without them. In my view, however, airstrikes without an effective ground force are unlikely to make any meaningful contribution to defeating Daesh, and there is no effective ground force.

The Commons backed airstrikes by 397 to 223, but like Corbyn and most Labour MPs, Starmer voted against.

* * *

Starmer had quickly established a reputation inside and outside Parliament. 'He was a thing among the membership,' says a veteran observer of the Westminster circus. 'A constituency fundraiser with Keir Starmer in his first year as an MP would sell tickets faster than one with any number of longstanding so-called shadow Cabinet heavyweights.' A colleague who had joined him for a day on the campaign trail recalls that 'the members of his local party obviously really loved him and knew him. There are some MPs who don't know who their members are.'

Others note that he is warmer in private than his often rather solemn public persona but that socialising in Parliament was not a priority. 'Off-duty he's actually quite light-hearted,' says one who knows him. 'But he is a serious guy. He wouldn't have four or five pints with the whips in the bar. And he'd want to get home – his family, his duties to his kids, he's not an absent parent.' Others praised his public-spiritedness. 'He's more interested in helping refugees, let's say, than in schmoozing in the bars,' said Siddiq.[19] 'I've seen him holed up in his office working hard while others are out partying on the terrace.'

Politically, though, Starmer was an enigma. He made no secret that he was a Corbyn-sceptic, even telling the 2015 Labour conference: 'JC is not the messiah, he hasn't got all the answers, and if you touch him you're not healed.' Beyond that, even close colleagues found him hard to place on the political spectrum. In early interviews, he fended off attempts to probe the question: 'People want to be paid properly for the work they do ... People want to live in secure housing they can afford – that's not about left and right, it's basic fairness and dignity,' he told *The Guardian* during the 2015 campaign. 'I do not need to have a label in order to make my mind up,' he said on another occasion.[20]

After the election, he regularly made clear that he had no time for the tendency of some in the party to pursue doctrine at the expense of victory, telling the *New Statesman* he would

> reject wholeheartedly any notion of a Labour Party that is not committed to returning to power at the first opportunity. Of course that needs to be principled power. But standing on the sidelines looking for the purest ideology is a dereliction of duty for any Labour member.

In a lecture to the Fabian Society, he spoke of a feeling within Labour that by the 2015 election the party had 'lost its way and turned into a pale imitation of itself. This was not a simple left/right divide; both those on the left and those on the right of our party were yearning for Labour to be more radical, more confident and, above all, more ambitious.' All true, no doubt, but a formulation that avoided placing himself anywhere on the scale.

In some ways, the fact that he was not aligned to a faction was an advantage for Starmer. 'While he is grounded in Labour tradition, he has not been grounded in the internecine warfare of Blairites versus Brownites,' notes one who knows the party well at all levels. '"Which position did you take in Ed versus David [Miliband], and how did you handle the 1988 presidency election in the National Union of Students?" He's avoided all that stuff.' For some, it also signalled a degree of political deftness. 'People thought he was inexperienced, but what he was actually being was cautious in very choppy political waters, which is what you'd expect from a sophisticated politician who doesn't share Jeremy Corbyn's view of the world,' says a senior colleague. At the same time, it left some colleagues scratching their heads. 'Keir has an incredibly impressive background,' said another MP at the time. 'But we still don't know what he thinks about stuff generally yet.'

The working assumption was that Starmer belonged somewhere in the amorphous soft left of the party, but some in the leader's team concluded that he was more moderate than that, and probably somewhere to the right of Ed Miliband. Despite this ideological divergence, Starmer and Corbyn got on reasonably well. They developed a functional working relationship, though interactions tended to be professional rather than pally. Both disliked confrontations. The Corbyn team was impressed with Starmer's discipline in sticking to lines that had been agreed by the shadow Cabinet.

This benign judgement became embarrassingly public when a document came to light in which Labour MPs were assessed for their fidelity to the socialist project and its leader. Ever alert to nuances of loyalty, opposition and betrayal, Corbyn allies had drawn up a list placing colleagues in one of five categories: Core Group, Core Group Plus, Neutral But Not Hostile, Core Group Negative and Hostile.

Some front-bench figures, including Chief Whip Rosie Winterton and shadow Minister for Mental Health Luciana Berger, were labelled Hostile, as was Sadiq Khan, by now the party's mayoral candidate. Starmer, however, found himself listed as Core Group Plus, placing him – at least in the eyes of the dossier's author – in Corbyn's loyal outer circle.

There were competing versions of how the list came to see the light of day. One was that several filing cabinets were left in a parliamentary corridor after a clear-out in the leader's office; another was that the document was left in a Westminster pub. A spokesman for Corbyn denied reports that the list had been drawn up by the leader's staff, but MPs on the list told reporters they believed it was 'kosher'.

Whatever its provenance, the list was a gift for Cameron, who had a field day at Labour's expense at Prime Minister's Questions. It was also a source of amusement to Corbyn critics on the Labour benches (John Spellar pinned a 'Core Group Negative' badge to his lapel, and another MP demanded an immediate upgrade to Hostile). The fact that it had diverted attention onto Labour's divisions away from the government's travails infuriated many in the party.

But the episode also demonstrated how adeptly Starmer had managed to gain the trust of the Corbyn operation without fully sharing its objectives. The dynamics of that relationship would be critical in the aftermath of the political earthquake that followed soon after.

CHAPTER 11

'AS DEMOCRATS, WE IN THE LABOUR PARTY HAVE TO ACCEPT THE RESULT'

Seventeen months after his arrival in Parliament, Keir Starmer found himself at the forefront of a debate that would for more than three years dominate not just politics but, it often seemed, much of national life. Its outcome would change British politics for ever.

Together with most of his party, Starmer supported the 2015 legislation for a referendum on Britain's EU membership in the early stages of its passage through Parliament. He abstained at the final reading, again in common with other Labour MPs. (Jeremy Corbyn, at that time campaigning for the Labour leadership, abstained throughout – even though, perhaps tellingly, he had voted for rebel Conservative backbencher David Nuttall's motion calling for a referendum in 2011.)

By the time the campaign got under way, Corbyn was leader and Starmer had taken up his post as a shadow Home Office Minister. Starmer's contributions to the campaign therefore focused on crime and security: he argued that EU criminal justice measures were crucial in the fight against organised crime, people trafficking, cybercrime and terrorism. He took the opportunity of restating his credentials as a former DPP. 'Anybody who's been involved in this on a practical, operational level recognises the risks here,' he told *The Independent*.

'It's a risk to the safety of people in this country.' Such warnings were dismissed as part of the Remainers' 'Project Fear' by the Leave campaign, which argued that co-operation with agencies in other countries would continue outside the EU, and that Europe's open borders were in fact the bigger threat to Britain's security. Whatever the merits of Starmer's argument, they did not prevail.

'Devastating result,' he tweeted the morning after the referendum. 'Now we must face the future with united determination to mitigate the impacts and heal the deep fractures in our society.' For Starmer and a large number of Labour colleagues, that future had to begin with the removal of their party leader.

Corbyn's performance during the campaign had been a lamentable disappointment to many on the Remain side, who felt his support had been half-hearted at best. He took little part in day-to-day campaigning and in his interventions seemed more preoccupied with the EU's need to reform than with its achievements. Twelve days before the referendum, on the Channel 4 show *The Last Leg*, Corbyn was asked how passionate he was about staying in the EU on a scale of one to ten. His matter-of-fact reply – 'seven, seven and a half' – epitomised his lukewarm approach.

Looking at Corbyn's history, his critics ought not to have been surprised. As a back-bench MP Corbyn often criticised the EU, denouncing a 'European bureaucracy totally unaccountable to anybody', opposing the Maastricht and Lisbon Treaties and declaring that he voted against joining the European Economic Community in the 1975 referendum. Even as recently as 2015, he had told the final hustings meeting of the Labour leadership contest that he did not rule out backing a Leave campaign if workers' rights and environmental protections were watered down. Remain campaigners worried that this ambivalence had communicated itself to Labour voters, and with some justification: on the day, Labour supporters were less likely to turn out than Tories, and more than a third of them voted to leave.

Corbyn's failure to rally Labour voters to the cause in greater numbers infuriated other senior figures in the party, but it also terrified them. Following David Cameron's resignation as Prime Minister the morning after the referendum, many feared a snap general election. With a leader so demonstrably unable to mobilise Labour support at the ballot box, they reasoned, the prospects for such a contest were not good. Cameron was eventually replaced the following month by Theresa May.

That weekend, Corbyn sacked his shadow Foreign Secretary, Hilary Benn, when the news broke that he was encouraging colleagues to demand a change of leadership. Nineteen further shadow Cabinet members quit, along with a number of more junior frontbenchers, including Starmer.

His letter to Corbyn is worth reproducing in full, since it reveals perhaps more than he intended:

Dear Jeremy

It is with deep regret that I am writing to resign as shadow Immigration Minister.

As soon as you were elected leader, I recognised and respected the mandate you had from members and undertook to serve and support you. To that end, I accepted the shadow Immigration post and have worked hard to deliver results for you and the party.

I have never spoken out publicly against you and I do not intend to do so now.

However, the EU referendum result was catastrophic for the UK, for our communities and for the next generation. We now face a very different future.

The challenge of leadership in this context is very different to the challenge only a year ago. It is clear that we need a much louder voice on the critical issues of renegotiating the UK's place in the world and mitigating the damaging impact of our exit from the EU.

In the last few days I have maintained my support for you, notwithstanding my reservations. However, the resignations across the shadow Cabinet and the shadow frontbench yesterday materially change this. It is simply untenable now to suggest that we can offer an effective opposition without a change of leader.

In the circumstances, I am duty bound to resign.

I do so with great sadness and deep regret.

Yours sincerely,

Keir Starmer QC MP

At first glance the letter seems simply polite. Whether out of courtesy or in order not to burn bridges, he has avoided being unduly or offensively critical: unfortunately, new circumstances mean we need a new leader. But on closer reading, the letter is non-committal to a fault. Starmer took the shadow home affairs job because he respected Corbyn's mandate, not because he endorsed what he was trying to do (not that he would ever say so 'publicly'). He had reservations but maintained his support, which he was ultimately withdrawing because all these other resignations made the situation untenable. In other words, he had not joined the front-bench team because he supported Corbyn, but he had not left it because he didn't. (He later offered another explanation: he resigned because of Corbyn's suggestion the day after the referendum that the government immediately invoke Article 50 of the Lisbon Treaty, the mechanism to begin the two-year departure process – a position on which Labour soon backtracked. 'When he said that, I felt he was in a fundamentally different place from me in terms of how we fight for the future of our country,' Starmer said.)[1]

The next day, Labour MPs overwhelmingly passed a motion of no confidence in Corbyn, who declared the vote 'unconstitutional' and refused to resign. In the subsequent leadership contest, Starmer was one of 172 MPs to nominate Owen Smith, who had resigned as shadow Work and Pensions Secretary after the referendum and emerged as the sole anti-Corbyn candidate. In a prelude to the long debate that would follow, Smith said that as leader he would press for a further public vote on the terms of Britain's EU exit.

But if Labour MPs longed to see the back of Corbyn, party members felt the opposite: at the end of July, they re-elected him with a landslide 62 per cent of the vote. With the leader clearly at odds with most of his parliamentary party, a long summer of infighting ensued.

Eager to build a team that could offer some semblance of competence and unity, Corbyn and his advisers – and especially his close ally, shadow Chancellor John McDonnell – were keen to have Starmer back in a high-profile position. Encouraged by the low-key nature of his resignation and the absence of hostility in his letter, they began to sound him out about the idea of joining the shadow Cabinet.

During the negotiations, which took place in August, it emerged that Starmer had two potential career moves in mind. One was to take over as shadow Home Secretary following Burnham's departure from the front bench to stand as Mayor of Greater Manchester. The other was to become shadow Brexit Secretary. The latter job was confirmed in the reshuffle that September.

As the leader of a pro-EU party, the Eurosceptic Corbyn had good reason to want an ardent Remainer in the Brexit post. 'The Corbyn political operation was smart enough to understand that it was leading a seriously Remain party, and it had a seriously pro-Remain spokesperson in Keir,' says one experienced Labour Kremlinologist. 'And that was a big advantage to them because he could shield them from everything they thought privately. They wanted him out there sending pro-Remain mood music.'

'I think without question it was a deliberate appointment,' agrees a well-placed former MP. 'That's not something you do accidentally. He [Corbyn] was helping tie his own hands so he didn't have to make any decisions. All the way through, Corbyn's strategy was to sit on the fence.'

The situation also presented Starmer with a big decision: should he remain on the backbenches or get back in the game by joining the team of a leader whom he had recently judged unsuited to the challenge of the times and unable to offer effective opposition? Unlike most of the colleagues who had quit in June, he decided to return. 'Brexit is so important, it would have been neglect of duty to simply sit it out,' he later explained.[2] With Corbyn re-elected, 'The right thing to do is to get behind the leader, and do the best job you can, and that's all I'm trying to do.'

But another reason was in play. Starmer told colleagues at the time that he believed the next leader of the Labour Party would come from within the shadow Cabinet – a line which caused resentment among some former frontbenchers, who felt it was a mistake to legitimise Corbyn's leadership. 'He realised that he was trading a little bit of credibility to get into the shadow Cabinet to try and influence the future,' says one who knows him. 'He'd weighed it up.'

Those around Corbyn were also in no doubt that this would have been part of Starmer's calculation: the successor would be chosen by a largely Corbyn-supporting membership who would look more favourably on a figure who had tried to make the project work than one who stayed on the sidelines. Indeed, Diane Abbott, whose position on Brexit was close to Starmer's, distrusted his motives and would regularly warn the Corbyn team that he was out to topple the leader.

(She would later confirm this in a BBC interview, saying she had been 'suspicious of him' and believed 'he had a project of his own to become leader of the Labour Party. I blame his mother for calling him Keir'.)[3]

One who knows the party well doubts that Starmer will have found the decision very hard:

> The mandate that Corbyn had after 2016 was so extraordinary that everyone just had to make do and make the best of this that they could. The most interesting politics to be found in the Labour Party at that point, outside the Corbynistas themselves, were to be found in those people who instead of waging unrelenting war on Team Corbyn were trying to understand the membership, understand the party, work out where the crossover between their position and the members lay and chart a course that could connect that together and bring Labour together.

And if personal ambition also played a part, that was no bad thing. This person continues: 'I think in recent years the Labour Party would have welcomed a little more ambition in its leaders.'

Even so, Starmer could not quite bring himself to voice unambiguous support for the man at the helm. Asked by Andrew Marr the weekend after the reshuffle if he thought Corbyn would make a good Prime Minister, the new shadow Brexit Secretary replied: 'Well look, we've had a leadership election, Jeremy won that, we accept it and we respect it.' That word again. 'Of course we want a Labour government, of course we want to support Jeremy to that end. He's won the membership, he now needs to win the country – he knows that, we know that and we need to work together on that.'

At the same time, Starmer was not entirely trusted by the Corbyn team. Sir David Lidington, who as Chancellor of the Duchy of

Lancaster in Theresa May's Cabinet was closely involved in the Brexit saga, remembers inviting Starmer to his office.

> I wanted to have a chat, to try and see, you know, 'where are you coming from on this?' But he wasn't allowed to come and see me one to one. They sent minders with him. He came into my office on the Upper Ministerial Corridor with Seumas Milne and somebody else, who sat there. It was like having a meeting with the Russian ambassador when he's got somebody from the FSB in the embassy to take a note of what he says. I saw Seumas sort of looking from one to the other of us, and I always felt that when the revolution came, in Seumas's mind, both of us were going in front of the firing squad, it was just a question of sequence.[4]

Starmer's opening move in his new job was to write to David Davis, the Secretary of State for Exiting the European Union, demanding that Parliament be given a vote on the government's Brexit plan before triggering Article 50. The letter also contained no fewer than 170 questions about ministers' intentions – a question for every day until 31 March 2017, the government's Article 50 target date, which suggests that the missive was more a political ploy than a genuine attempt to throw light on the subject. The range and detail of the questions ('In the event that there are "transitional arrangements" whereby the UK retains access to the single market while negotiating a longer-term trade deal, who will represent the UK at meetings of the WTO during that interim period, and how will the government ensure UK interests are protected if we are still being represented by the EU?'; 'What assessment has the government made of the fiscal impact of the different options it has considered for managing migration from the EU to the UK, and will it publish that assessment?'; 'Following Britain's departure from the EU, will football players with European passports be subject to the same work permit rules as currently apply to all other overseas players?') also signalled Starmer's strategy of bringing forensic, lawyerly scrutiny to bear upon every aspect of Brexit. Or, to his detractors, it was a sign that he would use questions on minutiae as a pretext for obstructing the effort to give effect to the referendum result.

Starmer's prosecutorial approach was rewarded with an early victory in Parliament. Davis had argued that getting the best deal with the EU would mean keeping the UK's negotiating position confidential, but the Scottish Nationalists, the Liberal Democrats and a number of Conservatives had supported Starmer's demand that MPs be allowed to vote on the government's opening terms. While the referendum result had to be accepted and respected, he told the Commons: 'That is not the end of the matter. The next question, and one that is increasingly pressing is: on what terms should we leave the EU? That question was not on the ballot paper.' The argument was resisted by Brexiteers – former Conservative leader Iain Duncan Smith urged Davis to 'resist the temptation to take advice from a second-rate lawyer who doesn't even understand the parliamentary process', a jibe for which he later apologised – but ministers judged that on this question, opinion in Parliament was with Starmer. The government accepted a motion that 'there should be a full and transparent debate on the government's plan for leaving the EU' and that MPs must be 'able properly to scrutinise that plan for leaving the EU before Article 50 is invoked', though in a way that respected the referendum result and did not undermine the government's negotiating position.

Pro-Europeans quickly decided they had found their champion. Laudatory media profiles began to appear, hailing Starmer as 'Britain's last Remaining hope' and 'the real Leader of the Opposition'. At a private event in Parliament, Starmer was seen to wince when someone greeted him as 'the man who'll make sure we stay in the EU'. The government benches also knew they were in for a hard time: 'You can't pretend he's not a serious person,' remarked a Conservative MP. At a time when the government had only a slim majority and many Tories were worried about Theresa May's plans, the shadow Brexit Secretary had become one of the most consequential political figures in the country.

The role of the Commons – and, by extension, the influence of the shadow Brexit Secretary – were further enhanced in January 2017, when, in a case brought by investment fund manager Gina Miller, the Supreme Court ruled that the government could not trigger Article 50 without authority from Parliament. It fell to Starmer to respond to the Bill the government subsequently introduced, which he conceded was 'very difficult' for the Labour Party. 'We lost the referendum,' he solemnly intoned.

> Yes, the result was close … Yes, technically the referendum is not legally binding. But the result was not technical; it was deeply political, and politically the notion that the referendum was merely a consultation exercise to inform Parliament holds no water … Had the outcome been to remain, we would have expected the result to be honoured, and that cuts both ways … as democrats we in the Labour Party have to accept the result. It follows that the Prime Minister should not be blocked from starting the Article 50 negotiations.

Starmer, along with Corbyn and most of his party, voted with the government to allow the Brexit process to begin, but not before extracting another concession from ministers: a commitment that the final agreement with the EU would have to be approved by both Houses of Parliament with a 'meaningful vote' – a phrase coined by Starmer – before it was concluded. With the government having also agreed to publish an official document setting out its plans, the shadow Brexit Secretary declared another success for his attritional approach.

'Just to be clear,' he told the Commons,

> nagging away, pushing votes and making the argument over three months, we have got a white paper, and it is important. Nagging away and making the arguments, we have got commitments about reporting back. Nagging away and making the arguments, we have got a commitment to the vote at the end of the exercise.

According to Starmer, this demonstrated how 'by chipping away and arguing away, we are making progress on accountability and scrutiny'. As would become clearer in the months that followed, 'nagging away' was not universally regarded as a laudable pursuit; one person's accountability and scrutiny looks to another like obstruction and delay.

With the Brexit process officially under way, attention began to focus on the terms of Britain's withdrawal and the substance of the country's future relationship with the EU. In her Lancaster House speech in January, setting out her negotiating priorities, Theresa May had ruled out membership of the single market and customs union, with no jurisdiction for the European Court of Justice, and declared that if the EU was not prepared to reach what the government considered an agreement, Britain would leave without one: 'No deal is better than a bad deal.'

In a speech of his own at Chatham House at the end of March, Starmer set out six tests that any deal would have to meet before Labour would support it. The agreement would have to ensure a 'strong and collaborative' future relationship with the EU; deliver the 'exact same benefits' as membership of the single market and customs union; ensure the 'fair management of migration'; defend 'rights and protections and prevent a race to the bottom'; protect national security and 'our capacity to tackle cross-border crime'; and 'deliver for all regions and nations of the UK'.

But while Starmer claimed that his tests were intended to protect 'core progressive values', others pointed out that one in particular was designed to be unachievable: it was, almost by definition, impossible that Britain could enjoy the 'exact same benefits' outside the single market as it did as a member. This observation was not confined to commentators and opponents: it was shared by Labour's international trade spokesman, Barry Gardiner, who, at a private event for a think tank a few months later, cheerfully declared it to be 'bollocks'.[5] Labour knew very well that

> we cannot have the exact same benefits and actually it would have
> made sense – because it was the Tories that said they were going to
> secure the exact same benefits – and our position should have been
> to say they have said they are going to secure the exact same benefits
> and we are going to hold them to that standard.

Starmer's relationship with Gardiner was fractious at the best of times. Gardiner was always instinctively closer to Corbyn's approach to Brexit than Starmer's, and their overlapping responsibilities had led to something of a demarcation dispute at the time of Starmer's appointment. The two scrapped regularly in meetings. Colleagues recall that on one trip to Brussels, the pair squabbled all the way out and all the way back, continuing their row in the pub afterwards.

Now Starmer was furious. He complained to Corbyn, who duly took the miscreant Gardiner to task ('We've had a conversation with him. It's quite clear he does support our strategy,' Corbyn later asserted). The shadow Brexit Secretary arguably had good reason to be cross. A form of words emphasising collaboration, rights and fairness was supposed to be something that any Labour MP could sign up to. The six tests had been designed not just to give Labour licence to vote against any deal that might emerge but to hold together a parliamentary party that was almost as divided on the issue as the Conservatives.

It was not the first occasion on which colleagues had raised Starmer's ire. He had been incensed when, in November 2016, McDonnell had said in a speech that 'Labour accepts the referendum result as the voice of the majority, and we must embrace the enormous opportunities to reshape our country that Brexit has opened for us' – a much more positive line than that agreed by the shadow Cabinet's Brexit subcommittee. Since the referendum, senior Labour figures had tried Starmer's patience by airing starkly conflicting views on practically all aspects of Brexit, including immigration and free movement, the future trading relationship and the desirability of a second public vote.

The party was forced to clarify its position when Theresa May unexpectedly called an early general election for 8 June 2017. May's plan had been to capitalise on the Tories' double-digit poll leads and expand her majority in Parliament in readiness for the forthcoming battle over the terms of Brexit. Her gamble was that former Labour supporters who had voted Leave in the referendum would swing behind the Tories as the only party fully committed to honouring the result.

Labour refused to accept her strategy. The party's manifesto promised that a Labour government would take Britain out of the EU and would 'seek to unite the country around a Brexit deal that works for every community in Britain'. They would replace Conservative plans with 'fresh negotiating priorities that have a strong emphasis on retaining the benefits of the single market and the customs union'. EU nationals living in Britain would have their rights guaranteed immediately, but freedom of movement would end.

Starmer was at pains to emphasise that Brexit itself was not at stake in the election. In an interview early in the campaign, he said Labour could not 'look like we are trying to rub out the result of the referendum'. Though he had wanted to remain, 'I accept the referendum was a referendum that was for real ... I'm not prepared now for the Labour Party not to genuinely accept the result. We asked for a decision and we got it.'[6]

All this made it difficult for May to sustain the argument that the election was all about defending the referendum decision. With both main parties apparently committed to going through with Brexit, voters focused on other issues – not least the Tories' hurriedly conceived plan to reform funding for social care, which prompted a mid-campaign U-turn that called into question May's claim to offer 'strong and stable leadership'.

Starmer spent most of the campaign knocking on doors with Labour candidates in marginal constituencies, where he claimed to find little discussion of Brexit. 'It's come up far less than I had thought it would, and that's across the country,' he reflected during a stop in the Midlands. 'It was billed as a Brexit election: in the end, it's an election that's turned into "What sort of Britain do you want to live in?" And therefore there's a lot of talk about the health service, about public services, about tax – about the basic deal between government and people.'[7]

However, Starmer was notably circumspect about the Labour manifesto as a whole, with its programme of nationalisation, tax hikes and spending increases. 'I think what's really important about this manifesto', he said,

is that it's opened a space for an honest discussion about the investment we need in infrastructure, in people, in skills, in the health service, in public services, and it's set out what we need to pay for it. That's a debate that I think we've all shied away from for a very long time in all political parties. And that's a debate that needs to be had.[8]

If May's judgement that a bigger majority would be needed to get a Brexit deal through Parliament was ultimately proved right, her 2017 gamble failed to pay off. Far from boosting her majority, the voters removed it altogether, returning a hung parliament with the Conservatives as the largest party, and forcing the Prime Minister into a deal with Northern Ireland's Democratic Unionists to keep the government in place. Labour gained an extra thirty seats, strengthening Starmer's hand in marshalling the opponents of May's Brexit plans.

* * *

As if he did not have enough to occupy him, after the election Starmer considered topping up his earnings once again with another part-time job in the legal world. He spoke to Mishcon de Reya, the law firm that had successfully represented Gina Miller over Article 50, about resuming the advisory role for which he had been paid £4,500 a month on top of his parliamentary salary until joining the shadow Cabinet the previous October. The firm confirmed talks were taking place, saying Starmer's 'wide experience and previous association with the firm would enable him to play a key and unique role in shaping the work of the academy, which leads new thinking and develops the potential of everyone in the firm'.[9]

The disclosure led to questions from Tory MP James Cleverly, who raised the possibility of a conflict of interest, given the firm's involvement in cases surrounding Brexit and the likelihood that Starmer 'will be personally involved with drafting and speaking on legislative amendments' on Britain's EU departure. Starmer's recent appointment to the Privy Council would give him access to confidential government briefings. The day after the news broke, Starmer decided he had enough on his plate after all, telling the firm he was grateful for their interest but 'given my other commitments, I have decided not to further the discussions'.

*   *   *

With attention largely focused on other issues, the Brexit policy in Labour's manifesto had been enough to get them through the election, but it did not end the ambiguities in the party's position. In the weeks following the election there was confusion over the single market and the customs union, with Starmer contradicting Corbyn and McDonnell by holding out the possibility of continued membership after Britain's EU withdrawal.

In a sign that Starmer was beginning to win the internal arguments within the shadow Cabinet, he announced at the end of August that Labour would seek a transitional deal with the EU on the existing terms of membership: 'That means we would seek to remain in a customs union with the EU and within the single market during this period. It means we would abide by the common rules of both.'[10] In her Florence speech the following month, Theresa May set out her own plan for an implementation period in which Britain would remain in the single market and customs union for two years. Starmer's proposal went further, saying this phase should be 'as short as possible, but as long as is necessary' – which suggested that under Labour, Britain could be following Brussels rules and paying into the EU budget for years after its departure in March 2019 – and that remaining permanently in a customs union with the EU was a 'possible end destination' for Labour. The party's uneasy truce was ratified when its autumn conference endorsed the policy. But as official negotiations with the EU intensified, the government's travails put Labour's internal disagreements in the shade.

There is no need to repeat here the long and tortuous battle within the government ranks that led to the Chequers compromise, the sub-sequent Cabinet resignations and the eventual conclusion of the With-drawal Agreement that was put before Parliament early in 2019. Three developments are more pertinent to us: the forces most hostile to Brexit winning the upper hand within Labour; the blocking of Theresa May's deal; and the ultimate outcome for Britain and Europe. Starmer's role was pivotal in all three.

In January 2018, the shadow Cabinet's Brexit subcommittee met to discuss a proposal that the party should support a permanent customs union with the EU. Starmer had been advocating the policy internally for several weeks and had presented a paper on the issue to the leader's office. Corbyn's team were worried that the idea would tie Britain too closely to the EU and look to Leave voters like a further dilution of Labour's commitment to honour the referendum result. At the meet-ing, to Starmer's surprise, participants were given numbered copies of an alternative paper aimed at deferring the issue and rejecting a Norway-style model which would leave the UK as a rule-taker and therefore fail to acknowledge voters' wish to 'take back control'. When Corbyn began to read aloud, Starmer interrupted, raging that the new paper was an insult to him and his team and had been 'sprung on us with no discussion, no consultation, no prior notice'. He would not be willing to defend this position in the media, he said.

'Jeremy started speaking, and Keir just said "enough", this was completely outrageous,' said one who was present.[11] Starmer was so incensed that some in the room feared he might resign. 'He looked close to telling them to shove it,' said another witness. 'I think Jeremy was slightly surprised at how angry Keir was.'

Others present backed Starmer's approach, and at the end of the meeting the leader's office paper was quietly collected and never seen again. A compromise was brokered whereby the leader would go along with Starmer on customs provided the policy also called for Britain to be exempt from certain single market rules on competition and state aid – rules which Starmer supported but Corbyn had always disliked.

The following month, Corbyn announced in a speech at a car factory in Coventry that Labour would seek to negotiate 'a new comprehensive UK–EU customs union to ensure that there are no tariffs with Europe and to help avoid any need for a hard border in Northern Ireland', dependent on Britain 'being able to negotiate agreement of new trade deals in our national interest'. At the same time, 'We cannot be held back inside or outside the EU from taking the steps we need to support cutting-edge industries and local business and stop the tide of privatisation and outsourcing, or from preventing employers being able to import cheap agency labour to undercut existing pay and conditions'. The deal was sealed.

The episode was just one flashpoint in a continuous tussle between the shadow Brexit Secretary and the team around the leader. A colleague recalls that Starmer would regularly 'grind them down with utter, deep application of logic, challenging a position and dissecting it with laser-beam analysis. Not just the forensic barrister but very deep drilling down into policy heft.'

Resisting the influence of more Brexit-friendly figures like Unite general secretary Len McCluskey, party chairman Ian Lavery, shadow Cabinet Office Minister Jon Trickett and senior Corbyn aides Karie Murphy and Seumas Milne became an unrelenting task. 'He'd get Jeremy in the room to agree a position, and then Jeremy's people would unpick it over the next few days, and he'd have to get Jeremy back in the room,' says one close observer. 'The fact that he got in the room in the first place is a testament to the fact that he just wouldn't relent. He was very, very patient and resilient. You've got to give him credit for the political grind, which few do give him credit for.'

Close Corbyn allies, on the other hand, felt Starmer sometimes irritated colleagues with his lawyerly approach and tendency to intellectual arrogance, often giving the impression that he felt he was the only one who really understood the nuts and bolts of the issue. Some also felt Starmer tried to run Brexit policy almost as a parallel operation: rather than working collaboratively, he would stay in a bubble with his staff and feed into the wider team only when necessary. He was also close to Simon Coveney, the Irish Foreign Minister, whom he consulted regularly on Brexit policy. Despite this somewhat semi-detached approach, however, members of the Corbyn team doubt that Starmer ever really came close to resignation. They reasoned that he would not readily have relinquished such a prime spot within Labour's Remain-backing majority and the broader liberal establishment, especially given his evident ambitions in the longer game.

Some believe Starmer's thinking on Brexit could have been influenced to some degree by his membership of the Trilateral Commission, a non-governmental group which serves as a talking shop for liberal internationalists. Founded in 1973 by the American banker David Rockefeller, it seeks to foster co-operation between Europe, North America and the Asia Pacific region. In April 2018, Starmer was listed as a member of the Trilateral Commission along with his friend David Miliband, the former Foreign Secretary who is now the handsomely paid head of the International Rescue Committee, a New York-based charity. During that year, the Trilateral Commission held meetings in Singapore, Beijing, California and Ljubljana, though it is not clear which of these gatherings Starmer attended, if any. Some within Labour circles are suspicious of Starmer's association with the group, seeing it as a vehicle to promote the interests of international financial elites.

Once Labour's position on customs was agreed, there were efforts on the Labour benches to soften the party's position still further. One group of younger pro-European MPs, including Chuka Umunna and Chris Leslie, derisively dubbed 'the shinies' by more jaded colleagues, argued that Labour should support an amendment to the Brexit legislation committing the government to joining the European Economic Area (EEA), thus keeping Britain in the single market but obliging adherence to many EU rules, including free movement of people. The party split three ways on the issue, with ninety Labour MPs defying instructions to abstain when the issue came to Parliament. Many of Starmer's colleagues believed he, too, would have backed a form of continued single market membership if Corbyn had not been implacably opposed.

'Almost everybody in the Labour Party has a view on Brexit,' Starmer said that spring.[12] 'But almost no two people have the same view. They all give me their opinions all the time in texts, in emails, in one-to-one conversations, in groups.' While two thirds of Labour voters backed Remain, two thirds of Labour MPs represented seats that voted to leave, which inevitably led to differences of opinion. Starmer's view had been informed by his 'strong belief that we cannot allow the Labour Party to divide and break up on this issue. We have got to hold the party together, and of course that means there are huge challenges.'

That is not to say that the shadow Brexit Secretary was a neutral arbiter between the various Labour views. Those close to the leadership noted that whereas he had initially been disciplined in sticking to an agreed line, Starmer became bolder in pushing the boundaries of Labour's position as time wore on. This was particularly true when it came to the debate over a second referendum. Deputy leader Tom Watson had sparked excitement by remarking at the end of 2017 that while Labour had not called for another public vote, 'When you're in complex negotiations on behalf of the nation you shouldn't rule anything out.' Corbyn, asked about his colleague's observation, replied:

'He did indeed say that, but our position is that we are not advocating a second referendum.' When it was later put to him that he was not saying he would never support another ballot, he said: 'We are not calling for one either.'

At this stage, Starmer was publicly resistant to calls for a further vote. At a meeting of the Parliamentary Labour Party in January 2018, he told colleagues that while he understood why people argued for a second referendum, there were serious practical problems, as well as

something more fundamental than that. If we sit here as a party aspiring to govern then we have got to recognise that if we spend all that time looking back in grief about what many of us didn't want to happen, thinking, 'How do we rub it out?' then we are unable to do what we need to do, which is to fight for the [final deal] that reflects what we stand for.

In a talk at University College London a few weeks later, Starmer went further, telling students that having campaigned to get people to vote in the referendum,

I'm not going to go back to those people and say, 'Now you've given me a result I didn't want I'm going to ignore it.' I think that would be really, really dangerous ... I think it's absolutely right that if we do have a referendum we abide by the result.

The official line, reiterated by McDonnell, was that 'all options are open' but that Labour's preferred route was to win a general election and change Brexit policy from within government. In March, Owen Smith breached this compromise position with an article in *The Guardian* arguing that 'we have the right to ask if Brexit remains the right choice for the country. And to ask, too, that the country has a vote on whether to accept the terms and true costs of that choice once they are clear.' Smith's stance was applauded by pro-Remain Labour colleagues, and his immediate sacking from the shadow Cabinet failed to end the debate.

A statement in July from the Unite union, Labour's biggest donor, that it was 'open to the possibility' of a popular vote depending on the political circumstances was interpreted as a further move towards support for another referendum ('Travel inside the Labour Party on this issue is only in one direction,' observed the independent People's Vote campaign eagerly). Later in the summer Barry Gardiner went off-script again: telling people they were 'stupid enough' to make the wrong decision 'undermines the whole principle of democracy in this country', he argued.[13] This drew another swift response from Starmer, who explained again that another referendum remained a possibility. If the deal was voted down, 'Parliament then decides what happens next and, in those circumstances, in my experience in the last few years, keep your options on the table, not off the table.'[14]

By the time London Mayor Sadiq Khan called in September for 'a public vote on any deal or a vote on a no-deal, alongside the option of staying in the EU', pressure was growing among grassroots members for an official shift in Labour's policy. Constituency parties and unions submitted more than 100 motions for debate at the autumn conference calling for a second referendum.

Despite Corbyn's and McDonnell's cautious approach, Watson was outspoken in support, arguing that he and his boss had been elected in 2015 to give Labour back to its members: 'So if the people's party decide they want the people to have the final say on the deal, we have to respect the view of our members and we will go out and argue for it.'[15] A YouGov poll found that 86 per cent of Labour members wanted a referendum once negotiations were concluded.

The idea worried some Labour strategists, who feared such a policy would alienate Leave voters and Remainers who wanted to get Brexit over with. It would also give potential Conservative rebels in Parliament a reason to back May's deal.

After much backroom wrangling, including a Sunday night meeting lasting into the early hours, the party thrashed out a form of words the leadership could live with: 'If we cannot get a general election, Labour must support all options remaining on the table, including campaigning for a public vote.' Starmer, who was instrumental in persuading activists in the meeting to accept the compromise, subsequently regarded it as a point of honour not to allow any slippage from the referendum commitment.

Exactly what the public would be voting on the second time around was left deliberately vague. Michael Crick, then at *Channel 4 News*, says he thinks Starmer has never forgiven him for his relentless pursuit of a clearer position. 'I doorstepped him three days running, working out what fringe meetings he was doing, then waiting for him outside,' Crick recalls.[16]

One of the doorsteps lasted about two minutes, along corridors and up and down stairs, and he got increasingly annoyed, though he was under enormous pressure at the time. And after his big speech we followed him into a room where I genuinely didn't realise the press weren't allowed. I think he thought we were persecuting him. We weren't. We were just chasing what was the really big story that week – Labour and the second referendum. He's never been very helpful since then. His press team never return calls or emails.

As the conference unfolded over that week, Starmer's intervention was decisive. On the Monday morning, McDonnell told ITV's *Good Morning Britain* that any such referendum would determine 'whether you accept the deal or not, or whether you send people back to negotiate a proper deal', not whether to stay in the EU after all. This echoed McCluskey, who had said the previous day: 'The referendum shouldn't be on "Do you want to go back in the European Union?" The people have already decided on that.'

Starmer contradicted this, saying the motion did not tie Labour to any position on the question in a second referendum. To the consternation of Corbyn's office but the delight of delegates, the shadow Brexit Secretary underlined the message in his conference speech the following day. 'It is right that Parliament has the first say' on a Brexit deal, 'but if we need to break the impasse, our options must include campaigning for a public vote.' He then added a line that had not been cleared by the leader's office and did not appear in the official text: 'And nobody is ruling out Remain as an option.'

This was a defining moment. The new stance, coupled with the policy of remaining in a customs union, widened the gap between the government and opposition approaches to Brexit and set the backdrop for the political battle that would follow. The tumultuous ovation in the hall cemented Starmer's status as the hero of Labour's anti-Brexit activists. And his extemporised departure from the agreed line in the full glare of a party conference confirmed colleagues' suspicions that he saw himself as Labour's next leader.

CHAPTER 12

'IF YOU WANT TO FIGHT FOR REMAIN, VOTE LABOUR'

Back in Westminster, to the nation's mounting exasperation, combat over Brexit resumed. The shadow Brexit Secretary made his presence felt in the proceedings. Whether he was doing so in the name of constitutional accountability or to frustrate Britain's departure from the EU at every turn was in the eye of the beholder.

In the two and a half years between the referendum and the debates on Theresa May's deal, Starmer engaged the government in a long series of parliamentary skirmishes on subjects including but not limited to: the procedure for invoking Article 50; the need for and timing of a meaningful vote on the Withdrawal Agreement and the future relationship; demands for a white paper on the government's negotiating plan; the role of Parliament in the event of no deal being reached; the procedure for updating Parliament on the state of negotiations; ministers' powers under legislation to translate EU law into UK law; the wisdom of fixing Britain's exit date in statute; the process for transferring powers to devolved Parliaments and assemblies. Starmer also used an arcane procedure known as a Humble Address, under which Parliament could vote to compel publication of confidential papers. In this way he forced the government to release civil service assessments on the impact of Brexit on different sectors of the economy and the

Attorney General's legal advice to the government on the protocol to prevent a hard border in Northern Ireland in the absence of a deal.

The tactic caused some consternation in Downing Street, as well as grudging respect for Starmer's effective deployment of an unorthodox political weapon. 'He certainly pursued that as an instrument of opposition in an effective way,' says a former minister.

> We had numerous discussions in No. 10 about what we do about this because there weren't obvious precedents. And it wasn't hardliners in the Cabinet – the civil service was pretty miffed about the idea that it could be insisted that they produce information that they might regard as sensitive. So Keir was good on that.

In the Commons, ministers occasionally vented their frustration at what they saw as blocking tactics. Brexit Minister Steve Baker accused Labour of using a strategy of 'demoralisation and delay' as a ruse to overturn Brexit. David Davis complained that Starmer's speeches were 'becoming rather repetitive – they are always crowing and carping'. Davis's successor, Dominic Raab, dubbed Starmer 'the prince of process', always arguing about 'protocol and procedure' rather than the substance of Brexit itself. After another Starmer lecture on the shortcomings of the government's plans, Raab archly observed from the despatch box, 'I gently say to the opposition that it is not entirely clear that it is Labour's overriding objective to give effect to the referendum.'

Even the Speaker, John Bercow, found his patience tested. When, during the course of a lengthy speech, Starmer proposed to give examples of EU agencies of which he thought the UK should remain a member after Brexit, Bercow interjected:

> Well, not many and not for long. The hon. Gentleman is a learned,

celebrated and cerebral individual, and I do not want to interrupt him, but the convention is that the reply is normally half the length of the statement ... I was a bit concerned when he said 'some examples', particularly as he is a lawyer.

Sir David Lidington, who as Chancellor of the Duchy of Lancaster faced Starmer in the Commons on a number of occasions, including the debate over the Attorney General's advice ('Those favourite gigs when every other Cabinet minister is for some reason unable to get a mobile signal') says that although he found the shadow Brexit Secretary 'intellectually formidable', he did not feel under huge pressure: 'He was sharp, he would assemble his case and present it, but his style of speaking was somewhat low-key.'[1] Unlike figures such as John Smith and Robin Cook, whose demolition of the government over the arms-to-Iraq affair remains a landmark in the history of parliamentary oratory, Starmer was not able 'to summon up the combination of forensic technique and intellectual analysis *coupled* with an ability to express outrage and channel anger at the government ... He didn't really rouse his own side. There was a bit of going through the motions when they were giving him support.' This echoes comments from other observers that the ability to inspire an audience is not among his natural gifts.

Starmer resisted the criticism that his aim was to obstruct. 'Every time somebody raises a legitimate question, it is suggested that they are somehow frustrating or undermining the process,' he said when proposing his motion for publication of the government's economic impact assessments. But that works both ways: anyone trying to frustrate or undermine the process would of course say they were raising legitimate questions in the name of democratic scrutiny. Which was the real motive?

Lidington believes there was an element of both.

I think he genuinely wanted scrutiny. But this is classic opposition. Tony Blair did this incessantly. You call for an inquiry, a reasoned amendment to the second reading of a Bill. Call for a review! These are all ways to prevent the opposition from being caught on the hook and have things quoted against it: 'You voted for this or that four years ago.'

Accordingly, Labour was preparing to vote against May's agreement with the EU well before it was concluded in November 2018. Shadow Foreign Secretary Emily Thornberry had become the latest front-bencher to provoke Starmer's ire when she told a Chatham House event in March 2018 that the deal was likely to be so vague that Labour might end up supporting it: 'If past evidence of the last few months is anything to go on, it's going to be a "blah, blah, blah" divorce,' she said. 'If you hold up "blah, blah, blah" to the six tests, it will probably pass it.' Starmer was once again reported to be 'furious' about the deviation from the agreed line, which he insisted had not changed. The shadow Brexit Secretary was adamant that his party was prepared to oppose the deal, even though it would mean Labour MPs walking into the same lobby as hardline Tory Brexiteers.

From the moment it was tabled, the prospects of May's Withdrawal Agreement winning parliamentary approval looked slim. Initially scheduled for December 2018, the vote was postponed for over a month to allow the government to seek reassurances from the EU over the most contentious element, the Northern Ireland 'backstop'. This specified that in the absence of a future trade deal, the whole UK would remain in a single customs territory with the EU, and Northern Ireland would stay in some aspects of the single market. Though the arrangement was intended to be temporary while alternatives were agreed, the UK would not be able to leave the backstop without EU agreement. A statement from Brussels that the backstop scenario would in practice last for the shortest possible time was not enough to convince MPs, who on 15 January 2019 voted down the deal by 230 votes, the biggest government defeat for over a century. All but three Labour MPs voted against the agreement. Starmer declared during the debate that Labour believed the deal was not in the national interest: 'It does not come anywhere near to meeting our tests, it will make the country poorer and more divided and it will not protect jobs and the economy.'

By the end of March, the May deal had suffered two further heavy defeats. The EU had granted an extension to the Article 50 departure deadline to 12 April, but the prospects of agreement in Parliament by this time looked remote. The Withdrawal Agreement had been opposed both by Conservative MPs who thought it tied Britain too closely to the EU after Brexit and by others who wanted to remain more closely aligned; a move in either direction would risk losing support from one wing or the other. Labour was in a similar position, with some MPs eager to get Brexit over with and a much larger group wanting a second referendum. Parliament held a series of 'indicative votes' on a wide range of Brexit propositions – including a customs union, EEA membership, a confirmatory public vote and revocation of Article 50 in the event of no deal – with the intention of revealing what kind of Brexit proposition could find a majority. In a demonstration of the prevailing political gridlock, every one of them was rejected.

After a seven-hour Cabinet meeting on 2 April, May announced that she would seek a further Article 50 extension to 30 June and invited Corbyn to take part in cross-party talks in an attempt to agree a unified approach. Following an initial meeting between May and Corbyn in Downing Street, the talks were continued in the Cabinet Office by a wider team from each side.

Starmer led the Labour delegation, which included McDonnell;

shadow Business Secretary Rebecca Long-Bailey; shadow Environment Secretary Sue Hayman; and Corbyn advisers Seumas Milne and Andrew Fisher. They would arrive at the entrance in 70 Whitehall, rather than the door of No. 10, to be escorted to the meeting room. The government side was led by Lidington and included his special adviser James Wild; Theresa May's chief of staff Gavin Barwell and communications director Robbie Gibb; Greg Clark, the Business Secretary; Julian Smith, the Chief Whip; chief Brexit negotiator Olly Robbins; and Steve Barclay, who had become the government's third Brexit Secretary following the resignation of Dominic Raab over the May deal the previous November. The long meetings were sustained by means of tea, coffee, luxury shortbread and samosas.

The talks opened with some optimism. After the initial round, 'We thought, you know, they are taking this seriously,' recalls Lidington. Barwell later said he thought it was 'perfectly possible' that an agreement could be reached and that the Labour team 'contained people who you felt, privately, actually wanted Brexit to go ahead, and wanted to find a way of doing it, but without Labour's fingerprints being on it'.[2]

The potential for a settlement on the future trading relationship was a particular focus of attention. One proposal under discussion was to sign up to a customs union until the general election and then – on the basis that no parliament can bind its successor – have each party outline its policy in its manifesto. 'That could be an agreement,' says another who was present, chuckling in retrospect at its implausibility.

You could vote for a customs union in this parliament to get it over the line, but then by the point at which you were implementing it, you have a different policy. That was where we were heading. It's clutching at straws. It was a demonstration of just how flexible we were trying to be to deliver this thing.

The government team quickly discerned, however, that some of their interlocutors were more willing to compromise than others. While those in Corbyn's immediate team 'were sending out signals in body language at the table but also in back-channel conversations that they wanted a deal', Starmer was insistent that any deal had to include the government accepting a customs union and a second referendum.

'We made it clear that we were prepared to guarantee them time and a vote on the second referendum at both the committee and report stages,' says one who was on the government side of the table.

> We took the view that if we got a Withdrawal Implementation Bill through second reading, there were going to be amendments on a second referendum anyway, and if we tried procedural manoeuvrings to block them the Lords would stick them in and send them back in any case. So we offered that, and we thought that was a pretty big deal.
>
> But Keir basically said no, you've got to do it the other way round. You have to have the referendum commitment written into the Bill when you introduce it, and you can have a vote to take it out later on. There's absolutely no way we could have done that. So I certainly thought, 'This guy is not serious, he does not want an agreement on this. He thinks he can contrive a way to bring down the government and then to have a second referendum.'

(Not everyone in the Labour team was equally enamoured of a public vote at this stage, however. According to one participant, at a time when Starmer happened not to be in the room, 'There was one moment where John McDonnell, whose position changed over time during those meetings, basically said, "At this point, I'm going to raise a second referendum." After a pause, he said, "OK, that's that raised. I said I'd do it, and I've done it."')

Another who was present remembers that Starmer conducted himself

> incredibly professionally, politely and with this overriding narrative that he's seriously engaging in the talks with a view to finding an agreement. It was done in a very grown-up way. He manages to fake genuine agreement, basically. But then in all these meetings, they would eventually come round to the area of people's votes – confirmatory referendum, as they described it.

The government team pointed out that if Downing Street offered a second referendum, they would have a good chance of passing the deal as it stood, with no need to compromise on the substance. 'But what they wanted was for us to make all these concessions, and at the end of that put that to a second referendum.'

If some on the government side doubted the sincerity of Starmer's approach to the talks, one incident crystallised their suspicions. As Barwell later recounted:

> We had an initial meeting, where we basically said to them, 'Download to us the things that would need to change for you to be able to live with this deal.' I was the secretary to the thing, so I sat there scribbling all these things down. We came back to them and said, 'Right, here's our first draft of what an agreement would look like.' They said, 'We don't like this, we don't like that, change this to that.' So we came back with a revised version. Keir picked it up and looked at it and said, 'Well, I don't like this wording on customs at all.' I was like, 'We just literally put in the wording on customs from Jeremy Corbyn's letter. You've just criticised your own language.' He looked slightly po-faced.[3]

When Barclay mentioned the incident in a Commons debate later in the year, Starmer denied it had taken place and demanded that the minister withdraw the allegation, which he duly did ('The shadow Secretary of State and I have always conducted our debates in the House with great courtesy, so in that spirit, of course I withdraw that'). But others who had been present in the negotiating room insist that it happened. 'Memories do get blurred with time, but certainly I can remember that meeting,' says Lidington. 'It's 100 per cent true,' says Gibb, for whom the event demonstrated 'the break between rhetoric and reality' that he perceived with Starmer.[4]

Reports that would appear in the media after each meeting were another powerful example of this. The two spokesmen worked together on how to communicate the progress of the talks to journalists. 'What we put out I would run past Seumas first, and Seumas would run what they were going to say past me,' Gibb recalls. But

> there were briefings to Norman Smith on the *Today* programme saying that the cross-party talks are going nowhere. I'd get a call from the BBC saying, 'I believe the talks are on the verge of collapse.' Well, who have you spoken to? 'Can't say. It's official sources.' It was completely disorientating. So I'd phone up Seumas Milne and say, 'What the hell's that about?' And he said, 'Well, it's not us briefing it.' What I think happened is that Seumas Milne and the leader's team were doing their best to keep discipline on their side. So the question is, who spoke to the journalists?

Gibb is convinced the negative briefings came from Starmer or his team, and that the mixed messages highlighted conflicting attitudes within the Labour delegation to the talks themselves. While with Starmer 'it was very clear that there was never any intention of supporting anything', Corbyn's office wanted to get a deal done 'because, well, you can argue about what their attitude to Brexit was, but at the very least I don't think they minded. They wanted to make progress. So there was obviously a division at the very heart of Labour during this period.' Lidington too sensed that 'the Corbynistas were much more likely to have been willing to do a deal' than Starmer. Indeed, some pro-Remain Labour MPs feared that Corbyn would ultimately whip them to back a deal they disliked and credit Starmer with preventing such an outcome.

Some who saw the process from the Labour side also believe that Starmer was the most deal-resistant of the party's negotiators, and that he prized the possibility of reversing Brexit through a second referendum above the chance to achieve a soft Brexit on negotiated terms. Other senior Labour figures tell it differently, however. One says that while Starmer doubted a deal was likely, 'he thought it was his duty to try and get one. They did go in with pretty earnest endeavour, and in their minds, they were prepared to defy the very strong Remainers in the Parliamentary Labour Party if they could have found a consensus that they thought was progressive.' But he soon decided that no such consensus would emerge:

> I think he was genuinely surprised just how little developed the thinking was about what an agreement might look like when they walked in the room. He was almost willing Theresa May on to get a team in place that could give Labour something where they could honour this mandate and the country could move on, but in the end they couldn't get there.

A key component of any compromise was a group of Labour MPs torn between their Leave-voting constituencies and their party's unwillingness to back a Tory-negotiated Brexit. According to one former Labour

MP, Corbyn's hope had always been that colleagues on his own benches would vote for the deal of their own accord in big enough numbers to allow it to pass without the party's official backing: 'Corbyn basically wanted to be in a position where it was all voted through but no one could accuse him of having voted for a Tory deal. He could sit on the fence; Starmer would be representing the Remainer majority of the Labour membership, and the MPs would vote it through.'

At one point in 2019, in order to give Labour MPs the cover they would need to back May's agreement, it was proposed that McCluskey would write a letter saying the referendum had to be honoured. This would have served as 'a nod and a wink' to backbenchers wanting to vote in line with their constituents' wishes. Had it come to a genuine choice between May's Withdrawal Agreement and a no-deal Brexit, according to one MP, 'a carefully worded letter from McCluskey would have emboldened some people to vote for a deal in that cliff-edge scenario, without any question'. There was even discussion within the Labour hierarchy about offering Labour MPs a free vote on the May deal with no enforced line from the party's whips. The MP goes on:

> I think it would have suited a lot of people for Brexit just to sneak through, with an intelligent, vocal but not overly organised resistance from people like Starmer and McDonnell and Abbott. That would have suited the Labour Party. To think that Corbyn would be capable of delivering that level of sophistication of political operation was perhaps the weakness of the logic.

In the event, the extensions to Article 50 meant the cliff-edge never arrived, the McCluskey letter was never written and the free vote was never offered. Only three Labour MPs supported May's deal on its first two meaningful votes, but many more found themselves in a quandary.

According to one insider, 'Nick Brown [Labour's chief whip] was absolutely ruthless in telling them, look, there'll be a general election fairly
soon, this government hasn't got a majority, if you want to stand as a
Labour candidate, you toe the line on this one.' Barwell has described
how, an hour before the third vote, the Prime Minister had eleven
Labour MPs in her study in an effort to persuade them to back the deal,
some of them in tears about the pressure they were under from their
own side. At the final vote, the number of Labour rebels supporting the
deal rose to just five. Gareth Snell, a Labour MP who changed his mind
and voted against the deal at the last minute, said his constituents expected him not to frustrate Brexit but there was 'increasing unpleasant
pressure on Labour MPs from the membership'.[5]

Not reported at the time was that in parallel to the official cross-party
talks, the two sides were surreptitiously holding a series of meetings in
Corbyn's own office. These discussions, held in Westminster's Norman
Shaw North building, took place in the absence of Starmer: only Milne,
Fisher and Murphy attended for Labour, with the government represented by Barwell, Robbins and Gibb. The six made what one participant describes as 'huge progress' in coming to an agreement over the
shape of a Brexit plan both sides could support. The idea, based on the
indicative votes that had taken place earlier, was that 'you would have
various options about how you would proceed with customs, various
options about how you proceed with the backstop and so on'. This
would result in an agreement which both Conservative and Labour
MPs would be whipped to support, outnumbering the rebels on either
side. During this time, there were two contradictory messages going to
the Prime Minister: one from those involved in the official cross-party
talks, and a much more optimistic one from the covert gatherings in
Corbyn's office.

As the main discussions wore on, however, it became clear that official agreement was unlikely on any terms that would get through Parliament. On 17 May, Corbyn ended the talks, saying they had gone as far as they could. The backchannel meetings closed at the same time. Seven days later, May announced that she would resign as Conservative leader the following month and step down as Prime Minister once the party had chosen a successor. Her parting thought: 'Compromise is not a dirty word.' The window of opportunity for a cross-party compromise on Brexit, always narrow, had closed.

*   *   *

The Brexit Party swept to victory in elections to the European Parliament; the Conservatives came fifth, and Labour was knocked into third place behind the pro-Remain Liberal Democrats. Boris Johnson became Prime Minister, beating Jeremy Hunt in the Tory leadership contest on a promise to leave the EU on 31 October, 'deal or no deal'. Parliament passed a law requiring the PM to seek a further extension if no deal was agreed by 19 October; twenty-one Conservative MPs who backed the move were expelled from the parliamentary party. Johnson announced a five-week prorogation of Parliament, a move later ruled unlawful by the Supreme Court. After unexpectedly cordial talks between Johnson and Irish leader Leo Varadkar, the government agreed a new deal that would scrap the unpopular backstop, taking the whole UK out of the customs union but leaving Northern Ireland following some EU rules, meaning some checks would be necessary on goods between Northern Ireland and Great Britain but not on the Irish border. Commitments on continued alignment with EU regulations were scrapped from the Withdrawal Agreement and moved to the non-binding political declaration on the future relationship, which now envisaged a free trade agreement rather than any closer association

– a harder Brexit than May had proposed. When the new deal was put before Parliament on 19 October, effectively the new deadline day, MPs instead voted to delay approval and force a third Brexit postponement. Johnson reluctantly complied and ten days later, at the fourth time of asking – once the EU had agreed to push the departure date to 31 January – Parliament agreed to his motion for a general election.

It was during this dramatic period, with any prospect of Labour backing a Tory deal having vanished, that the party's anti-Brexit forces began to dominate. Labour's performance in the European Parliament elections, in which it won just 14 per cent of the vote, prompted senior figures, including Emily Thornberry, Shami Chakrabarti and Diane Abbott, to call for a shift in the party's position towards a second referendum in any circumstances.

Starmer led the charge, tweeting: 'It's no use trying to hide from these very disappointing results. We need to reflect hard and listen to our members, supporters and voters. The only way to break the Brexit impasse is to go back to the public with a choice between a credible Leave option and Remain.' Crucially, McDonnell, who had by now developed a close alliance with Starmer over Brexit policy, also signalled a shift in his position. The shadow Chancellor said that since at this point the Tories looked unlikely to back an election given their own recent drubbing at the hands of the Brexit Party, 'Our only option now is to go back to the people in a referendum.'[6] Some Labour MPs in Leave-voting constituencies disagreed – Gloria De Piero warned that reversing the 2016 result 'would be an effective ending of Labour's historic coalition of working-class, middle-class, city and non-city voters'[7] – but Corbyn agreed to move. 'It's clear that the deadlock in Parliament can only be broken by the issue going back to the people through a general election or a public vote. We are ready to support a public vote on any deal,' he wrote to MPs.

A further step was taken during the Conservative leadership contest, when Corbyn challenged the final two contenders to put any deal to a referendum. 'In those circumstances, I want to make it clear that Labour would campaign for Remain against either no deal or a Tory deal that does not protect the economy and jobs.'

Starmer's immediate priority was to prevent a no-deal Brexit – something Johnson, unlike his predecessor, seemed perfectly willing to countenance. A plan to pass a vote of no confidence in the government and install the opposition leader as caretaker Prime Minister was abandoned when it became clear the other parties would not accept the idea of Corbyn in No. 10. An alternative was needed.

Much of Starmer's summer holiday in Devon was spent climbing a hill in search of a mobile phone signal and 'standing in the rain with one or two disinterested sheep' while co-ordinating tactics with allies across Parliament. Informal contacts between Starmer and discontented Tories had been going on for more than two years, but at this point the tempo changed significantly, according to those involved. The threat of a no-deal exit, as well as suspicions that Johnson would prorogue Parliament and thereby thwart moves to prevent it, had brought into the picture a number of Conservative MPs, including former ministers, who had never previously rebelled. In mid-August, MPs from all parties met formally in Westminster, some breaking their holidays, to agree the strategy for what became the Benn Act – proposed by former shadow Foreign Secretary Hilary Benn and dubbed the 'Surrender Act' by Johnson – which forced the Prime Minister to ask the EU for a further delay.

'By that stage, Starmer had the upper hand,' says one former Labour MP. 'Corbyn had almost lost interest. All Corbyn wanted was a way out, a general election.' Starmer's next battle was over the stance Labour should take when such an election arrived. After talks with union heavyweights at the TUC conference in July, Corbyn announced a new approach: in government, Labour would negotiate a new deal with the EU and put it to a referendum alongside the option to remain. Which side the party would officially take in such a referendum was still an open question.

The convoluted new position was 'a massive compromise hugely to do with the balance of powers among the trade union general secretaries', according to one well-placed observer of Labour's internal machinations.

> [It was] to do with Len McCluskey wanting Leave to be respected; the other major unions wanting a path to a people's vote or whatever it was going to be called; and the tension at the heart of Corbyn World over how to play the politics of Remain after Britain had voted to leave.

Starmer probably concluded that 'any form of words, however laughable or compromised, that moved Labour in the direction he wanted was progress and therefore should be taken. As long as you won the essential principles of the thing, how much did it matter that everything else was a mess?'

Once again, there was pressure for the party to go further: this time to oppose Brexit altogether. Watson urged members to sign the 'Remain Declaration', calling on Labour to become 'the party of Remain'. McDonnell also urged a shift in stance: 'I've said look, we need to express a view now which is clearly, as I said, I will vote Remain, I want to campaign for Remain,' he told *The Andrew Marr Show*. 'But what Jeremy is rightfully doing … let's talk to people, bring them together, build consensus and then go for it, and that's what he's doing at the moment.'

Resistance continued from those around Corbyn, but the shadow Brexit Secretary was firmly on the side of the Remainers. If it came to another referendum, he said in an interview that summer, 'I would campaign for Remain because I don't think there's a deal that is as good as the deal that we've got.' Internally, he pushed as strongly as he could for Labour to commit to supporting Remain in any subsequent referendum. All talk of respecting the 2016 result had been abandoned.

As in previous years, the issue came to a head at the Labour conference in September. As well as a statement of the official policy from the party's National Executive Committee and a supportive motion proposed by party members, delegates debated an alternative proposition, also backed by dozens of constituency parties, that would have committed Labour to 'reflect the overwhelming view of its members and voters' and therefore 'campaign energetically for a public vote and to stay in the EU in that referendum'.

Though he did not explicitly call for delegates to back the Remain motion, Starmer left little doubt as to his position. At a People's Vote rally during the opening weekend of the Brighton conference, he declared that in a referendum, 'I will campaign for Remain alongside millions of other people in this country, because it's not just a technical question of whether you want to be in or out of the EU, it's about what sort of country we want to be.' In an interview afterwards, he said a majority of Labour members wanted to remain, and 'we've got to listen to what they've got to say about it'.

Winding up the impassioned debate from the conference platform, Starmer reminded the party whom they had to thank for the evolution of its policy. 'Last year I stood before you and said nobody was ruling out the option of Remain,' he said. 'We've come a long way.' While he respected those who took a different view, 'You know where I stand on the question of Remain. I've said many times that I will campaign for Remain.' He announced that an incoming Labour government would legislate for a public vote immediately upon taking power and hold it within six months. Labour now had a simple message: 'If you want a referendum, vote Labour. If you want a final say on Brexit, vote Labour. If you want to fight for Remain, vote Labour.'

Amid chaotic scenes and a heavily disputed show of hands, the motions endorsing the party's official line were carried and the pro-Remain policy narrowly defeated. Starmer admitted he was disappointed by the result. 'What Jeremy's trying to achieve, in fairness is – given the divisions across the country – somebody's got to be prepared to say: "We'll have a referendum to find a way through and I'll stay above that" … I personally think it's better to campaign for Remain and that's what I've said.'[8] In practice, though, this is what would happen. Starmer went on:

> I have got a pretty clear idea of where the members are on this, and therefore I think it is very likely that the members will want us to campaign for Remain. We campaigned for Remain in 2016, we are currently campaigning for Remain against any Tory outcome, and it seems to be obvious where the members are on this.

In November, with the election campaign under way, Labour's election manifesto duly spelled out the party's position:

> Labour will give the people the final say on Brexit. Within three months of coming to power, a Labour government will secure a sensible deal. And within six months, we will put that deal to a public vote alongside the option to remain. A Labour government will implement whatever the people decide.

The Labour deal would include a permanent customs union and close alignment with EU rules – neither of which would amount to Brexit at all in the eyes of many Leave voters.

During the campaign, Corbyn confirmed the position he would take, or rather decline to take, in a referendum campaign: 'I will adopt, if I am Prime Minister at the time, a neutral stance so I can credibly carry out the result of that to bring our communities and country together rather than continuing an endless debate about the EU and Brexit' he told a BBC *Question Time* audience.

The policy did not make for an easy campaign for Starmer. An uncomfortable interview with Susanna Reid and Piers Morgan on ITV's *Good Morning Britain* was par for the course:

Susanna: What are you going to campaign for in that second referendum?

Starmer: Well in a sense, what I campaign for is secondary, because what we're saying is it's for the country now to decide. We're saying less power to politicians, that's where we've been stuck for three and a half years.

Susanna: Hang on, hang on. Yes, but I need to know, if I'm voting for you, what do you believe in? Do you think we should leave or remain?

Starmer: The Labour Party says we're going to put this choice before you.

Susanna: But if I'm voting for you as my political representative, for instance, as one of your voters, do you want to leave or remain?

Starmer: I've said many times what my personal position is.

Susanna: You want to remain.

Starmer: But that's missing the point.

Susanna: So am I voting to stay in the EU?

Starmer: Can I just finish this?

Susanna: Sorry, it's just that we're running out of time, and I want to be clear what Labour's policy is. Are we leaving or remaining?

Starmer: We are going to, within six months, have a referendum, and we're going to say, 'Here's the best deal that can be secured,' and it's going to go up against Remain, and we're going to let the public decide the answer to that question.

Susanna: And it will be such a good deal that you yourself would vote against it?

Starmer: We're duty bound to get the best possible deal, of course we are.

Susanna: How can it be a really good deal if you're going to vote against it?

Starmer: Well, we're duty bound to get the best deal that we can, and I think that's something that secures our economy and is consistent with the Good Friday Agreement.

Piers: Why would the EU give you a good deal if they know that you're going to actively campaign against it?

Compared to the crisp Conservative slogan – 'Get Brexit Done' – Labour's policy became an object of derision among the electorate. In research conducted by this author, voters mocked the prospect of Labour ministers going to Brussels to negotiate a new deal and then coming home to campaign against it.[9] They found the idea of a Prime Minister remaining neutral on such a fundamental question simply ridiculous. Many former Labour voters were appalled that the party had, as they saw it, done everything in its power to prevent the 2016 result from being honoured and was now seeking to reverse it.

Starmer, however, was already looking to the future. By the time the election was called, he had assembled an informal team of advisers including Claire Ainsley, then director of the Joseph Rowntree Foundation think tank and author of *The New Working Class: How to Win*

Hearts, Minds and Votes, and Morgan McSweeney, head of Labour Together, an activists' network dedicated to exploring new ideas on the future of the left. Starmer had also begun to hold dinners with journalists where discussion would range well beyond his Brexit brief – a sure sign that his horizons had shifted.

On 12 December 2019, Boris Johnson's Conservatives won the general election with an eighty-seat majority. Labour lost sixty seats, its worst performance since 1935. Jeremy Corbyn announced his resignation. On 23 January 2020, Johnson's Withdrawal Agreement became law, and eight days later the UK left the European Union.

* * *

Though voters on all sides were desperate to get it over with, Brexit was not the only reason for Labour's defeat: many saw a divided party with a fanciful manifesto and a leader they did not want within a country mile of No. 10. But in an election resulting from parliamentary stalemate over a decision voters had made three years earlier, the opponents of Brexit had drawn a clear dividing line on the biggest issue of the day, to the great benefit of the Conservatives. 'What Brexit did was shift votes to the Tories,' says John Mann, now Lord Mann, the Labour MP for Bassetlaw until 2019.[10] 'What Corbyn did was stop people voting Labour. So if it had been a non-Brexit election, Johnson versus Corbyn, the Tories would have got fewer votes from Labour. And that would have saved quite a few Labour seats.'

Recollections vary on how and why this dividing line came to be drawn. Even those who saw events unfold at first hand dispute exactly what happened and the extent of Starmer's role. Some assert that he wanted to support a soft Brexit compromise deal, became convinced no such outcome was possible given the parliamentary arithmetic and concluded a second referendum was the only way to resolve the matter. The other interpretation is that despite saying he respected the 2016 result, he helped erect one obstacle after another to its implementation, rejected the prospect of compromise and tried to reverse a decision that he had never truly accepted. 'Starmer has a constituency that was more than 70 per cent Remain,' observes Mann.

> So does Corbyn. So does Abbott. So they're surrounded in every part of their life by people who voted Remain. It was fairly obvious to me what the result would be, but I suspect people like Starmer were shocked at just how big the Tory victory was [in 2019]. But there was no attempt to talk to voters in the north of England by anybody outside the north of England. It just wasn't happening.

For a senior figure from Theresa May's Downing Street, the explanation is that Starmer is 'probably brilliant on the tactics, hopeless on the strategy'. His plan

> was not to get what he would regard as the best Brexit for Britain with different priorities; it was to have no Brexit for Britain. And what he ended up with was a massive majority for Boris and the hardest of all hard Brexits. Strategically it was a stupid decision. He managed to make life very difficult for the government, but to what end?

Some players put the failure to support a soft-Brexit deal down to a series of tactical miscalculations. 'When I met different groups from the Labour Party, they would all say to me they were on the cusp of winning,' says Lidington. 'One would say, "We're going to sweep this for Norway-Plus," and then another lot would say, "No, it's all moving towards a second referendum," so they did not believe they would need to compromise with the government.' Another senior Tory involved in the process thinks Labour was in a similar position to the EU itself:

> On the one hand they wanted to get the closest possible relationship, but at the backs of their minds they believed the Remainiacs who were coming across to say, 'We're on the verge of stopping Brexit altogether.' And they went for that hardcore 'stop Brexit altogether', which was a gamble that didn't pay off.

A veteran Labour strategist argues that many in the party failed to see the wood for the trees:

> You could talk to Labour MPs about who their voters were and how much they wanted to get Brexit done, and they'd say, 'Yes, but the Prime Minister hasn't yet given us a guarantee on the third codicil.' You'd think, 'There are two different planets here.' It was only after-wards when they sat back and it was too late that they realised they should have taken the deal.

At the same time, whatever position the party took would have cost votes among those who disagreed, and 'you can't predict with exacti-tude which group of voters you're going to lose from which position in advance and compare it on a spreadsheet to another group. So maybe there's an argument there for Labour just doing what it wants to do.'

Another argument is that the Labour leadership were too ready to concede to Johnson's demand for an election. 'Jeremy was in the bunker with Karie Murphy and Seumas Milne,' says a former Labour MP on the moderate wing of the party.

Incredibly, they'd persuaded themselves we would sweep to victory. It was fantastical, and Keir knew it was fantastical, but he went along with it because he knew we would lose, then there would be a leadership election and it would be very likely he'd become leader of the Labour Party. He knew there were some of us who didn't want to have an election and we were on a free vote. The significant thing is that this vote needed a two thirds majority to pass. I think if it had just been most of the Tories and the Corbynistas it might not have passed. Keir said it was inevitable, but nothing is inevitable. I think that was a selfish approach.

Insiders say it would be unfair to blame Starmer for the untidy policy which Labour took to the people in 2019, given the array of views within the party and even within the shadow Cabinet. 'He's sufficiently aware to know that something that you need a flowchart to understand is bad policy,' as one colleague puts it, but there had to be a position for Labour to unite around. Some suspect he had strong reservations about Corbyn's decision to agree to an election. But by contributing to the impasse in Parliament, and with his outspoken support for holding a new referendum and remaining in the EU – a stance that infuriated many Labour voters in Leave-voting constituencies and confounded colleagues on his own benches who would have preferred the party to back a deal when it had the chance – Starmer surely helped to create the circumstances of Labour's rout.

Some suspect Starmer's own personal ambition helped explain his pursuit of the referendum-and-Remain policy. 'I'm not very impressed with him,' says one former Labour MP who lost his northern seat in the 2019 debacle.

Some of us had decided that if we had to have Brexit it should be a soft Brexit. But Starmer got into bed with the People's Vote people so as to get votes for the leadership among members of the London Labour Party. And he wouldn't do a deal with Theresa May, which was there to be done and would have meant a soft Brexit. So what happens? May has to resign, we get Boris and we get a hard Brexit. All because he wanted to get himself elected leader.

Lidington, a former Remainer who was closely involved in trying to pass the May deal that would have kept Britain more closely aligned with the EU than the deal ultimately concluded by Johnson, reflects that whatever the mix of motives, 'Starmer is one of the authors of a very hard Brexit. There is no doubt in my mind about that.' Starmer's personal campaign to remain in the EU had ended in defeat. But a vacancy had opened up for which he would apply with enthusiasm.

CHAPTER 13

UNDER NEW MANAGEMENT

Shortly before six o'clock on the morning of Friday 13 December 2019, *The Guardian* website published a shortlist of Labour MPs who it believed might stand to succeed Jeremy Corbyn as party leader. With the final election results just in and the scale of Boris Johnson's stunning victory at the polls clear, six names were mooted: Starmer, Emily Thornberry, Rebecca Long-Bailey, Angela Rayner, Jess Phillips and Lisa Nandy. *The Guardian*'s instincts about who in the Labour Party might be considering putting themself forward would prove almost entirely accurate. Five of the six on its list did indeed throw their hats into the ring. Only Rayner decided not to do so, opting to contest another elected position, the deputy leadership, instead. A further candidate, Clive Lewis, would join the leadership contest, though his bid was soon scuppered.

At his own count in Islington in the early hours, Corbyn had acknowledged that his party's woeful performance signalled the end of his four years in charge. He would not lead Labour into the next election, he said, but he would not resign immediately either, as his predecessor, Ed Miliband, had done in 2015. Instead, he requested that the party embark on a 'process of reflection' – with him in charge – while it chose a new leader. Many within Labour and outside it thought this ill-advised and self-indulgent. They believed Corbyn's continued presence at the top of a battered organisation, which had lost sixty MPs and now had just 202 members in the House of Commons, prevented it from making a clean break with the immediate past. Yet Corbyn would not be moved.

Four days after the election, on 16 December, Frank Dobson's funeral was held at St Pancras Church in Starmer's constituency. Among the hundreds of people who gathered to pay their respects were many of Labour's best-known figures, including Corbyn, Tony Blair, Neil Kinnock, Ed Miliband, Jack Straw, John McDonnell, Andy Burnham, Sadiq Khan and Emily Thornberry. Dobson's son, Tom, delivered the eulogy, but, as Dobson's successor, Starmer was also invited to give a spoken tribute to him. One attendee remembers that other mourners were less than impressed. 'He talked about his selection and how he'd got to know Frank, and it just didn't strike the right note,' this person recalls.

It was a funeral. It wasn't a political event. It was a church. And he referred to Frank being an atheist, and I thought that was a bit simplistic. Frank was extremely interested in religion, he was a trustee at York Minster, he was very well read in religion, and he knew a lot about it. I felt sorry for the priest who had to pick up from there. I remember Chris Bryant saying afterwards, 'Keir seemed to talk mostly about himself,' and I thought that captured it rather well.

The starting gun to mark the beginning of the contest to succeed Corbyn had been fired, and those who wished to replace him set to work scrambling their teams and preparing their campaigns. Remarkably, Starmer apparently decided to use the funeral for these purposes. 'After the funeral we all tottered off to the big hotel next door,' reports the same source.

It was very nice, actually. There were vast quantities to drink, but it was a very highly charged event because it wasn't just that Frank had died and had a lot of friends, we had also just lost the election. So it was a sort of wake for something in the party as well as a wake for Frank. These two sad events came together. But I remember Keir was lobbying people in the queue going in and running down Emily Thornberry. He was doing a bit of canvassing. I thought that wasn't quite the thing.

Party rules dictated that each candidate who intended to stand would be required to secure the blessing of 10 per cent of the party's MPs or MEPs – this was set at twenty-two MPs or MEPs – by 13 January. If they managed to clear this hurdle, they would then need to add to this support from at least 5 per cent of Labour's constituency parties or other affiliated groups, such as trade unions, by 15 February. Those with sufficient backing to make it onto the final ballot paper would then face a vote by full party members, union affiliates and registered supporters, a group which numbered 784,181 eligible voters in total. The new leader would be announced on 4 April. In between, there would be hustings and televised debates around the country. The contest would be a marathon rather than a sprint.

Emily Thornberry, who had served as shadow Foreign Secretary since 2016, was the first contender out of the blocks, announcing her candidacy two days after Dobson's funeral, on 18 December. She was joined the next day by Clive Lewis, Corbyn's shadow Treasury Minister. On 3 January, backbenchers Lisa Nandy and Jess Phillips announced their respective campaigns. On 4 January, Starmer declared his hand with a three-pronged approach. First, he released a video online in which 'ordinary' Labour supporters waxed lyrical about his record in the law and politics over the previous three decades. That day he also visited the Brexit-backing town of Stevenage in Hertfordshire. He rounded off the start of his campaign launch by writing a piece for the *Sunday Mirror*. Under the headline 'It won't be a decade before Labour wins a general election if we unite', he spelled out his objectives as the candidate who could bring Labour's pro- and anti-Corbyn factions together. These included continuing 'the moral fight against poverty, inequality and injustice', and campaigning for 'peace and justice around the world with a human rights approach to foreign policy and international relations'. His slogan was 'Another Future Is Possible' and many people appeared to agree, for he was the bookmakers' clear favourite to succeed Corbyn from the start. The last candidate to announce their bid was Rebecca Long-Bailey, a Corbynista who had been the shadow Business Secretary since 2017. She made her pitch in an article published in *Tribune* magazine on 6 January.

In an early indication of how one-sided the contest would turn out to be, Starmer gained the backing of forty-one MPs – almost twice the number required to get onto the ballot – within four days of announcing his launch. He was well ahead of his rivals from the word go. In the same timeframe he also won the endorsement of the trade union Unison, which had 1.3 million members. Comprising a wide range of public sector employees, Unison had backed Corbyn's leadership bid in 2015 and it was considered vital in helping to select the next Labour leader. Announcing Unison's support for Starmer, its general secretary, Dave Prentis, commented:

We believe – if elected by the membership – Keir Starmer would be a leader to bring the party together and win back the trust of the thousands of voters who deserted Labour last month. Keir has a clear vision to get Labour back to the winning ways of the past. He is best placed to take on Boris Johnson, hold his government to account and ensure Labour can return to power.

Usefully for Starmer, given the continued presence of the party's left-wing Momentum faction, he also recruited Simon Fletcher to his campaign team at this early stage. Fletcher was Corbyn's former chief of staff who ran his successful leadership bid in 2015.

Starmer launched his campaign formally at the Mechanics Institute in Manchester on 11 January, delivering a speech in which he said 'factionalism has to go' if the party was to recover from its latest election defeat. He said Labour also needed to be a 'very effective opposition' against Boris Johnson, describing him as 'a man of no principles, no moral compass, who will go anywhere to stay in power'. Yet he was careful to recognise Corbyn, saying he

> made our party the party of anti-austerity, and he was right to do so. He made us the party that wanted to invest more heavily in our public services, and he was right to do so. We must retain that. We build on that and don't trash it as we move forward.

Starmer knew that worshipping at Corbyn's altar was obligatory if he was to get enough votes to lead the party himself. He may have been right that Boris Johnson 'will go anywhere to stay in power', but in praising Corbyn, who had just presided over Labour's worst showing at a general election for almost a century, he showed that he was prepared to do whatever it took to win power in his own party.

On 13 January, Clive Lewis withdrew, unable to muster enough support among the parliamentary party. The remaining five candidates (four women plus Starmer) each had sufficient backing to make it to the second round. The first hustings took place in Liverpool on 18 January. The event was dominated by the issues which had caused such division within the party over the previous few years, namely anti-semitism and Brexit. Then, Jess Phillips, with twenty-three MPs supporting her – just one more than the threshold required – withdrew her candidacy on 21 January, leaving a field of four. It would not be accurate to say that the race had attracted much interest nationally by this stage, certainly when compared to the 2015 contest eventually won by Corbyn, which was characterised by a surge of more than 100,000 new members joining the party. Naturally, however, with the country still absorbing the consequences of Johnson's handsome eighty-seat majority and the prospect of a new Tory government, Labour's internal battles were hardly likely to electrify the general public.

For Starmer, the contest was brought to an abrupt halt in early February when his mother-in-law, Dr Barbara Moyes, died in hospital following an accident. He had to step away from his political commitments to be with his family, and in doing so he missed a hustings event held in Nottingham on 8 February, at which the Labour MP Jim McMahon stood in for him. Other candidates might have been concerned at not being able to appear at this event, yet Starmer's absence had little, if any, effect on his campaign. As the short-priced favourite, his lead always seemed unassailable. On 15 February, Emily Thornberry was eliminated from the race after failing to achieve enough support from local constituency parties. She had thirty-one constituencies to her name, two shy of the thirty-three required. Not having received any backing from Labour Party affiliates, which represented the other route to the final ballot, her ambitions to lead were finished. This left Starmer – who had by this point secured the backing of eighty-eight MPs (42 per cent of the parliamentary party) – to fight it out with Long-Bailey and Nandy. Theirs were the three names on the ballot papers that were sent out to the hundreds of thousands of Labour Party members and supporters in late February.

There were several obvious differences between the three remaining candidates. The most obvious was that Starmer was the only man among them. This mattered given that there had never been a female Labour leader before. He was also seventeen years older than Long-Bailey and Nandy, both of whom were born in 1979 and were therefore aged only forty. This generational difference undoubtedly gave rise to the feeling in the two women that they might be able to appeal to younger members more easily than Starmer, but at the same time being older allowed Starmer and his team to play the 'experience' card, presenting him as someone who had already held high public office as DPP. His near thirty-year career in the law also allowed him to outgun his rivals financially. Over the course of his campaign, Starmer attracted donations of just over £700,000 in cash and services, significantly more than the other candidates. The vast bulk of this money – £580,000 – came from thirty-five individual donors. Various small businesses came up with just under £50,000, while three trade unions – Unison, USDAW and Community – bankrolled Starmer to the tune of just over £80,000 in cash and practical support.

His old friend and colleague Helena Kennedy was instrumental in helping with these financial efforts, organising one highly lucrative event at Doughty Street Chambers. Bill Bowring was among those invited. 'I saw Keir at his fundraiser at Doughty Street Chambers,' Bowring says. 'I remember asking him if he still had a copy of the report of the Haldane Society mission to Northern Ireland and he said if he did, he couldn't find it, so I sent it to him. Lots of barristers and solicitors were there.' Indeed, many of these legal figures dug deep to help out. One, Robert Latham, a Doughty Street human rights lawyer like Starmer, gave him £100,000. This sum was matched by the Labour peer Lord

Alli. Kennedy also hit the phones for Starmer as a phone bank volunteer, regaling Labour members with tales of his legal achievements and overall competence.

Just before the first of four televised debates was held, in the second week of February, Starmer announced the ten pledges on which he would focus if he were elected leader. He tweeted: 'My promise to you is that I will maintain our radical values and work tirelessly to get Labour into power – so that we can advance the interests of the people our party was created to serve.' He based these promises on 'the moral case for socialism'. The first covered 'economic justice', in which he would increase income tax for the top 5 per cent of earners and reverse cuts in corporation tax. The second area was 'social justice', in which he said he would abolish universal credit, 'defend our NHS' and axe university tuition fees. His third vow related to 'climate justice'. His fourth pledge concerned 'promoting peace and human rights'. By this, he said he meant 'no more illegal wars' and a review of arms sales. The idea of 'common ownership', in which public services including 'rail, mail, energy and water' are in public hands, was his fifth promise. His sixth guarantee was to 'defend migrants' rights', including a promise to 'defend free movement as we leave the EU'. The seventh pledge was to 'strengthen workers' rights and trade unions'. Next, he said he would promote the 'radical devolution of power, wealth and opportunity', including scrapping the House of Lords. 'Equality' was pledge number nine and 'effective opposition to the Tories' was the final promise. In this, he said he would provide 'forensic, effective opposition' in Parliament and would 'never lose sight of the votes "lent" to the Tories in 2019' while swearing to take 'robust action to eradicate the scourge of antisemitism' and to 'maintain our collective link with the unions'.

On the surface, some of the items on this political shopping list probably appeared reasonable or even appealing to moderate Labour members.

Yet on closer examination, there is no doubt that they incorporated a nakedly left-wing agenda which might potentially generate support from the more extreme element of the party too. Renationalisation, the extension of union power and significant tax increases were all things of which Jeremy Corbyn would doubtless approve. At the same time, the 'no more illegal wars' statement was obviously designed to prove that Starmer was cut from very different cloth to another ex-Labour leader, Tony Blair, whose decision to join the invasion of Iraq in 2003 lingered long in the memory and had turned him into a hate figure for many.

The notion that the pledges were a ruse on Starmer's part to secure the Corbynista vote, become leader and then return Labour to the centre ground cannot be dismissed. Others at the time believed that Starmer was in fact harking back to his days on *Socialist Alternatives* magazine and genuinely held a desire to take Britain as far to the left as Corbyn had intended to had he won power. What most people agreed is that Starmer's politics are ambiguous, with neither the hard left nor the centrists necessarily claiming him as one of their own in any distinct sense. Immediately after Starmer became leader, James Schneider, Corbyn's former head of strategic communications, wrote:

> Keir Starmer is not a ghoulish neoliberal, reactionary authoritarian, or a lover of war, but he isn't a socialist. Hard to place, he appears to be on the progressive end of social reformism, the nicest possible part of the establishment. He has no strong allergy to being near socialist ideas, but they aren't to his taste or style.[1]

Starmer, in fact, has often referred to himself in public as a socialist, though, as has been pointed out by others many times before, Labour is not and never has been a socialist party per se; rather, it is a party which has socialists in it.

Perhaps the only real difficulty that Starmer encountered during the campaign related to the money his team received from friends and supporters. As with any donation to any MP, Starmer had a 28-day window in which to declare each one in the House of Commons Register of Members' Financial Interests. Yet some rivals concluded that he was being rather slippery by taking advantage of this allowance, pointing out that some of his donations might not be publicly known by the time members cast their vote. Starmer was breaching no rules by taking his time to publish the names of his donors, but the MP Jon Trickett, for example, who was pro-Rebecca Long-Bailey, thought it was below the belt. 'Delaying publishing donations until the vast majority of people have voted is entirely undemocratic,' he said.[2]

On 4 March, Starmer and Long-Bailey gave journalist Andrew Neil separate interviews which were broadcast on the BBC. Neil challenged Starmer about the donations. Yet so, too, did Long-Bailey when she spoke to Neil. She told him: 'I think there's always an assumption that you don't get nothing for nothing in this world. And those who donate to your campaign will expect to be repaid in some way in the future.' She also criticised Starmer for having what she thought was a somewhat vague set of policies, despite his having published his list of ten pledges. 'I don't know what Keir's policy ideas are, if I'm honest,' she said.

I know he says he wants to adopt the same values that the [Labour Party] has, but what does that mean in practice? I hope that he keeps to our values and our principles. I think we need to see more detail. We need to see more meat on the bone in terms of what Keir believes in – and indeed about all of the candidates.

As the campaign neared its conclusion, Starmer gave an interview to the *New Statesman*. In fact, this 5,000-word profile piece, which included on the record quotes from friends including Gavin Millar, was almost certainly crafted with Starmer's help as he edged closer to the finishing line untroubled by either of his younger rivals. In it, he revealed himself to be more 'metrosexual' than perhaps anybody realised, as he confessed to 'moisturising nightly'. This was the cause of much mirth from some newspaper journalists, including at the *Daily Mail*, where he was instantly hailed as 'Mr Moisturiser'. In the *New Statesman* interview, he also spoke of his wife's Jewish faith, which is a product of her father, a Polish Jew who emigrated to Britain and married her mother, who converted. 'It's very important that [my children] understand the history of their granddad,' Starmer said. 'Occasionally on a Friday night we'll have prayers with him.' Although he was scrupulously careful not to criticise Corbyn's leadership during the contest, remarks such as this hinted that he was prepared to acknowledge that antisemitism had contributed to Labour's catastrophic loss in 2019, and he clearly wanted to purge it from the party.

By the morning of Saturday 4 April, Britain was in lockdown because of the Covid-19 crisis. The planned conference which was to be held in London to announce the new Labour leader was cancelled. Instead, the party relayed the result over its social media feeds. Starmer won in the first round, having received 275,780 votes (56.2 per cent of the available vote). Rebecca Long-Bailey was a distant second with 135,218 votes (27.6 per cent). Lisa Nandy trailed in third place with 79,597 (16.2 per cent). Starmer also achieved the most support from both the constituency parties and affiliates, having secured 374 constituencies and fifteen affiliates. Long-Bailey ended with the backing of 164 CLPs and seven affiliates. Nandy had clocked up seventy-two constituency parties and four affiliates. In a pre-recorded speech which was distributed online, Starmer spoke of the 'honour' of his victory but, inevitably, it was bittersweet as he was also forced to acknowledge that public life had 'all but come to a standstill'. The matter of the new Labour leader's identity suddenly appeared to be rather trivial in comparison to a potentially lethal disease which threatened millions of people around the world. (In this respect, the result arguably had echoes of Iain Duncan Smith's election as leader of the Conservative Party in 2001. Duncan Smith's victory was due to be announced on 12 September but was delayed because of the 9/11 terror attacks in the United States.) Just as had been the case when he became DPP, Starmer had competed among a relatively weak field of candidates and won. Now he had to try to restore morale and order to his divided party before embarking on the matter of readying it for the next election. In this, he would be helped by his new deputy leader, Angela Rayner, who had also been voted into her post that day, with just over half of the available votes.

It has been noted before that people who aspire to the highest office in the land have experience of trauma or tragedy which perhaps drives them on to succeed. An assessment of those who have been in power over the last thirty years shows this to be more than a theory. Boris Johnson's mother, Charlotte, had a nervous breakdown when he was ten and was committed to the Maudsley Hospital in London for nine months with depression, rupturing his childhood. His parents later divorced. Theresa May was an only child whose mother had MS and whose father died after a car crash in 1981, when she was in her mid-twenties. Her mother died the following year. David Cameron's father, Ian, was born with both legs deformed and endured repeated operations in an attempt to straighten them and ease his pain. Gordon Brown was kicked in the head during a school rugby match aged sixteen, leaving him blind in his left eye and fearful of losing his sight in his right eye. Tony Blair's father suffered a stroke when Blair was ten, which ended his own political ambitions to stand as a Conservative candidate and had a big impact on family life. John Major's father, who was sixty-three when Major was born, suffered poor health and then bad luck in business, which forced the family to move to a cramped flat in Brixton. Such setbacks tend to leave a mark on a person's character, instilling in them a desire to achieve. The difficulties of Starmer's mother, which dogged his own life to some degree, are by now well known, suggesting that he also has the sense of validation that comes from political power running through his veins. Having become Leader of Her Majesty's Opposition after just five years in Parliament, the next task confronting him was to try to rebuild the Labour Party into a credible government-in-waiting.

*   *   *

Jeremy Corbyn's people had left their lair in a shambles. The Thames-facing rooms that comprise the Leader of the Opposition's office were strewn with paper and even discarded clothes. Old letters and draft speeches were crammed into drawers, cupboards and crates or simply left lying around. A printed email chain detailing a plot to depose former deputy leader Tom Watson after the election before last was found in a desk. The whole mess was consigned to the shredder.

The metaphor for the job that faced the new tenant was too perfect. Starmer had taken over a party that was divided, disorganised and demoralised and the voters' verdict on it had been stark. It was time to start again.

The job of recreating Labour began with the appointment of Starmer's front-bench team. John McDonnell and Diane Abbott resigned before they were pushed, while Corbynites Jon Trickett, Ian Lavery and Richard Burgon were relieved of their duties along with Barry Gardiner, the new leader's old antagonist. The return of Ed Miliband, Lord Falconer and David Lammy – who shortly afterwards joined Starmer as an unpaid associate tenant at Doughty Street Chambers – also suggested a change of direction from the Corbyn years. But the reshuffle hardly amounted to a wholesale clear-out: of the thirty-two members of Starmer's first shadow Cabinet, twenty-five had been on Corbyn's front bench at the 2019 election.

Some Labour figures welcomed this as a sign that Starmer would try to unify the party's competing tribes rather than wage war on the defeated left. The divisions of the previous five years had been brought painfully into focus by the leak of an 860-page dossier, compiled in the last months of Corbyn's leadership, claiming to document evidence of a 'hyper-factional atmosphere' in party HQ, which had supposedly impeded the handling of disciplinary complaints, particularly those relating to antisemitism. The report even stated that 'some employees seem to have taken a view that the worse things got for Labour the happier they would be, since this might expedite Jeremy Corbyn's departure from office'. The document had been compiled as evidence for the Equalities and Human Rights Commission, which was conducting an inquiry into Labour's approach to antisemitism, but would not now be submitted.

The leak sparked a fresh outburst of infighting. Twenty-nine left-wing MPs – including four members of Starmer's new front-bench team – called for the document to be published in full, while opponents of Corbyn condemned it as an attempt to divert blame for the handling of antisemitism complaints away from the leadership and onto party staff.

Starmer tried to calm the situation, ordering a review into how the document came to be commissioned and leaked while stressing the need for unity. 'We have to stop the factionalism in our party. We have to create a different culture,' he told members in a video call. 'If we carry on taking lumps out of each other we are heading for a loss at the next general election.'³ Nevertheless, the dossier row highlighted what would become a persistent tension: maintaining a united party on the one hand and showing voters that Labour had changed on the other.

Though always politically active, Starmer had not spent his life steeped in Labour's internal politics. Since his selection as a parliamentary candidate, however, he had become acquainted with the sectarian struggles that preoccupy many of its members at all levels, from the smallest ward of a local constituency party to the shadow Cabinet and the National Executive Committee. Even in Holborn & St Pancras, elections to minor committee posts had often turned into ferocious ideological struggles. Camden Momentum, the local branch of the left-wing group set up to support Corbyn's leadership, urged Labour members to vote against Starmer in the leadership election, claiming he was making an 'opportunistic tilt to the left' despite failing to 'engage with, encourage or welcome the left at the local level'. Controlling the Labour Party's levers of administrative and organisational power would be crucial, and on this front, he was able to make early progress.

Centrist candidates swept the board in by-elections to the NEC that took place alongside the leadership contest. Together with the leader, deputy leader and three front-bench representatives, this meant there was already a 'Starmerite' majority on the ruling body that had recently been dominated by the left. The value of this was quickly seen when it approved David Evans, Starmer's preferred candidate, to take over as the party's general secretary following the resignation of Corbynite Jennie Formby. Evans quickly launched a review of Labour's organisational structure, bringing in Bob Kerslake, former head of the civil service, to lead the project.

If the party's internal mechanics seem to outsiders to be bewildering, impenetrable and irrelevant, they are an inescapable part of life inside Labour. One who is familiar with their mysteries says the importance of these apparently humdrum developments should not be underestimated:

> Most leaders have to wait several years for an NEC majority or a general secretary of their choosing. Corbyn doesn't get his until after his 2016 re-election as leader. Blair had to negotiate almost every single general secretary there ever was between the different factions, and I don't think he ever got his first choice. Whereas Keir, right off the bat, managed to push through his first choice. And that speaks to the efficacy of the political operation around him.

An ally adds:

> There were so many different parts of the party that were preparing for life after Corbyn that there was always going to be energy that could be tapped there. And critically, he's just not that interested in the internal workings of the Labour Party to have spent a whole lot of time with a spreadsheet thinking about who he needed to speak to and who he needed to get on board. His politicking in that respect was far more natural and probably more effective for that.

Colleagues say Starmer also brought a new level of discipline to proceedings. 'All the meetings, which had previously been a shambles, are now being run properly,' said Falconer.[4] 'The Corbyn Cabinet was full of people intervening on topics which had fuck all to do with the topic they were talking about, and high levels of abuse or obsequiousness. That doesn't happen any more.'

On one issue in particular, Starmer was determined to show an early and decisive break with the past. In his victory speech in April, he had described antisemitism as 'a stain on our party' and promised to 'tear out this poison by its roots and judge success by the return of Jewish members and those who felt that they could no longer support us'. The words echoed those of Chief Rabbi Ephraim Mirvis, who wrote during the general election campaign that 'a new poison – sanctioned from the top – has taken root in the Labour Party'. Shortly after his election, Starmer called Mirvis to mark Yom Hashoah, the day when Jewish communities commemorate the victims of the Holocaust. Mirvis tweeted:

> Thank you to Sir Keir Starmer for his personal call today to convey his solidarity with the Jewish community as we mark Yom Hashoah. I welcomed hearing directly of his commitment to take the necessary action to root out antisemitism from the Labour Party as a top priority. It is heartening that the task of rebuilding the Jewish community's trust in the Labour Party has begun.

Determined to match words with action, Starmer sacked Rebecca Long-Bailey for sharing online an interview given by actor Maxine Peake, in which Peake claimed police techniques that had led to the killing of George Floyd in Minneapolis had been 'learnt from seminars with Israeli secret services' ('Maxine Peake is an absolute diamond,' the shadow Education Secretary had averred). The decision infuriated the left, but Starmer was unrepentant, saying it had been wrong to share an article containing antisemitic conspiracy theories. 'I've made it my first priority to tackle antisemitism and rebuilding trust with the Jewish community is a number one priority for me,' he added.[5] Jewish groups welcomed the decision and Labour MP Margaret Hodge, who had been among Corbyn's sternest critics, tweeted: 'This is what a change in culture looks like. This is what zero tolerance looks like. This is what rebuilding trust with the Jewish community looks like.' Shortly afterwards, Labour agreed to pay substantial damages and offered an unreserved apology to seven former employees who sued the party for making false and defamatory comments about them after they criticised the leadership's handling of antisemitism complaints in a BBC *Panorama* programme.

More Jewish leaders recognised the change of approach. Lord Triesman, Lord Mitchell and Lord Turnberg returned to the Labour Party, having left over antisemitism under Corbyn. Former Chief Rabbi Lord Sacks, who had previously described Corbyn as an antisemite who had 'given support to racists, terrorists and dealers of hate', said the party was 'doing better' under Starmer.[6] 'The first thing is they have acknowledged the problem and its scope. And the second thing is that the leader has shown that he is willing to take responsibility. And thirdly he has reached out to the Jewish community in a way that the Jewish community feel very reassured by.'

A critical test came in October, when the EHRC published its report into the party's handling of antisemitism complaints during the Corbyn era. Starmer had always intended this to be the defining moment at which the party could deal decisively with the issue, acknowledge past failures and begin to restore its reputation. The Commission's findings were unequivocal and devastating. It concluded that the Labour Party was responsible for three breaches of the 2010 Equality Act relating to harassment, political interference in antisemitism complaints and failure to provide adequate training to those handling such complaints. The body said its analysis pointed to 'a culture within the party which, at best, did not do enough to prevent antisemitism and, at worst, could be seen to accept it'.

Starmer said, 'I found this report hard to read. And it is a day of shame for the Labour Party. We have failed Jewish people, our members, our supporters, and the British public.' He accepted the report in full and without qualification and promised a culture change within the party, adding that if there were still those 'who think there's no problem with antisemitism in the Labour Party, that it's all exaggerated, or a factional attack, then, frankly, you are part of the problem too, and you should be nowhere near the Labour Party either'.

Step forward Jeremy Corbyn. 'One antisemite is too many,' he wrote in response to the report. 'But the scale of the problem was also dramatically overstated for political reasons by our opponents inside and outside the party, as well as by much of the media.' Corbyn was immediately suspended from the Labour Party – a decision taken by the general secretary, David Evans, which Starmer made clear he supported. 'I can't tell you how disappointed I was,' he said later.[7] 'Because the words he used, what he said, coming from the former leader of the Labour Party in response to that report were just about as bad as you can get.'

Though Corbyn was readmitted to the party the following month, the leader decided to withhold the Labour whip from his predecessor until he apologised for claiming that the scale of antisemitism had been exaggerated. 'I'm the leader of the Labour Party, but I'm also the leader of the Parliamentary Labour Party,' Starmer tweeted in explanation of his decision. 'Jeremy Corbyn's actions in response to the EHRC report undermined and set back our work in restoring trust and confidence in the Labour Party's ability to tackle antisemitism.'

The left's response was fierce. Corbyn began legal action. Former party chair Ian Lavery said the refusal to let the former leader sit as a Labour MP looked like 'a vengeful, divisive, provocative sort of move from Keir Starmer' who was conducting a 'personal and political vendetta' and behaving as though the party was 'a tin-pot dictatorship'. Len McCluskey bewailed 'an act of grave injustice which, if not reversed, will create chaos within the party'. Momentum condemned the decision and a number of constituency Labour parties passed motions of solidarity with Corbyn. The simmering row also prompted a 'digital walkout' from an online NEC meeting by thirteen left-wing members, who were also cross at the leadership's support for appointing moderate Margaret Beckett as its chair in preference to the hard-left Ian Murray of the Fire Brigades Union, the former vice-chair whom they considered next in line. Howard Beckett, assistant general secretary of the Unite union and no relation, incongruously raged: 'Today the entire left walked out of the NEC. We won't stay silent on Keir Starmer's factionalism any longer.' (Margaret Beckett was elected unanimously in their absence.)

While there is truth in the adage that divided parties do not win elections, it is also the case that a good row can be useful for a new leader – provided the voters believe the leader is on the side of the angels and, crucially, the leader wins the row. For this reason, it is unlikely that Starmer did much fretting over a showdown with elements of his party angry about his action to tackle one of its biggest failings. Nevertheless, apart from the political benefits and the simple belief that it was the right thing to do, there was another reason, closer to home, why dealing with antisemitism was near to his heart.

In an interview for the Limmud Festival of learning in December, Starmer spoke again about the Jewish heritage of his wife's family. Victoria's father had been born Jewish and had roots in Poland, while her mother, who had recently died, had converted to Judaism. Starmer said that they were bringing up their two children 'to recognise the faith part of their grandfather's family, and it's very important. Just carving out that tradition, that bit of faith on Friday is incredibly important, because we get together, and we do Zoom prayers now.' Though by no means a secret – indeed, he had spoken about it earlier in the year during the leadership campaign – the fact of Starmer's Jewish family ties came as news to many people, including some close colleagues.

In the early months of his leadership, then, Starmer had set a new tone on antisemitism, dealt decisively with transgressions and in so doing begun to rebuild relations with the Jewish community. But all this raised a question which was regularly asked by his opponents: if Starmer so deplored Labour's record on the issue under Corbyn, why did he spend four years in his shadow Cabinet?

The question was put to him directly at the Limmud Festival. 'I thought it was better to stay and try and change things; others thought it was better to leave,' he said. 'I thought it was better to make the arguments that needed to be made in the shadow Cabinet. I took the view that if you are in a party you stay in and fight for change; other people took a different view.'

Colleagues insist that Starmer did indeed challenge the leadership on the issue. He pushed for the party to adopt the International Holocaust Remembrance Alliance's widely recognised definition of antisemitism, which had been resisted by Corbyn allies, and to establish a streamlined complaints procedure that would allow members to be summarily suspended or expelled for extreme breaches of the rules. 'He got criticised for not speaking out loudly enough, but he challenged Jeremy on it at the shadow Cabinet, and it was contrary to his personal political interests at the time to do it, so fair play to him,' says a colleague.

Lord Mann, who became an adviser to the government on antisemitism after stepping down as Labour MP for Bassetlaw in 2019, says he understands Starmer's decision to stay in the shadow Cabinet:

> It's a tactical question, so I don't criticise him over that. He did speak out; I'd have liked to hear him louder. There are lots of people who should have spoken up more and earlier. But the Jewish community will judge him on what he does now when he's got power.[8]

So far, the former MP gives Starmer good marks on this front:

> He's sufficiently linked in with the Jewish community to understand the issue and the nuances of the issue. He's copied the Blair guidebook on being party leader. Rule number one: you can show how good you are as leader by leading your own party. Show your leadership qualities on things you can actually do something about, so it's not just all promises of what you would do if you were in power. He knows he'll get kudos from doing it, but he also knows it's the right thing to do. So you're going to do it and you're going to give it particular attention to make sure you do it well.

Another insider concurs. 'You can always say, "You should just resign and have nothing to do with it," and that's a respectable position to take,' she says.

> But the path he took has actually led to the problem being addressed in very dramatic terms. Biting your tongue is never an easy thing to do but it worked out to the advantage not just of Keir politically but of everyone who is decent and wants to see antisemitism destroyed.

Expelling a former leader and sacking a prominent frontbencher were dramatic proof of Starmer's determination to rid the party of one of the most toxic features of the Corbyn years. Showing that the party had changed in other respects would be a much harder slog. While Starmer himself was manifestly a different kind of leader from his predecessor, rescuing the Labour brand would mean putting clear red water between the new leadership and the old regime.

Again, the mission was complicated by the awkward fact that Starmer had spent four years in Corbyn's senior team, effectively campaigning to make him Prime Minister – a connection which Labour's opponents were clearly determined to exploit for all it was worth. When Starmer asked at Prime Minister's Questions in July about the threat Russia posed to Britain's national security, Johnson retorted that the new Leader of the Opposition had 'sat on his hands and said nothing while the Labour Party parroted the line of the Kremlin, when people in this country were poisoned on the orders of Vladimir Putin'. Starmer pointed out, quite truthfully, that he had spoken out strongly against the Salisbury attack of 2018, in which an assassination attempt by Moscow operatives upon a former Russian military officer resulted in the death of a British woman. Starmer said at the time that the attack 'deserves to be condemned by all of us without reservation', that he believed responsibility lay with Russia and that he supported the actions then Prime Minister Theresa May proposed in response. This stance differed somewhat from that of Corbyn, who questioned the conclusion that Putin's government was responsible and even suggested a sample of the nerve agent used in the attack be sent to Russia so the Kremlin could confirm whether or not it was theirs. Corbyn's response had dismayed many of his own MPs and confirmed many voters' doubts about the approach a Labour government would take to security and defence. Starmer tried to dismiss Johnson's attack – 'In case the Prime Minister has not noticed, the Labour Party is under new management' – but he knew that moving on from the Corbyn era would take more than a slogan.

'Let's be brutally honest with ourselves,' he told his first Labour conference as leader. 'When you lose an election in a democracy, you deserve to. You don't look at the electorate and ask them: "What were you thinking?" You look at yourself and ask: "What were we doing?"' Being serious about winning meant dealing with the things that had driven people away from the party. 'Never again will Labour go into an election not being trusted on national security, with your job, with your community and with your money.'

He saw that this was not primarily to do with Labour's policies so much as its values. Many voters, including former Labour voters, believed that the party had come to see the world in a completely different way from them. Episodes like the response to the Salisbury attack suggested a reluctance to stand up for Britain. Corbyn's refusal to sing the national anthem at public events like the Battle of Britain memorial service and his equivocal attitude to terrorists – he notoriously talked about inviting 'friends' from Hezbollah and Hamas to Parliament, among many other incidents – were a disturbing sign for many former Labour voters. There was a widespread feeling that Labour under Corbyn treated longstanding supporters outside its metropolitan enclaves with disdain, and even seemed rather to dislike the country it claimed to want to govern.

Starmer soon set about the long task of trying to change this perception. 'I'm really proud of my country and I wouldn't be leader of the Labour Party if I wasn't patriotic,' he said on a 'Call Keir' video meeting with voters in Bury soon after becoming leader.

> In the Labour Party we should be proud of being patriotic. We're all working, knocking on doors in the rain or shine, to try to put in place a team that can go into government to improve the country we live in because we love the country we live in. I don't think we should shy away from that.

The new patriotism strategy scored an early hit in the shape of a front-page splash in the traditionally Conservative *Sunday Telegraph* on the seventy-fifth anniversary of VE Day in May 2020, in which Starmer wrote in praise of the generation who had 'protected our country in its darkest hour'. The piece, which was accompanied by a photograph of a saluting, medal-bedecked old soldier, also noted the effect of the coronavirus crisis in care homes, the debt the country owed to key workers and the need to tackle longstanding injustices, but in a way that would have been unthinkable under the party's previous leader.

To Westminster observers, this manoeuvre signalled a new level of ambition and professionalism. As one Labour strategist puts it:

> They understood – where do you go? Go to the *Telegraph*. What do you do? You hit them on the elderly. How do you do it? With a veteran. And for everyone in Westminster who rolled their eyes at the so-called obviousness of it, it has been a long time since the Labour press operation ran something as effective as that. So if I was Tory HQ, I'd be concerned about the lethality of what that represented.

But despite this promising early success, the interaction of patriotism, values and history soon proved difficult territory for Starmer. The Black Lives Matter protests that followed the killing of George Floyd also in May 2020 were an early example. Asked during a radio phone-in whether he approved of protesters in Bristol pulling down a statue of the slave trader Edward Colston and dumping it in the harbour, Starmer said:

> It shouldn't have been done that way. Completely wrong to pull down a statue down like that. Stepping back, the statue should have been taken down a long, long time ago. We can't, in 21st-century Britain, have a slaver on a statue … The statue should have been brought down properly, with consent, and put, I would say, in a museum.

The following day, in common with a number of other public figures and left-leaning politicians, he 'took a knee' in support of the BLM movement. But rather than do so in public, he tweeted a photo of himself and deputy leader Angela Rayner kneeling on the floor of an otherwise empty meeting room in Parliament with the caption: 'We kneel with all those opposing anti-Black racism. #BlackLivesMatter.' The approach suggested an attempt to balance the sensibilities of left-wing activists with the views of the wider public, who were much more sceptical about BLM and its aims. Soon afterwards, the attempt came to grief.

Asked in an interview what he thought of BLM's calls to 'defund the police', Starmer was unequivocal:

> That's nonsense, and nobody should be saying anything about de-funding the police. I would have no truck with that. I was Director of Public Prosecutions for five years, I worked with police forces across England and Wales, bringing thousands of people to court, so my support for the police is very, very strong and evidenced in the joint actions I've done with the police. There's a broader issue here, the Black Lives Matter movement, or moment if you like, interna-tionally, is about reflecting something completely different, and it's reflecting on what happened dreadfully in America just a few weeks ago and acknowledging that as a moment across the world. It's a shame it's getting tangled up with these organisational issues, with the organisation Black Lives Matter.[9]

This forceful and evidently sincere pronouncement chimed with what the public might have expected from a responsible political leader: ac-knowledgement that a serious issue had been brought into focus but rejection of a protest movement's more extreme demands. The left took a rather different view. BLM tweeted: 'As a public prosecutor, Sir Keir Starmer was a cop in an expensive suit', and a number of Labour MPs criticised his choice of words: '#BlackLivesMatter isn't just a moment, it's a movement,' said Streatham MP Bell Ribeiro-Addy.[10] 'It's clear that if we want to see real change, it's going to take sustained pressure from below.' His old adversaries at Camden Momentum demanded that the NEC pass a vote of no confidence in the leader. An endorsement from Nigel Farage ('Heartily agree with @Keir_Starmer's condemnation of the Black Lives Matter organisation') did nothing to reassure his critics.

In the days that followed, Starmer expressed contrition for the language he used. 'I meant "moment" as in "a defining moment", a turning point, and I genuinely think that reflects the sentiment that many, many black community leaders have expressed in recent weeks,' he said, adding:

I was absolutely not pandering to a racist vote. I was trying to recognise the significance of what was happening and express a determination that it should be a turning point, and to join with those across the Black Lives Matter movement who desperately do want it to be a turning point ... If people thought it meant something else, then of course I regret that.[11]

A caller on his LBC phone-in show suggested his offending comment might be 'indicative of unconscious dismissive language and attitudes' of the kind that feed structural racism in society and asked if he would consider taking unconscious bias training. Starmer said he was introducing such training for all Labour Party staff and that he would take the course himself as soon as he could fit it in. Asked by host Nick Ferrari if he thought he needed it, he replied:

I think everybody should have unconscious bias training. I think it is important. There is always the risk of unconscious bias, and just saying, 'Oh well, it probably applies to other people, not me' is not the right thing to do, so I'm going to lead from the front on this and do the training.[12]

(The implication of his remarks – that all voters need instruction to overcome their inherent racism – will not have been lost on those who heard them.)

The response to Starmer's comments on BLM were nothing to the row that followed the leak of an internal document recommending that the party associate itself with the union flag. Based on research by a branding agency called Republic, the presentation stated that 'belonging needs to be reinforced through all messengers' and that 'communicating Labour's respect and commitment for the country can represent a change in the party's body language'. Among other advice on restoring economic credibility and regaining the trust of once core voters, it suggested that 'the use of flags, veterans, dressing smartly at the war memorial etc give voters a sense of authentic values alignment'. The recurring theme of patriotism, together with interventions such as a political broadcast in which Starmer promised to 'rebuild our country' while standing next to the flag, suggested the advice was already being acted upon.

The backlash from the left was immediate and ferocious. Clive Lewis, a black MP who had served as shadow Business Secretary under Corbyn, said, 'It's not patriotism; it's Fatherland-ism. There's a better way to build social cohesion than moving down the track of the nativist right.'[13] He was not alone. Social media was awash with condemnation of Labour's supposed embrace of nationalist bigotry, and a barrage of comment pieces in left-leaning papers demanded to know what the point of the left was if it was going to walk and talk like the 'far right'. Other commentators, by no means confined to the right, mused upon the left's apparent disdain for the flag and the history of Britain, and wondered how deep the Starmerite conversion to patriotism really went.

Perhaps most damning of all was the verdict of a member of staff at Labour HQ, who said of the leadership: 'They don't believe any of this stuff; they're saying whatever they think will get them votes.' The unearthing by the Guido Fawkes website of the earlier mentioned *McLibel* video, in which Starmer mused, 'I got made a Queen's Counsel, which is odd since I often used to propose the abolition of the monarchy,' hardly authenticated his apparently newfound patriotic credentials.

Starmer stood his ground, at least to a degree. 'The union flag represents the country that Labour wants to govern, and that Keir wants to be the Prime Minister of. It's a symbol of the country we want to lead,' said his spokesman. 'You can call that patriotism, you can call it whatever you want, but that's what we stand for.' At the same time, he tried to distance himself from the document that had caused the fuss, which was 'produced by an external agency about the Labour Party … the recommendations in that report are their recommendations. It is not right to say it was presented as our strategy.'

When opportunities arose for Labour and its leader to display their attitude to national security, the resulting message could perhaps be described as ambiguous. In September 2020, Starmer ordered his MPs to abstain on the second reading of the Overseas Operations Bill, which was designed to protect British soldiers and veterans from prosecution over actions taken while serving abroad. Critics of the bill were concerned that it might deny justice to victims of alleged torture and war crimes, and – given Starmer's earlier work as a human rights lawyer – many were surprised at his stance on the issue. Nineteen Labour MPs defied the instruction and voted against, including three frontbenchers who lost their jobs as a result. Thirty-seven members of the Holborn & St Pancras Labour Party wrote to the *Camden New Journal* to vent their displeasure at their MP's stance and remind him that his leadership election platform had included a commitment to 'no more illegal wars'. Two months later Starmer and his party changed tack and opposed the legislation at its final stage in the Commons.

In October, the leadership faced an even bigger rebellion over the Covert Human Intelligence Sources Bill, also known as the 'Spy-cops' Bill, which gave legal protection to undercover agents forced to commit crimes while on secret operations. Thirty-four Labour MPs voted against the legislation despite again being whipped to abstain – a directive which allowed Conservative Home Secretary Priti Patel to say, 'Their leader may have changed, but Labour still can't be trusted on national security.'[14] On the other hand, Labour won an unintended endorsement on the issue when a speech from shadow Defence Secretary John Healey, affirming the party's 'non-negotiable' commitment to Britain's independent nuclear deterrent, was greeted by a piece in the *Socialist Worker* complaining that 'Starmer's Labour backs arms bosses, nukes and war'.

There were also tentative efforts to move away from the Corbynite approach to the economy. Starmer's suggestion that the government should 'look at the idea of a wealth tax' was swiftly abandoned despite support for the idea from the party's left. He told the Confederation of British Industry conference in November that he wanted a new partnership between Labour and business, saying he was 'under no illusion about the work we have to do if we're to win back your trust … When a business is failing it is often because the management is failing. The Labour Party is now under new management.'

These attempts by Starmer to show himself as a different kind of leader and change some of the more electorally damaging perceptions of his party's brand caused consternation in parts of the left. As we have seen, the Haldane Society of Socialist Lawyers banned Starmer

from membership on the grounds that he was 'demonstrably not a socialist'. Some in the Labour movement began to complain that since the
leadership contest little or nothing had been heard of his ten pledges,
which had been carefully calibrated to secure the support of a membership still largely loyal to Corbyn.

One such figure was Unite leader Len McCluskey. 'The fact is that
Keir Starmer ran on a radical programme, some might say a Corbyn
programme, and of course I keep this to hand,' he told an interviewer
from *The Observer* in August 2020, flourishing Starmer's campaign
leaflet. 'For me, he has to recognise that the ship he is sailing, if it lists
too much to the right, then it will go under.' As for the union's status as
Labour's biggest donor, 'It would be a mistake if anybody took Unite
for granted.' Two months later, its executive voted to cut funding to the
party by around £150,000.

Some senior party figures saw this as a small price to pay for a bit
of distance between the Labour Party and one of the most outspoken
supporters of Corbyn's socialist policies. As centrist Labour MP Ben
Bradshaw put it: 'I don't think this will bother Keir Starmer one bit, in
fact I think he'll probably welcome a bit of distance from the man who
has done our movement so much damage.'[15]

But the left remained vocal enough to remind outsiders that the
Labour Party as a whole had not been transformed overnight by Corbyn's departure. Starmer's own deputy, Angela Rayner, widely regarded as a more left-leaning figure than the leader himself, undermined
the new message of statesmanlike moderation by shouting 'scum' at
Conservative MP Chris Clarkson during a speech in the Commons,
earning a stern rebuke from the Deputy Speaker, Eleanor Laing: 'We
will not have remarks like that from the front bench: not under any
circumstances, no matter how heartfelt they might be – not at all.'
Labour MPs including Diane Abbott and Dawn Butler spoke out in

support of the blockading of newspaper presses by the protest group Extinction Rebellion. A Labour Party report titled 'Remaking of the British state: for the many, not the few', commissioned under Corbyn but not made public until ten months into Starmer's leadership, proposed the abolition of the honours system and gallantry medals for the military; reparation payments to former colonies; the scrapping of trade union laws; and the disestablishment of the Church of England. Labour MP Nadia Whittome declined to condemn protesters in Bristol who injured police officers and set police vehicles on fire while demonstrating against the Police, Crime, Sentencing and Courts Bill, while sixteen Labour city council candidates signed an open letter blaming the police for 'excessive force'. Shadow Culture Minister Alex Sobel dented his leader's efforts to reposition Labour as a pro-business party, saying on a podcast about the environment:

> When I first came in as an MP [in 2017] I was like, I'm not taking meetings with any of these people, these people are the enemy, you know? I'm a socialist, my job is to transform society … Now I take the meetings because I'm like, we haven't got enough time, you know? That's still my dream, but we aren't going to have time to do that and save the climate.[16]

As former MP Ian Austin put it: 'Keir Starmer is trying to drag the Labour Party back to common sense but keeps being undermined by this sort of silly infantile nonsense most people grow out of as teenagers.'[17]

How damaging are these repeated departures from the authorised message? One experienced campaign professional who has worked on both sides of the Atlantic says they can be a chance to show who is in charge:

There you can learn from both Biden and Blair, which is the clear position of, 'I lead the Labour Party, I lead the Democratic Party, the Labour Party is me, the Democratic Party is me. It's not what these other guys say.' You could equally paint a picture of Tory grassroots sentiment that was anathematic to mainstream voters if you brought those qualities to the fore and there was a weak Tory leader who wasn't standing in contravention of them. As long as your leader looks like they're in tune with the voter, the voter, I think, ignores or can dismiss the rest of the stuff.

True enough, provided the leader's own position – and their persona – is well enough established. In the early months in the job Starmer had managed to show that he was not like Jeremy Corbyn. But this left another question: who are you, then? Answering this and persuading voters that Labour had changed and was now a serious alternative government would be hard enough at the best of times – let alone during a global pandemic.

CHAPTER 14

CAPTAIN HINDSIGHT

tarmer had pictured the scene of his leadership election triumph many times: applause, flags, media, thousands of cheering supporters. 'It would have been the moment to turn and face the country,' he said.[1] 'What I didn't imagine was facing the country standing in my own living room with a camera and microphone for company.'

His victory speech, delivered in front of closed window shutters in his north London house, marked the beginning of a year in which he would not address a real public event or shake a single voter by the hand. During a deadly pandemic this misfortune barely registered on the scale of human hardship, as Starmer himself readily acknowledged. Even so, lockdown had created the worst possible campaigning conditions for a new political leader needing to introduce himself to the country.

Starmer had planned to launch his leadership with a long nationwide tour of former Labour seats, a demonstration that he was eager to listen and rebuild trust with the people and places the party had lost. This was swiftly abandoned and replaced with a series of town hall-style meetings on Zoom, the video calling platform, during which Starmer would listen to voters' views and answer their questions. As isolated workers all over the world were finding, such virtual encounters were better than nothing but no substitute for genuine human interaction. This was a real drawback for the Starmer project, which would depend on grasping the reasons for the breakdown of Labour's relationship with its former heartlands.

For Lord Mann, who stood down in 2019 and whose Bassetlaw constituency was subsequently won by the Conservatives, this should be the main lesson for Starmer from Labour's election defeat. 'He should certainly have spent more time in the north understanding those issues,' he says.[2] 'And that is the learning point for him. He's got to spend a ridiculously large amount of time understanding those issues, because my seat was everything his constituency isn't. You need to stand in other people's shoes.' Only so much of this could be done through the wonders of technology. 'A Zoom call is not going to get many people in the Bassetlaw constituency. I would state that as a fact rather than a criticism that he hasn't done it. And he's lost some time because of that.'

One Labour strategist who has seen Starmer in action believes direct encounters with the public not only show him at his best but are crucial to the development of his own thinking:

He listens. He doesn't listen like Ed Miliband listens, which is listening whilst waiting for your turn to speak. There's two types of listening by politicians. Type one is listening so that you can then tell the voter what you think and what they now think too. And version two is listening because you're trying to understand the voter's perspective so you yourself can go away and have a think about that. And understanding that persuasion rarely comes from the impassioned arguments in the moment but rather from reassurance and trust that is built over a longer period of time.

Confined to his top floor at home ('The children are now in charge of the house and I'm in the loft,' he confessed),[3] Starmer broke up long days on screen or phone with regular jogs. He hosted the shadow

Cabinet meeting on Zoom at 9.30 a.m. every Tuesday. As well as limiting his contact with potential voters, the restrictions made it harder for Starmer to cement relationships with his colleagues in Parliament. With much parliamentary business being conducted remotely, MPs and staff no longer bumped into each other in the Commons tearoom, the voting lobby or the party's Southside HQ in Victoria Street. 'It does matter,' said a friend of Starmer's,

> because even being able to say to your party members, 'Oh, I mentioned your campaign to Keir,' those little fleeting things, being able to say, 'Oh, congratulations on that speech you made or the birth of your daughter.' Those sorts of things really matter to generating that sense of team, and we've not been able to do it … It has caused difficulty, especially with new MPs who didn't get a chance to get to know Keir before Covid.

The national crisis created by the pandemic meant Starmer was constrained not just physically but politically. In his living-room victory address, he acknowledged that the government faced a huge responsibility,

> and whether we voted for this government or not, we all rely on it to get this right. That's why in the national interest the Labour Party will play its full part. Under my leadership we will engage constructively with the government, not opposition for opposition's sake. Not scoring party political points or making impossible demands. But with the courage to support where that's the right thing to do.

Unusually for a new party leader, the first order of business was not to begin plotting against his main opponent but to call him to discuss how they could work together. Starmer spoke to the Prime Minister by telephone soon after arriving in his new office on 4 April 2020, the two agreeing to meet the following week in Downing Street to discuss how best to tackle the Covid crisis. The appointment could not be kept. The following day, 5 April, Johnson was admitted to hospital having tested positive for the virus. In a tweet, Starmer wished him a speedy recovery. After a week, including three nights in intensive care, the PM was released to recuperate at Chequers. Looking haggard, he released a video thanking the NHS for saving his life and praising nurses and doctors for looking after him 'when things could have gone either way'.

With a critically ill Prime Minister and the pandemic claiming more than 1,000 lives a day, Starmer correctly sensed that there was no public appetite for party politics. Nor did he disagree with the thrust of the government's approach: those who questioned the policy of extended lockdowns were to be found on the Conservative benches, not Labour's. Instead, he chose to focus on the question of competence, asking detailed questions about ministers' handling of the crisis and the basis of their decisions.

However, Johnson's illness, followed by the birth of baby Wilfred Lawrie Nicholas Johnson at the end of April, meant that Starmer had to wait until he was a month into the job to confront his opposite number at Prime Minister's Questions. He opened their long-awaited encounter by welcoming the PM back to Parliament and congratulating him on the arrival of his son. Then came the punch:

When the Prime Minister returned to work a week ago Monday, he said that many people were looking at the 'apparent success' of the government's approach, but yesterday we learned that, tragically, at least 29,427 people in the UK have now lost their lives to this dreadful virus. That is now the highest number in Europe and the second highest in the world. That is not success, or even apparent success, so can the Prime Minister tell us: how on earth did it come to this?

He followed up by interrogating the figures on deaths in care homes, the rate of testing, the abandonment of contact tracing and the supply of personal protective equipment for NHS staff. He accused the government of being 'slow on lockdown, slow in testing, slow on the supply of PPE'.

Starmer's performance pleased the critics. The BBC's Laura Kuenssberg described the encounter as 'the lawyer versus the showman'. Joe Murphy of the *Standard* wrote:

> The word 'forensic' is the one that everyone will use about Sir Keir's silky performance at the despatch box. It was indeed. Yet the word doesn't actually begin to capture the quietly terrifying force of a skilled former chief prosecutor assembling all the evidence and nailing it piece by damning piece to the accused.

Starmer's early outings as Labour leader helped to draw a contrast with both his opponent and his predecessor. The fearsome political interrogator Andrew Neil tweeted that it was 'clear that the United Kingdom now has a functioning, probing, measured, informed official opposition. The government will need to raise its game.' Dominic Grieve, a fellow lawyer who had worked with Starmer in the previous parliament in his days as a Tory Brexit rebel, says the Labour leader's parliamentary performances have shown him to be the 'complete antithesis' of the Prime Minister.[4]

His forensic skills as a prosecuting lawyer sometimes come to the fore, and he's pretty good at puncturing Johnson's braggadocio, helped by the fact that there's an empty House of Commons so that the claque who makes the noise in the background isn't there. So Johnson looks like a person in some difficulty with the law sitting in the witness box being cross-examined.

For his part, Starmer tried to avoid being characterised as a perennial lawyer. He explained on *Desert Island Discs* that he did not approach politics like a day in court. 'They are completely different. If you're a lawyer it's based on the facts, it's a proper argument, there's a judge who makes the decision. In politics it's completely different because it's a different art of persuasion.'

Johnson himself mentioned Starmer's lawyerly credentials at every opportunity, whether because he believed it would be an effective line of attack with voters or because he simply thought Starmer would find it annoying. During a bad-tempered exchange over school reopening plans in June, the PM declared:

> The right hon. and learned Gentleman still cannot work out whether he is saying that schools are not safe enough or that we should be going back more quickly. He cannot have it both ways. It is one brief on one day and another brief on the next. I understand how the legal profession works, but what the public want to have is some consistency.

He tried a similar jibe the following week, concluding an answer to a question on the same subject with a brisk, 'Mr Speaker, your witness.'

In the early days, the public liked what they saw of their serious new Leader of the Opposition. By early June 2020, YouGov found more voters thinking Starmer was doing a good job than those who felt the same about Johnson, and that people were more likely to agree than disagree that Starmer looked like a Prime Minister-in-waiting. Labour's polling deficit against the Conservatives, which had stood at twenty-four points when Starmer took over, had almost closed by early autumn. This success was short-lived. In principle, the idea that the country needed a decent, grown-up opposition holding the government constructively to account during the crisis was surely correct. In political terms, this would prove a much harder strategy to implement than it sounded.

Starmer and his party supported the government's overall approach to the pandemic: lockdowns, school closures and generous financial support for jobs and businesses. After the emergency provisions in the Coronavirus Act were passed in one day without a vote in March 2020, Labour under Starmer did not oppose their renewal six months later and voted to extend them further the following March.

This, however, left plenty of scope for him to criticise. The supply of PPE, the arrangements in care homes, the calculation of official mortality figures, the test and trace programme, the support for self-employed people and new job starters, the timing of the end of the furlough scheme, the school reopening plans, the protection for those using public services, the procurement contracts for safety equipment, the guidelines for employers, the changes to universal credit, the quarantine for international travellers, the government's messaging and communications, the leaks of government plans, the council funding, the school exam marking, the NHS capacity planning for winter, the free school meal provision, the exit strategy from lockdown and the immigration surcharge for NHS and care workers from overseas (on which he was able to claim the credit for a change in policy) were all subjected to Starmer's stern scrutiny. His reproaches were usually delivered more in sorrow than in anger, but there was an echo of Brexit-era Starmer: assurances of support on the overall destination but quibbles about every single step along the way.

Starmer's repeated complaint that the government had been slow in all the major decisions – slow into lockdown, slow on testing, slow with PPE, slow with an exit strategy – developed into a kind of mantra as the weeks wore on and he repeated it in interview after interview. To large parts of the public this began to sound more like carping from the sidelines than constructive opposition. Even non-Tories were often inclined to give the government the benefit of the doubt as it battled to contain a national crisis in unprecedented circumstances. Few thought a Labour government under Starmer would be handling the situation any better.

His approach also clearly irritated Johnson. At PMQs on 8 July, he replied to a question from Starmer on the spread of infections in care homes by saying:

> The reality is that we now know things about the way the coronavirus is passed from person to person without symptoms that we just did not know. That is why we instituted the care home action plan on 15 April. That is why we changed the procedures. Perhaps he did know that it was being transmitted asymptomatically – I did not hear it at the time. Perhaps Captain Hindsight would like to tell us that he knew that it was being transmitted asymptomatically.

The moniker would be used again and again to characterise Starmer as an armchair critic who enjoyed the luxury of retrospective complaint without the responsibility of making decisions based on limited information.

But while some began to see Starmer as a nit-picking opportunist, many on his own side felt the opposition leader was giving the government too easy a ride. Starmer's observation in PMQs that the expansion of critical care capacity in the NHS had been an 'amazing piece of work' prompted a storm of protest on Twitter from those who blamed the government for Britain's escalating death toll. Alastair Campbell, Tony Blair's former press secretary, wrote that the opposition should 'show no mercy' in challenging ministers, even during a crisis.[5]

The Labour leader ordered his MPs to abstain in Commons votes on the 'rule of six' for private gatherings, a 10 p.m. curfew for pubs and the tier system, under which different restrictions would apply to different parts of the country depending on the local prevalence of the virus. This decision brought predictable scorn from the Prime Minister, who declared that 'Captain Hindsight is rising rapidly up the ranks and has become General Indecision'.[6] It was also condemned by the more unlikely figure of former England footballer Gary Neville, who complained that Labour was not doing its job of protecting the disadvantaged: 'They know that the economic support isn't in place aligned with those restrictions, which means you've got to take a position and be bold and go against it, you cannot abstain … You're the opposition, don't sit in the stand.'[7] After a successful campaign led by another footballer, Marcus Rashford, to persuade ministers to continue the provision of free school meals during the summer holidays, a poll found voters thinking the Manchester United forward was doing a better job of holding the government to account than Starmer.

Starmer was also regularly criticised for demanding new measures when the government was already widely expected to announce them at any moment. The most glaring example was in January 2021, when interviews in which he called for a new national lockdown and the closure of schools within the following twenty-four hours were broadcast after government sources had briefed the media that exactly such an announcement was imminent. Starmer's office said the interviews were recorded before the move was confirmed, but the charge remained that his position was always that the government should be doing more of what they were doing anyway, but faster: questions about the effectiveness of restrictions or the wider consequences of lengthy lockdowns went unasked by the official opposition.

Nevertheless, Starmer did occasionally take the opportunity to give the government a good kicking. During the first lockdown, when millions were prevented from travelling even to visit sick relatives or attend funerals, Johnson's chief adviser, Dominic Cummings, was accused of breaking the law by driving his family from London to his parents' home in Durham so that their young son could be looked after while both he and his wife were ill. The incident provoked a furious reaction from much of the public and the media – including right-leaning newspapers – and some Conservative MPs, as well as the government's opponents. Starmer said: 'If I were Prime Minister, I'd have sacked Cummings,' and raged that it looked like 'one rule for the Prime Minister's advisers, another rule for everybody else'. Combined with recent missteps over the easing of restrictions and slow progress on testing and tracing, the incident led to a collapse in approval of the government's management of the crisis. 'I am putting the Prime Minister on notice that he has got to get a grip and restore public confidence in the government's handling of the epidemic,' he said.[8] 'There is a growing concern the government is now winging it. At precisely the time when there should have been maximum trust in the government, confidence has collapsed.'

He was able to adopt a similar tone of outraged indignation after Johnson was forced to cancel plans to ease restrictions over the 2020 Christmas break, under which up to three households would have been allowed to meet indoors for the first time in months. Starmer, who had called unsuccessfully for a 'circuit breaker' lockdown to check a rise in Covid cases earlier in the autumn, demanded a review of the festive relaxation, prompting the Prime Minister to say in the Commons: 'I wish he had the guts to just say what he really wants to do, which is to cancel the plans people have made and to cancel Christmas.' Three days later, on 19 December, Johnson announced that the spread of a dangerous new variant of the virus had forced him to reverse the decision and introduce new, tougher rules for much of the country. Having warned of such an outcome, Starmer said that the measures were necessary and that he supported them.

> But there is no getting away from the fact, and what angers people the most and frustrates me the most, is that, yet again, the Prime Minister waited until the eleventh hour to take this decision. It was blatantly obvious last week that the Prime Minister's plan for a free-for-all over Christmas was a risk too far. And yet, rather than listening to concerns and taking them seriously the Prime Minister did what he always does. Dismissed the challenge, ruffled his hair and made a flippant comment ... It is an act of gross negligence by a Prime Minister who once again has been caught behind the curve ... We have a Prime Minister who is so scared of being unpopular that he is incapable of taking tough decisions until it is too late.

If Starmer was sometimes able to articulate people's frustration over incidents like the Cummings debacle and the Christmas U-turn, the pandemic's unrelenting dominance of the news made it even harder than it usually is for an opposition party to win attention for its own agenda. A rare opportunity came with the leader's speech to Labour's 'virtual' party conference, in which, as previously noted, he told his party it had deserved to lose the election. He also declared: 'I want this to be the best country to grow up in and the best country to grow old in. A country in which we put family first. A country that embodies the values I hold dear: decency, fairness, opportunity, compassion and security' – most of which were values that many voters had not associated with Labour for some time. As well as its attempt to position Labour as the party of the family, the speech was also noted for its ambition. Starmer went on:

> In 1945, Attlee had to build a society fit to reward the sacrifices of the war. In 1964, Wilson had to make the 'white heat of technology' work for working people. In 1997, Blair wanted to extend the new era of opportunity to everyone. In the seventy-five years since the historic victory of 1945 there have only been three Labour winners. I want to be the fourth.

But as the second wave of the pandemic gathered pace during the autumn, such promising themes were soon submerged in the all-Covid news cycle. By the turn of the year, left-leaning commentators and some in Parliament began to wonder aloud when Starmer would begin to set out a compelling vision of Labour as an alternative government. 'It's all tactics, no strategy,' said one Labour MP.[9] 'Keir and his people are not political and they're making increasing missteps because they don't have an analysis about where they ultimately want to get to.'

Labour figures briefed friendly media sources that there was, in fact, a plan. Starmer was approaching his leadership in phases: having established himself as a serious figure at the head of a constructive opposition, he would now begin to set out Labour's own priorities.

A New Year speech in which Starmer called for a reversal of planned hikes in council tax, and an extension of the temporary uplift in universal credit and the ban on home repossessions introduced early in the pandemic – a continuation of his party-of-the-family theme – was well received by the leader writers. *The Times* judged it 'a powerful statement of intent' and declared that Starmer had 'earned a proper hearing'. A lecture by shadow Chancellor Anneliese Dodds, designed to expound Labour's newfound commitment to fiscal responsibility, was described by Philip Collins of the *New Statesman* as 'crushingly, almost preternaturally, dull', which was surely progress given the party's reputation for financial recklessness.

In February, in what was billed as his most important speech to date, Starmer set out his own broader analysis, designed to rival the narrative that had helped the Conservatives win and consolidate power before and after 2010. While David Cameron and George Osborne had successfully claimed that their policies represented a return to sound economic management after years of Labour overspending, Starmer argued that the pandemic had disproportionately affected the UK because Tory austerity had weakened the foundations of British society, and that the post-Covid reconstruction presented an opportunity for change. The centrepiece of his speech was a proposal for British Recovery Bonds, through which savers would be able to invest in the country's recovery, along with state-financed start-up loans for 100,000 new small businesses: 'An example of the active, empowering government I believe is needed if we're to build a more secure economy.'

But such interventions failed to gain traction, and the idea of British Recovery Bonds sank without trace. Criticisms soon resurfaced, boosted, as we have already seen, by the row over the notorious 'flag memo'. As can sometimes happen in politics, the theme of Starmer's lacklustre leadership gathered momentum and became self-perpetuating as more commentators chimed in. Starmer needs more than a list of Tory failures, they chorused. He needs to be a better storyteller. He hasn't convinced people that Labour have really changed. He needs to be bolder and surprise people. He should hit the government harder. He should stop nagging and nit-picking. He's letting Boris off the hook. He sounds shifty and opportunistic. He's commentating on events, not leading. He needs to show passion. He lacks the killer instinct. His forensic arguments don't win over the crowd. He has no alternative plan. His shadow Cabinet is all but anonymous. He's alienating his supporters on the left. He's in thrall to Labour's woke wing. He's abandoned the working class. He is Miliband 2.0. He's letting focus groups determine his strategy. He hasn't got a strategy, only tactics. He's being hard on Labour and soft on the Tories.

Above all, they said, the party under Starmer doesn't seem to know what it is for. 'We don't hate Jews any more, vote Labour' wouldn't do as a slogan, as pundit Dan Hodges pitilessly put it.[10] 'Does anyone know what the Labour Party is doing?' the comedian Mark Steel was moved to ask in his *Independent* column. 'Are they still going? Maybe they were wound up in November and have retrained as yoga instructors or pig farmers.'

Such complaints were not confined to the columnising class. Labour MPs and even shadow Cabinet members regularly grumbled to reporters about their leader's shortcomings. 'People are starting to get restless and wanting to know what we stand for.' 'He comes over as solid but too risk-averse and frankly a bit boring.' 'Starmer just isn't very political. He spent too long doing a politically neutral job as Director of Public Prosecutions and that has made him risk-averse.' 'It seems to me that we've got one of the most incompetent governments we've ever had, who are managing the pandemic in a dreadful way, and all too often we're just agreeing with them and giving them carte blanche.' 'If we had an election tomorrow then [Tottenham MP] David Lammy would get a majority of 100,000 or whatever, but that doesn't help us in seats like Grimsby.' 'They think they understand the red wall, when really all they understand is Westminster game-playing and a couple of postcodes in Camden.' In early February the Socialist Campaign group, comprising left-wing MPs, unions and party members demanded an emergency conference to discuss what it called the 'crisis' in the party. Critics also pointed to evidence from NEC elections suggesting the party's membership had fallen by just under 57,000 – around 10 per cent, or nearly 250 a day, to 495,961 – since Starmer became leader. The party's finances had also taken a hit: donations totalled just over £15 million during Starmer's first year in charge, compared to £21.8 million in the first twelve months under Corbyn.

Some in the party were also distressed at the abandonment of what they still considered a fruitful campaign issue: Brexit. In December 2020, Starmer whipped Labour MPs to vote for the deal Boris Johnson and the EU reached on Christmas Eve, arguing that while a better deal should have been negotiated, Parliament now faced a binary choice:

A thin deal is better than no deal, and not implementing this deal would mean immediate tariffs and quotas with the EU, which will push up prices and drive businesses to the wall. It will mean huge gaps in security, a free-for-all on workers' rights and environmental protections, and less stability for the Northern Ireland protocol.[11]

Party figures explained that the issue had to be put to bed: they could not hope to win back lost voters while still apparently refusing to accept their decision on EU membership, emphatically confirmed at the 2019 election. Starmer later signalled that he would not seek to restore freedom of movement – abandoning one of his ten leadership election pledges – saying any Labour government would inherit the agreement as it now stood: 'I don't think there's scope for major renegotiation,' he said.[12] 'We've just had four years of negotiation. We've arrived [at] a treaty and now we've got to make that treaty work.' Thirty-seven MPs defied his order to back Johnson's deal, and many wanted to continue the battle. 'The idea that the Brexit issue is done and dusted is for the birds,' said Richard Corbett, a former Labour leader in the European

Parliament.[13] 'Just as with Covid, Labour must highlight Johnson's incompetence and malevolence, and point to how the damage can be rectified.' Exeter MP Ben Bradshaw, a centrist, said Starmer had been right to focus on Covid during the crisis, but 'it is not going to be sustainable not to talk about Brexit for very much longer. Otherwise, what's the point of being the opposition?'

How far these criticisms were justified – and even the fact that many of them were mutually contradictory – effectively ceased to matter. The idea that Starmer's leadership was struggling became an established fact, an embedded part of the political narrative. He was also the victim of more tangible misfortunes. In October 2020, he collided with a Deliveroo cyclist while en route to his Kentish Town tailor in his Toyota RAV4 ('How did you not see me?' called the aggrieved victim before being taken to hospital with an injured arm. The police decided to take no action.)

A more politically embarrassing incident followed when a misunderstanding at PMQs led Starmer to initiate a stand-up row with Johnson in the Commons voting lobby. In response to a question on coronavirus travel restrictions, Johnson said:

> If we had listened to the right hon. and learned gentleman, we would still be at the starting blocks, because he wanted to stay in the European Medicines Agency [which had taken much longer than the UK medicine regulator to authorise Covid vaccines] and said so four times from that despatch box.

Starmer hit back furiously: 'Complete nonsense. Don't let the truth get in the way of a pre-prepared gag: the Prime Minister knows that I have never said that, from this despatch box or anywhere else, but the truth escapes him.'

Conservative MP Mark Francois happened to be sitting behind Johnson. 'I said to him, "Did he say it?" and Boris said, "Yes." So I texted my researcher and said, "PM certain he said it. Find the quote!" He found the extract from Hansard,' he recalls.[14] Francois made a point of order at the end of PMQs, declaring that Starmer had indeed said, on 31 January 2017, 'Why would we want to be outside the European Medicines Agency, which ensures that all medicines in the EU market are safe and effective?' After the session, Francois says,

> I walked out of the chamber to the Members' Lobby. As I came out, I saw the PM and Trudy, his PPS, standing with Starmer basically wagging his finger at him very aggressively, red in the face, and he's almost shouting at him. And he's saying, 'I never said that; that's wrong.' The PM stood his ground. He didn't overreact. He just said, 'Look, Keir, check the record.' Denis Healey's first law of politics is 'when you're in a hole, stop digging'. Keir Starmer was in the cab of a JCB. It's lucky for Keir nobody took a photo.

Back in his office, Starmer watched the exchange again and realised what had happened. As his spokesman later explained, he had 'misheard' and thought Johnson had said he wanted to join the EU vaccination programme. 'Keir accepts that, on this occasion, the Prime Minister was referring to old comments about the European Medicines Agency, and Keir admits he was wrong and made a mistake in his response.' The incident crowned a terrible week for Starmer, which also saw the leaked flag memo and the emergence of the video in which he talked of his former republican sympathies. It also provided further material for the satirists. 'I guess it's fitting that the Labour leader has finally mildly lost his rag in a misunderstanding over the European Medicines Agency and the EU's vaccine programme. And no doubt he ran the full gamut of emotions from shirty to tetchy,' mused *The Guardian*'s Marina Hyde.

Perhaps the biggest obstacle to Labour's attempts to gain ground on the government was altogether out of Starmer's hands. By November 2020, the taskforce established by Johnson under venture capitalist Kate Bingham had secured 350 million doses of vaccines under development. On 2 December, the UK became the first country in the world to approve the Pfizer-BioNTech vaccine, and the first inoculations took place six days later. Two more vaccines, from AstraZeneca and Moderna, were approved by early January. By Starmer's first anniversary as Labour leader some 27 million people had received at least one dose, making the UK's programme one of the most successful in the world. Polls found that close to nine in ten voters approved of the scheme, a remarkable score for any government endeavour.

The success of the vaccine rollout eclipsed Starmer's continued criticism of the government's handling of the pandemic. More seriously for Labour, it blunted the party's whole political attack on Johnson's Conservatives. 'If there is one thing that the Labour Party absolutely does not want right now it is a sudden and sustained display of competence on the part of this government,' said a gleeful minister.[15] 'Yet that's exactly what they're now facing.'

Added to this was the fact that with Conservative Chancellor Rishi Sunak spending on an unprecedented scale and Johnson's government loudly committed to 'levelling up' previously neglected parts of the country, Labour's habitual anti-austerity message had become redundant. As one senior party figure put it:

We are facing a very difficult fight over the next few years, where the Tories are going to spend lots of cash in seats they won, stick a picture of the MP next to a bypass or bridge with a grinning Boris on the leaflets and say: 'The Labour MP never got this done in twenty years, look what a difference I've made.' I've not heard a single answer to how we combat that.[16]

Starmer was not without his defenders. His allies were at pains to emphasise the progress he had made considering the battering the party had received at the 2019 election. Having inherited what one senior aide described as a 'burning skip of a party', the new leader's task effectively combined Tony Blair's reinvention of Labour in the 1990s with David Cameron's rebranding of the Tories after 2005. 'If we'd been a car, we'd have been scrapped,' said one shadow minister. Voters had begun to lose trust in Labour before they had heard of Jeremy Corbyn; a swift transformation of the party's fortunes was never realistic. While Starmer represented a return to decent, grown-up politics, most people were simply not that interested in what the opposition had to say, especially during a national crisis when they were willing the government to succeed – a government which under Johnson's premiership still felt relatively new, despite the Conservatives' decade in office.

Even so, there was no escaping the fact that the more voters saw of Starmer, the less impressed they seemed. The 48 per cent of voters who told YouGov that they thought he was doing his job well in the summer of 2020 proved to be a peak. The number declined steadily over the autumn, falling to 26 per cent by the following April; nearly twice as many said they thought he was doing badly. Overall, the Conservatives had once again opened a consistent lead in the polls.

But the state of the parties would soon be tested not in opinion surveys but at the ballot box. The May 2021 local elections would see contests for councils, mayoralties and police and crime commissioners throughout Britain, as well as elections to the Welsh Assembly and the Scottish Parliament.

In what may be a Westminster record, the time-honoured game of expectation management – in which the parties compete to say how badly they expect to do in the hope of achieving what will then look like a comparative success – began as early as January, when Labour sources began to brief that they anticipated a 'vaccine bounce' for the Tories. The party's internal projections suggested its aim should be to minimise losses. 'There are no signs in any of the polling we have seen that we are going to make any advances whatsoever,' said a well-placed insider.[17]

The stakes were raised further when Mike Hill, the MP for Hartlepool, stood down over allegations of harassment, triggering a by-election in a formerly solid Labour seat which the party had held only narrowly in 2019. Ominously for Starmer, however, the vote for the Brexit Party in the heavily Leave-voting constituency had been nearly three times the size of Labour's majority over the Tories; with no such party to split the pro-Brexit vote, the result this time might look every different.

Traditionally, the date of a by-election is decided by the party holding the seat; perhaps fatefully, Starmer decided it would be held alongside the other contests on 6 May, which would make the result the lead story of election night. Another big judgement call was for the party's NEC to draw up a 'longlist' consisting of only one candidate: Dr Paul Williams, a Remain-voting supporter of a second referendum who had been the MP for nearby Stockton South until the voters decided otherwise in 2019. Starmer would visit the constituency three times before polling day.

Launching his party's national campaign, Starmer proclaimed that 'every vote for the Labour Party is a vote for nurses' pay, for NHS staff' – arguably an odd choice of theme, since none of the hundreds of candidates up for election in May would have any power over such questions were they to be elected. For several weeks, though, the Tories themselves seemed eager to supply the opposition with extra material. It emerged that David Cameron had privately lobbied ministers and senior civil servants to give Greensill Capital, a firm in which he had an interest and which subsequently collapsed, access to a coronavirus bailout scheme. It was reported that Johnson had said he would rather see 'bodies pile high in their thousands' than take the country into a third lockdown before agreeing to do so the previous autumn. Dominic Cummings, who had left his role as Johnson's chief adviser in November, claimed an anonymous Conservative donor had paid £58,000 towards the cost of refurbishing the PM's Downing Street flat before being reimbursed by Johnson, a loan which he had failed to declare.

Starmer did his best to capitalise, switching the focus of Labour's message to 'the return of Tory sleaze', but to little avail. A visit to the wallpaper department of the Manchester branch of John Lewis, a playful attempt to highlight the story that Johnson had spent £840 on a single roll, was roundly ridiculed. ('Starmer seems to think his only role is to catch Boris Johnson out over some perceived failure, ill-judged remark or flaw in his procurement of soft furnishings. And then to follow it up with an infantile stunt,' thundered the following day's *Sun*.) Gallingly for Starmer, YouGov gave the Conservatives an eleven-point lead, with more voters having a favourable view of Johnson than his opponent, even though more than half of respondents said they considered the Tories 'very sleazy and disreputable'.

Starmer's campaign didn't get any happier. On Good Friday, he posted a video of his visit to Jesus House, a prominent church in London, which Boris Johnson and the Prince of Wales had both visited in the preceding weeks. Starmer described Jesus House as 'a wonderful example of a church serving their community' by hosting a vaccine centre and running a food bank. The video also showed Starmer and local MP Dawn Butler praying with pastor Agu Irukwu.

A backlash from this wholesome scene followed when it emerged that Pastor Irukwu had opposed same-sex marriage and, in 2006, written to the *Telegraph* along with other churches opposing equalities legislation, fearing that it would curtail religious freedom. *Guardian* columnist Owen Jones was among those demanding that Starmer repent: 'Unless the Labour leadership wants to make it clear it doesn't care about LGBTQ people, it needs to apologise.' Rather than explain that he took a different view from the pastor on some questions and reiterate that the church was doing good work that he wanted to encourage, Starmer repudiated the whole event. 'I completely disagree with Jesus House's beliefs on LGBT+ rights, which I was not aware of before my visit,' he tweeted. 'I apologise for the hurt my visit caused and have taken down the video. It was a mistake and I accept that.'

The pastor later explained that the Labour Party had initially approached Jesus House with an email highlighting the church's efforts to promote vaccine take-up and asking if Starmer could come and see for himself. He added that the incident had led to appalling abuse of the church on social media:

> Some of the language that has been directed at us can only be described as vile, abusive, hateful, and possibly criminal. It is tantamount to cyberbullying and the timing of this attack during Easter, one of the most important events in the Christian calendar, was particularly upsetting for us as a congregation.[18]

To cap it all, one sunny April day in Bath, Starmer was thrown out of a bar. 'Get out of my pub!' shouted Rod Humphris, the landlord, as the Labour leader stepped into The Raven. 'That man is not allowed in my pub!' He continued his tirade. 'You have failed me. I've been a Labour voter my entire life, you have failed to be the opposition. You have failed to ask whether lockdown was functioning.' As someone whose business had been closed by government edict for much of the preceding year, he had not been impressed with Starmer's stance. 'Thousands of people have died because you failed to do your job and ask the real questions ... Why have we just accepted lockdown?' Video of the altercation, which was reminiscent of the satirical drama *The Thick of It*, was seen by millions. Starmer said afterwards that he profoundly disagreed with Mr Humphris's view and that 'the vast majority recognise the lockdown is necessary and the restrictions are necessary'. True though that may have been, the encounter seemed to sum up the fortunes of an increasingly beleaguered leader.

As the elections approached, Labour campaign sources complained that the party was 'skint' and that canvass returns were 'abysmal' outside the party's safe areas. A shadow minister returning from by-election duty said things did not feel good. 'A lot of it is body language. People don't want to speak; they close the door. People who have been Labour in the past say they haven't made up their minds.'[19] Starmer's final round of media interviews felt like a pre-emptive post-mortem. He would take full responsibility for the results, he said, 'Just as I take full responsibility for everything that happens in the Labour Party under my leadership.' On the *Today* programme two days before polling day, he said his job was

to rebuild the Labour Party out of that devastating loss in 2019 and put us in a position to win the next general election. I said on the day that I was elected that that was a mountain to climb. It is, we're climbing it, and I've got a burning desire to build a better future for our country, and Thursday is a first step towards that better future. But I don't think anybody realistically thought that it was possible to turn the Labour Party round from the worst general election result since 1935 to a position to win the next general election within the period of one year. It was always going to take longer than that.

EPILOGUE: 'CHANGING THE THINGS THAT NEED CHANGING'

The Conservatives won Hartlepool with a 16 per cent swing and a majority of 7,000. The Tory Mayor of Teesside was re-elected with nearly three quarters of the vote, and his counterpart in the West Midlands was returned to office comfortably. Labour lost control of councils including Durham, Plymouth, Sheffield and West Lancashire. Tory gains included Dudley, Harlow, Northumberland and Nottinghamshire. Labour wins in London, Wales, Bristol, Liverpool, Manchester and West of England mayoral contests could not disguise the party's latest pounding. Tracy Brabin's election as Mayor of West Yorkshire meant another testing by-election eight weeks later in her former constituency of Batley & Spen – a contest in which Labour squeaked home with a majority of 323, down from 3,525 in 2019.

In his ritual TV interview the morning after the May local elections, Starmer looked rattled, perhaps even slightly manic. 'We have changed as a party, but we've not made a strong enough case to the country. We've lost that connection, that trust, and I intend to rebuild that and do whatever is necessary to rebuild that trust,' he insisted.[1] Quite what that would entail was unclear – at least, it seemed, to him: 'Changing the things that need changing. That is the change that I will bring about.'

There followed a predictable round of recrimination and soul searching. Starmer's allies echoed the need for change and argued a swift transformation in Labour's fortunes had always been unrealistic, while figures from all wings of the party bemoaned its lack of message and direction. Some argued that an existential crisis was at hand: Tony Blair warned that parties have no divine right to exist and that Labour needed 'total deconstruction and reconstruction'. Starmer's leadership was called into question. Was it still possible to see him entering No. 10? Was he the new Neil Kinnock, who was unable to win himself but who laid the foundations for eventual victory under new leadership? Or could he even follow in the ignominious footsteps of George Lansbury, who, in 1935, became the last Labour leader to step down without fighting a general election?

At the time of writing, these questions naturally remain unanswered. And as the past few years have shown time and again, making predictions about politics is a fool's errand. But now we know more about the man, we can better assess how he measures up to the historic task he faces.

Starmer is not what Napoleon would call a lucky general. The pandemic constrained him politically and practically, making it even harder than it usually is for an opposition leader to set out his stall. But sometimes in politics you have to make your own luck, and Starmer has often been the author of his own misfortune. Having said he would take responsibility for the May election results, he removed his deputy, Angela Rayner, from her role as party chair and campaign co-ordinator – an apparent buck-passing manoeuvre that resulted in a furious backlash, a shambolic reshuffle and a further weakening of his authority. His left-wing leadership election platform left him open to accusations of betrayal and limited his mandate for change. His preoccupation with party unity has often meant hedging and backtracking, depriving the party of a sense of direction and often leaving Starmer with the worst of all possible worlds. His efforts to project Labour as a patriotic party of mainstream values culminated in him telling voters they should all have unconscious bias training to counter their innate racism. To take another small but telling example, it comes to something when a British political leader finds himself apologising for visiting a church at Easter. Starmer has repeatedly spoken of doing what it takes to win, without spelling out what he thinks this might be. The result is a party united only in discontent.

Through his determined efforts to eradicate antisemitism from the Labour Party, Starmer has already rendered the country a valuable service, albeit one that ought never to have been needed. But after passing that early test of leadership, his progress seemed to stall. Reassembling Labour's voting coalition means reversing a decline that has taken place over a generation, not just a couple of recent elections. The mountain Starmer faces means that winning at the first time of asking would be an electoral feat to surpass those of Attlee and Blair. He will not be cheered by the irony that it falls to him to wrest millions of working-class voters from the clutches of Alexander Boris de Pfeffel Johnson, Old Etonian.

Is Starmer the man to do it? Many have their doubts. Mark Seddon, the former editor of *Tribune*, has known every Labour leader since James Callaghan and worked for Gordon Brown in his role as UN special envoy for global education and as a member of his Economic Policy Commission. He was also an elected member of Labour's ruling National Executive Committee during Blair's leadership. He voted for Starmer to become leader in 2020 but now speaks for many disillusioned supporters. 'Pandemic or no pandemic, we simply don't know what Sir Keir believes in,' he says.[2]

He seems to lack the prerequisites that could be found in different measure in all of the previous Labour leaders I have known and worked for. Where some verve, colour, charisma, inner steel and morality – and above all humour – could seriously wing the absurd Beano comic character currently inhabiting No. 10 Downing Street, there is none. What passion there is manifests itself in petulance and anger, often directed towards people on his own side. The public seems to have made up its mind about Sir Keir, fairly or unfairly, or maybe even both. It may not be Sir Keir's fault that Labour is now largely a party of loyal-to-the-last Wales, cities and university towns. It is nearly suffocated in Scotland; in retreat in historic old coalfields and middling towns. The rot is now so deep that even many of life's natural optimists ask the question: can anyone begin to lead Labour back from the wilderness? Sadly, if there is that someone, it seems increasingly unlikely that it will be Sir Keir.

The proximate cause of Labour's 2019 slump – though not the root – was the combination of Brexit and Corbyn. Starmer did everything in his power to prevent the former and, as a loyal member of his shadow Cabinet, campaigned to make the latter Prime Minister. Given the nature of the task he faces, such credentials do not seem promising. But this need not mean his fate is sealed. As one experienced strategist says:

It matters far more to Westminster watchers that Starmer was Mr Remain than it does to Red Wall voters who will be making their decision on him, not based on what happened a pandemic ago with regards to a referendum campaign and the internal politics of the Labour Party thereafter. After all, politics is always like, 'What have you done for me lately?'

And as for his predecessor, 'Voters will just say, "I didn't like that guy, but I like this one," or they'll say, "We still haven't forgiven you for Corbyn," in which case it doesn't work for anyone.'

Those who have known Starmer well, both in Parliament and in his life before politics, often speak of his character, as well as his intellect. But when it comes to his predicament, their compliments can be as instructive as others' criticisms. 'I feel his integrity very strongly,' says Lord Goldsmith, who has known Starmer since his time as Attorney General in the Blair government.[3]

> His decency I feel very strongly. But it's interesting that after he'd been DPP he didn't go about as Mr Rentaquote, which some people have done. He wasn't looking for opportunities to have people talking about Keir Starmer. I would say he is genuinely concerned about doing the job well and not promoting himself.

Admirable no doubt, but not necessarily a recipe for political success.

The May election trouncing spurred Starmer to greater efforts on the self-promotion front. The opening move was an interview on Piers Morgan's *Life Stories*, in which he spoke tearfully about his mother's illness and other episodes from his family life (a gambit also employed by Gordon Brown shortly before he was turfed out of Downing Street in 2010). Even if publicity of this kind succeeds in making voters feel they know him better, to have any chance of success he will need to be bolder politically.

'I remember Gordon Brown, really early on before Labour was in power, on a tour,' says a senior Labour figure with long experience of campaigning.

> It was a tour of the south-west and he was getting out to the places he

wasn't comfortable in. And I thought, that looks very confident, and you learn something from it. You look at your weaknesses and you address them. Margaret Thatcher was brilliant and Tony Blair was brilliant at that. That is the determining factor for Keir Starmer. He's spent most of his time as an MP in his comfort zone. You cannot win by staying in your comfort zone. So that is the big test. By definition, that's not easy, and that will be really fascinating to see. Plenty of others have failed that test.

If he has not so far been a dazzling figure on the platform, this need not rule him out of contention. 'Will he ever be an orator like Neil Kinnock? Who will ever be that?' says Goldsmith.

Neil is very special. It's very hard to achieve that particular style of oratory, which we all admire enormously, but it's a particular talent. I don't think we know that. I think let's wait until there have been live events when he's got the opportunity to really engage with a crowd. I think that's important to see.

A somewhat bland persona, meanwhile, can actually be a reassuring feature for leaders on the left. 'I think he comes from that grand old tradition of the Labour Party that some of its most radical figures in substantive terms look like its most establishment people in terms of their profiles,' says an old party hand.

You can be a much more radically successful leader for the Labour Party if you feel like much more of an establishment person, whereas Labour leaders who delighted in their taking-to-the-barricades personas haven't made it to No. 10. He has something in common with those Labour leaders who went on to become Prime Minister because his objective hasn't been, 'I have a lifelong ambition to be leader of the Labour Party.' It's more, 'I have a lifelong ambition to be a Labour Prime Minister.'

To come close to achieving this, Starmer will need to show he is in charge. After the May elections he reorganised his top team, replacing his political and communications directors, moving his chief of staff to a new role and appointing Deborah Mattinson, a pollster close to Gordon Brown, as his new director of strategy. But Starmer will also need to be prepared for more bruising political battles. 'I think ultimately the decision will be, is he going to face down the hard left and reposition the party, or is he going to try and bring both sides together and negotiate through the power of logic and intellect?' says a colleague.

> We haven't really seen which course he wants to take yet. He's obviously fallen out with them about Corbyn's behaviour over antisemitism. But when they come to making calls on the economy or security or foreign affairs, for him to win an election he's going to have to fall out with them comprehensively, and I'm not sure whether he's got the bandwidth to do that.

Peter Mandelson and Alastair Campbell like to remind the left of the inescapable truth that Labour's record in the last eleven elections reads, 'Lost, lost, lost, lost, Blair, Blair, Blair, lost, lost, lost, lost.' The thing about Blair was not just that he took Labour towards the centre, though he did, but that he relentlessly put voters' priorities ahead of his party's, and made sure he won the battles that ensued. In doing so, he showed who was in charge and reinforced his status as a leader.

It is time for Starmer to follow this example. 'Let Reagan be Reagan' was the famous mantra of White House allies who felt the 40th

President was at his best when he followed his instincts. 'Let Starmer be Starmer' may turn out to be terrible advice but that, for what it's worth, is mine. If what then comes to the fore is the radical left-wing lawyer of old, voters can at least decide if that's what they want. But if his true aim, tempered by experience, is to turn Labour back into a party that speaks for the country and can be trusted with government, he must fight for it every day and face down anyone who stands in his way. After all, he has nothing to lose.

ENDNOTES

CHAPTER 1: 'THE POSHER THE VOICE, THE MORE VULGAR THEY ARE'
1   Interview with Andrew Cooper, 5 January 2021.
2   *Profile*, BBC Radio 4, 26 September 2009.
3   Interview with Tony Alston, 7 January 2021.
4   'Keir Starmer: "My mum's health battles have inspired me"', *Ham&High*, 27 March 2015.
5   Interview with Diana Watson, 6 January 2021.
6   *Profile*, BBC Radio 4, 26 September 2009.
7   *Political Thinking with Nick Robinson*, BBC Radio 4, 9 March 2018.
8   *Today*, BBC Radio 4, 19 December 2019.
9   Interview with Nicky Kerman, 25 January 2021.
10 Interview with Politico, 23 September 2019.
11 Interview with Bruce Reed, 25 January 2021.
12 Keir Starmer interview with the *Sunday Times*, 11 April 2021.
13 'Sir Keir Starmer, Leader of the Opposition', *Desert Island Discs*, BBC Radio 4, 15 November 2020.
14 *Political Thinking with Nick Robinson*, BBC Radio 4, 9 March 2018.

CHAPTER 2: SCHOOLBOY SOCIALIST
1   As quoted in Derek Gillard, 'Education in England: A History', 2018.
2   Charles Moore, *Margaret Thatcher, The Authorized Biography, vol. 1* (London: Allen Lane, 2013).
3   Interview with David Jones, 8 January 2021.
4   *Daily Mail* editorial comment, 25 September 2009.
5   Interview with Andrew Sullivan, 14 December 2020.
6   Interview with Andrew Cooper, 5 January 2021.
7   Interview with Peter Wheatley, 18 February 2021.
8   Interview with Mark Dixon, 18 February 2021.
9   'Hello: MP Keir Starmer', *On the Hill*, 22 November 2015.
10 Interview with Graham Best, 20 February 2021.
11 Jon Pike, tweet, 2.56 p.m., 4 January 2020, https://twitter.com/runthinkwrite/status/1213474320699338752
12 'The chairman's amicable dinner', *Reigatian Magazine*, 2014.
13 Reigate Grammar School website, 13 January 2017.
14 Interview with Politico, 23 September 2019.

CHAPTER 3: KING OF MIDDLE-CLASS RADICALS
1 Interview with David Griffith, 14 December 2020.
2 *Today*, BBC Radio 4, 19 December 2019.
3 Interview with John Erskine, 8 January 2021.
4 Interview with Adam LeBor, 18 December 2020.
5 'Sir Keir Starmer, Leader of the Opposition', *Desert Island Discs*, BBC Radio 4, 15 November 2020.
6 Email from Prof. Clive Walker, 9 December 2020.
7 Interview with Ken Macdonald, 2 March 2021.
8 Geoffrey Robertson, *Rather His Own Man* (London: Biteback, 2019), p. 152.
9 Keir Starmer, St Edmund Hall website.

CHAPTER 4: ALTERNATIVES
1 'Vice Man Jailed', *The Times*, 13 August 1985.
2 Interview with Andrew Cooper, 5 January 2021.
3 *Profile*, BBC Radio 4, 26 September 2009.
4 *St Edmund Hall Magazine*, 1986–87.
5 Interview with Richard Barbrook, 26 February 2021.
6 Benjamin Schoendorff, tweet, 1.05 p.m., 18 December 2019, https://twitter.com/b_schoendorff/status/1207285746467520512
7 *Profile*, BBC Radio 4, 26 September 2009.
8 Interview with Peter Tatchell, 23 February 2021.
9 Interview with Hilary Wainwright, 12 February 2021.
10 Interview with Andrew Coates, 2 February 2021.
11 'Has Keir Starmer got what it takes to save the Labour Party?', *Sunday Times*, 15 March 2020.
12 Interview with Colin Wells, 14 December 2020.
13 Robertson, *Rather His Own Man*.

CHAPTER 5: SOCIALIST LAWYER
1 Interview with Colin Wells, 14 December 2020.
2 Interview with Bill Bowring, 16 December 2020.
3 Interview with Peter Tatchell, 23 February 2021.
4 Email from Sarah Spencer, 25 March 2021.
5 *PR Week*, 23 June 1989.
6 *The Guardian*, 15 August 1989.
7 *The Guardian*, 24 August 1989.
8 Robertson, *Rather His Own Man*.
9 *Law Gazette*, 12 February 2021.

CHAPTER 6: UPHOLDING THE RULE OF LAW
1 As quoted in 'Upholding the rule of law?', Haldane Society, April 1992.
2 Quoted in *The Observer*, 29 November 1992.
3 Interview with John Hendy, 1 April 2021.
4 *The Independent*, 6 April 1993.
5 'Undercover Policing Inquiry: Starmer urged to give evidence', *The Guardian*, 4 February 2021.

CHAPTER 7: DOUGHTY STREET
1 'He has an ability to motivate and is not easily cowed. If there is a row with the government he will fight his corner', *The Guardian*, 1 August 2008.
2 Interview with Ken Macdonald, 2 March 2021.
3 'Legal Aid in 21st-century Britain', *The Guardian*, 12 March 2009.

4   *The Independent*, 19 July 2004.
5   'Sir Keir Starmer slammed for trying to block death penalty for two killers who murdered ex-BBC newsreader', *Sun on Sunday*, 8 March 2020.
6   Interview with David Blunkett, 22 April 2021.
7   Keir Starmer interview with *The Times*, 4 March 2003.
8   Keir Starmer, 'Human rights and terrorism: A rugged terrain', *Socialist Lawyer*, April 2007.
9   'Lawyers create waves with specialist aims', *The Times*, 13 July 2000.
10 As quoted in 'Keir Starmer: Who is he, really?', Tortoise Media, 23 March 2021.
11 Interview with Ian Paisley Jr, 19 April 2021.
12 'Sir Keir Starmer, Leader of the Opposition', *Desert Island Discs*, BBC Radio 4, 15 November 2020.
13 'Keir Starmer selects EU anthem at Desert Island Picks event', *Camden New Journal*, 26 June 2019.
14 'Register of Members' Financial Interests – introduction to the registers for the 2019 parliament'.

CHAPTER 8: 'CREDIBLE AND TRUE'

1   'Sir Keir Starmer, Leader of the Opposition', *Desert Island Discs*, BBC Radio 4, 15 November 2020.
2   Interview with Ken Macdonald, 2 March 2021.
3   Interview provided by Nazir Afzal, 7 April 2021.
4   'Think about criminals' human rights orders DPP', *Daily Mail*, 4 November 2009.
5   Interview with Dominic Grieve, 19 February 2021.
6   Kelvin MacKenzie evidence to the Leveson Inquiry, 9 January 2012.
7   'Journalist's conviction quashed as judge questions law used in Operation Elveden', *The Times*, 27 March 2015.
8   'My mentor died a broken man after Starmer's groundless prosecution', *Evening Standard*, 12 May 2021.
9   'Keir Starmer takes Labour adviser role and hints at career as MP', *The Guardian*, 28 December 2013.
10 Interview with Daniel Janner, 7 December 2020.
11 Interview with Harvey Proctor, 19 April 2021.

CHAPTER 9: 'ONE OF THE STARMERS SHOULD BE AN MP'

1   Interview with Bruce Reed, 25 January 2021.
2   'Keir Starmer, "My mum's health battles have inspired me"', *Ham&High*, 27 March 2015.
3   Interview with Bill Bowring, 16 December 2020.
4   'The trouble with Kids Company', *The Spectator*, 14 February 2015.
5   'Ex-law chief Keir Starmer: "I'll work to tackle London's housing crisis if I'm made an MP"', *Evening Standard*, 8 September 2014.
6   Email from Jon Holbrook, 5 February 2021.
7   'People make assumptions about me which turn out to be wrong', *Ham&High*, 11 December 2014.
8   'Keir Starmer: "2015 will be a defining election … I can't walk away from it"', *The Guardian*, 19 December 2014.
9   Interview with Michael Crick, 15 April 2021.

CHAPTER 10: CORE GROUP PLUS

1   'Labour's Keir Starmer: "If we don't capture the ambitions of a generation, it doesn't matter who is leading the party"', *The Guardian*, 9 April 2016.
2   'Labour should forget "Blairism" and reclaim Blair's early radicalism', *The Guardian*, 12 May 2015; 'Labour activists urge Keir Starmer to stand for party leadership', *The Guardian*, 15 May 2015.

3   Letter from Starmer to Narice Bernard, seen by research team.
4   Interview with Michael Crick, 15 April 2021.
5   'Who is Andy Burnham? Labour leadership contender guide', BBC News, 30 July 2015.
6   Interview with Dominic Grieve, 19 February 2021.
7   'High Speed Rail (London–West Midlands) Bill, Hansard, vol. 607, 23 March 2016.
8   'MPs split over plans for £7,000 salary hike from IPSA', Ham&High, 9 June 2015.
9   'Andy Burnham: "The real me comes out when I'm angry"', The Guardian, 14 November 2020.
10 'Former Director of Public Prosecutions calls for victims' law', The Guardian, 3 February 2014.
11 'Labour's Keir Starmer: "If we don't capture the ambitions of a generation, it doesn't matter who is leading the party"', The Guardian, 9 April 2016.
12 'Investigatory Powers Bill', Hansard, vol. 607, 15 March 2016.
13 'Starmer: Privacy is always a key consideration', Daily Politics, 6 June 2016.
14 'Snooper's Charter is "unlawful" and must be overhauled, Labour's Diane Abbott says', The Independent, 22 December 2016.
15 'Labour MP Keir Starmer tours UK to find "firm but humane" migrant policy', Evening Standard, 7 January 2016.
16 Hansard, vol. 605, 10 February 2016.
17 'Diane Abbott: Labour must never try to outdo the Tories or UKIP on immigration', LabourList, 16 November 2016.
18 'Airstrikes in Syria are lawful, but I'll be voting against them', The Guardian, 30 November 2015.
19 'Keir Starmer: the Brexit opponent making Labour heard on Europe', Financial Times, 16 October 2016.
20 Ibid.

CHAPTER 11: 'AS DEMOCRATS, WE IN THE LABOUR PARTY HAVE TO ACCEPT THE RESULT'

1   'Keir Starmer MP: Choosing ideological purity before power is a dereliction of duty', New Statesman, 25 July 2016.
2   'Keir Starmer interview: "Winning elections is all I'm here for, that's why I came into it"', The Guardian, 24 March 2017.
3   Newsnight, BBC, 19 October 2020.
4   Interview with David Lidington, 18 February 2021.
5   'Labour's Barry Gardiner rubbished key Brexit policy', BBC News, 10 April 2018.
6   'Labour would end free movement but not "sever ties" with EU, says Starmer', The Guardian, 25 April 2017.
7   'Labour's 2015 election result is no yardstick for success, says Starmer', The Guardian, 19 May 2017.
8   Ibid.
9   'Keir Starmer in talks for role with law firm that represented Gina Miller', The Guardian, 24 July 2017.
10 'No "constructive ambiguity". Labour will avoid Brexit cliff edge for UK economy', The Guardian, 26 August 2017.
11 'Keir Starmer clashed with Corbyn on Brexit "to brink of resignation"', The Guardian, 18 September 2018.
12 'Keir Starmer: "We cannot allow Labour to break apart over Brexit"', The Guardian, 24 March 2018.
13 'Brexit: Barnier warns UK against blaming EU in event of no deal', Irish Times, 21 August 2018.
14 'Keir Starmer: second Brexit referendum should be kept on table', The Guardian, 23 August 2018.
15 'Tom Watson tells Corbyn: "We must back members on new Brexit vote"', The Guardian, 22 September 2018.
16 Interview with Michael Crick, 15 April 2021.

CHAPTER 12: 'IF YOU WANT TO FIGHT FOR REMAIN, VOTE LABOUR'
1 Interview with David Lidington, 18 February 2021.
2 'Brexit interview: Gavin Barwell', UK in a Changing Europe, 1 and 25 September 2020.
3 Ibid.
4 Interview with Robbie Gibb, 15 February 2021.
5 'Only two more Labour MPs switch sides to back May's Brexit deal', *The Guardian*, 29 March 2019.
6 'Corbyn backs referendum on Brexit deal after EU election exodus', *The Guardian*, 28 May 2019.
7 'This isn't about Brexit. Backing Remain now would wreck Labour', *The Guardian*, 27 May 2019.
8 'Keir Starmer eyes anti-Brexit long game', Politico, 23 September 2019.
9 'Was it really "Brexit wot lost it" for Labour?', Lord Ashcroft Polls, 17 December 2019.
10 Interview with John Mann, 22 February 2021.

CHAPTER 13: UNDER NEW MANAGEMENT
1 'Bridging the gap: Corbynism after Corbyn', Verso blog, 6 April 2020.
2 'Jon Trickett hits out at "undemocratic" Keir Starmer amid leadership donations row', PoliticsHome, 3 March 2020.
3 'Keir Starmer warns Labour members to stop taking "lumps out of each other"', HuffPost, 16 April 2020.
4 'Keir Starmer: "The government has been slow in nearly all of the major decisions"', *Financial Times*, 6 May 2020.
5 'Labour's Rebecca Long-Bailey sacked in antisemitism row', BBC News, 25 June 2020.
6 'Rabbi Sacks believes Labour is finally taking antisemitism seriously: Keir Starmer is willing to take responsibility', *Evening Standard*, 18 September 2020.
7 'Starmer says Corbyn's response to antisemitism report "as bad as you can get"', *Belfast Telegraph*, 29 November 2020.
8 Interview with John Mann, 22 February 2021.
9 *BBC Breakfast*, 29 June 2020.
10 Bell Ribeiro-Addy MP, tweet, 4.59 p.m., 29 June 2020, https://twitter.com/BellRibeiroAddy/status/1277632852969078784
11 'Labour leader Keir Starmer appeals to black people not to leave the party', HuffPost, 2 July 2020.
12 *Nick Ferrari at Breakfast*, LBC, 6 July 2020.
13 'Leak reveals Labour plan to focus on flag and patriotism to win back voters', *The Guardian*, 2 February 2021.
14 'Sir Keir Starmer hit by series of Labour resignations over Covert Human Intelligence Sources Bill', Sky News, 16 October 2020.
15 'Keir Starmer would "welcome a bit of distance" from Len McCluskey as union cuts funding, says Labour MP', *The Independent*, 7 October 2020.
16 'Labour MP apologises for saying he once saw business as "the enemy"', *The Guardian*, 20 March 2021.
17 'Labour frontbencher under fire after calling businesspeople "the enemy"', *The Sun*, 29 March 2021.

CHAPTER 14: CAPTAIN HINDSIGHT
1 'Keir Starmer: I won't be defined by our past leaders', *Evening Standard*, 1 May 2020.
2 Interview with John Mann, 22 February 2021.
3 'Keir Starmer: I won't be defined by our past leaders', *Evening Standard*, 1 May 2020.
4 Interview with Dominic Grieve, 19 February 2021.
5 'With so many coronavirus deaths, Labour should not be holding back', *The Guardian*, 22 April 2020.

6 Hansard, vol. 685, 2 December 2020.
7 'Gary Neville says government "out of their depth" – while Labour "let opposition have a clear run" – in scathing attack on country's politicians over coronavirus', *Manchester Evening News*, 6 December 2020.
8 'Keir Starmer: "Boris Johnson has to get a grip and restore public confidence"', *The Guardian*, 2 June 2020.
9 'Decent, competent, cautious, but Starmer still has to prove he can inspire victory', *The Guardian*, 2 January 2021.
10 'Dan Hodges: Starmer lacks belief, drive and hunger. And the British people can smell it…', *Mail on Sunday*, 27 March 2021.
11 'European Union (Future Relationship) Bill', Hansard, vol. 686, 30 December 2020.
12 'Keir Starmer ditches EU free movement pledge as a lost cause', *The Times*, 11 January 2021.
13 'Keir Starmer facing pressure to end silence on Tory Brexit failures', *The Guardian*, 13 February 2021.
14 Interview with Mark Francois, 4 March 2021.
15 'Johnson is on the crest of a vaccine wave. Labour will just have to ride it out', *The Guardian*, 3 February 2021.
16 'Keir Starmer to launch fightback with Labour policy blitz', *The Guardian*, 12 February 2021.
17 'Labour failing to win back enough Tory voters, officials warn', *The Guardian*, 27 January 2021.
18 '"We have felt prosecuted, judged, and sentenced unfairly": Jesus House hits back after Keir Starmer apologises for visiting church', Premier Christian News, 7 April 2021.
19 'Tories confident of election "hat-trick" in Hartlepool, Teesside and the West Midlands', *The Times*, 5 May 2021.

EPILOGUE: 'CHANGING THE THINGS THAT NEED CHANGING'
1 BBC News, 7 May 2021.
2 Interview with Mark Seddon, 28 May 2021.
3 Interview with Peter Goldsmith, 19 April 2021.

INDEX